# PRESS ON

# PRESS ON

*Messages on Faith, Hope, and Charity from*

## JOSEPH B. WIRTHLIN

DESERET
BOOK

SALT LAKE CITY, UTAH

*For Elisa*

**Library of Congress Cataloging-in-Publication Data**

Wirthlin, Joseph B., 1917-
    Press on : messages on faith, hope, and charity / Joseph B. Wirthlin.
       p.   cm.
    Includes bibliographical references and index.
    ISBN 978-1-59038-834-1 (hardback : alk. paper)
    1. Christian life—Mormon authors.   I. Title.
    BX8656.W58 2007
    289.3'32—dc22                             2007021169

Printed in the United States of America
Publishers Printing, Salt Lake City, Utah

10   9   8   7   6   5   4   3   2   1

# CONTENTS

# CONTENTS

# FOREWORD

Long before my father was ordained an apostle, he had found the secret to happiness and success—service to God and his fellow man. Since his youth, he has possessed a determined work ethic that has characterized him as a husband, father, friend, and servant of the Lord. His absolute integrity is legendary and an example to all. His straightforward focus in adhering to gospel principles has allowed him to touch the lives of many. His compassion for all inspires others to reach above and beyond their potential. His quick wit, sense of humor, and simple approach to life have given him the ability to reach many through his messages. Dad's simple faith and love of the Lord drive him to be his best, and he wants the same for those around him. His humble and guileless approach to life have been felt by many in ways that have taught the Master's plan and soothed many broken hearts.

My father's love of sports, especially football and running, is evident in this book, in the many talks he has given, and elsewhere. His youthful participation in athletics taught him that in life you must be in shape, not only physically but also spiritually, if you are to have any hope of accomplishing your stewardship.

Anyone who knows Dad at all knows that the best decision he ever made was to marry Elisa Young Rogers in the Salt Lake Temple. The example of their marriage, with their absolute devotion to each other and their unwavering adherence to gospel principles, has established a standard that is envied by the members of their own family as well as anyone else who has observed them. Mother's support and devotion—always willing to travel on a moment's notice to diverse places around the world—have enabled them to teach many about an ideal marriage relationship. Now in the sunset of his own mortality, Dad has faced his greatest test, the passing of his beloved Elisa. His reaffirming, pure testimony of the reality of the resurrection, borne in general conference less than two months following her passing, was one of his greatest moments, one that will be remembered for years to come. That testimony serves as the final chapter of this book.

In the aftermath of Mother's death, Dad is now, as never before, putting into practice the many principles he has taught over the years—the importance of putting one foot in front of the other, of never giving up, of doing the best you can, and of pressing on in the face of whatever adversity life throws at you.

My father has never asked for nor sought any notoriety by virtue of his sacred calling. He has only sought to build the kingdom and serve his Master, whose work this is. In Dad's mind, he is no more important or greater than the humblest deacon. He has always taught on a level for all to understand by sharing stories from everyday life, much as the Savior did during His mortal ministry. Dad has an uncanny ability to lift while teaching, gently inspiring Saints everywhere to face and overcome their challenges and rise to greater heights.

I think the one scripture that sums up my father's life and ministry comes from the words of Nephi: "Wherefore, ye must press forward with a steadfastness in Christ, having a perfect brightness of hope, and a love of God and of all men. Wherefore, if ye shall press forward, feasting upon the word of Christ, and endure to the end, behold, thus saith the Father: Ye shall have eternal life" (2 Nephi 31:20).

Such is Dad's faith, and such is his prayer for us all.

JOSEPH B. WIRTHLIN JR.

# ACKNOWLEDGMENTS

As with all works not officially published by the Church, the contents of this book reflect my personal views and do not necessarily represent the official doctrines of The Church of Jesus Christ of Latter-day Saints. However, I have always attempted to be in harmony with the standard works and the words of our living prophets. Any errors to be found herein are my sole responsibility, and I hope they will be looked upon with kindness.

I wish to express my deep appreciation to the excellent design and production staff at Deseret Book, led by Cory Maxwell, who has encouraged this book from the beginning. He has been expertly assisted by editor Richard Peterson. Thanks also to designer Richard Erickson and typographer Tonya Facemyer for their work. I have been greatly blessed over the years with an able and talented secretary, Ann Pickrell, whose good judgment and skill has been indispensable. And this book would not be a reality were it not for the prodding and persistence of my grandson Matthew for whom I am grateful.

Finally, I wish to thank my Brethren, whose testimony, example, commitment to the Lord, and patience with me is profound. I love them and sustain them with all of my heart.

# PRESS
# ON
## WITH FAITH

# 1

# "FOLLOW ME"

## *"Straightway Left Their Nets, and Followed Him"*

They were fishermen before they heard the call. Casting their nets into the Sea of Galilee, Peter and Andrew stopped as Jesus of Nazareth approached, looked into their eyes, and spoke the simple words, "Follow me." Matthew writes that the two fishermen "straightway left their nets, and followed him" (Matthew 4:20).

Then the Son of Man approached two other fishermen who were in a ship with their father, mending their nets. Jesus called to them, "and [James and John] immediately left the ship and their father, and followed [the Lord]" (Matthew 4:21–22).

Have you ever wondered what it must have been like to have lived in the days of the Savior? If you had been there, would you have heeded His call "Follow me"?

Perhaps, a more realistic question might be, "If the Savior were to call you today, would you be just as willing to leave your nets and follow Him?" I am confident that many would.

But for some, it may not be such an easy decision. Some have discovered that nets, by their very nature, are sometimes not so easy to leave.

Nets come in many sizes and shapes. The nets that Peter, Andrew, James, and John left were tangible objects—tools that helped them earn a living.

We sometimes think of these four men as modest fishermen who did not sacrifice much when they left their nets to follow the Savior. To the contrary, as Elder James E. Talmage has observed, Peter, Andrew, James, and John were partners in a prosperous business. They "owned their boats and gave employment to other men." According to Elder Talmage, Simon Peter "was well to do in a material way; and when he once spoke of having left all to follow Jesus, the Lord did not deny that Peter's sacrifice of temporal possessions was . . . great" (*Jesus the Christ,* 204).

Later, the net of wealth entrapped a rich young man who claimed that he had obeyed all the commandments from his youth. When he asked the Lord what else he might need to do to gain eternal life, the Master said, "If thou wilt be perfect, go and sell that thou hast, and give to the poor, and thou shalt have treasure in heaven: and come and follow me." When the young man heard that "He went away sorrowful: for he had great possessions" (Matthew 19:21–22).

## Entangling Nets

Nets are generally defined as devices for capturing something. In a narrower but more important sense, we might define a net as anything that entices or prevents us from following the call of Jesus Christ, the Son of the living God.

Nets in this context can be our work, our hobbies, our pleasures, and, above all else, our temptations and sins. In short, a net can be anything that pulls us away from our relationship with our Heavenly Father or from fellowship in His restored Church.

Let me give you a modern example. A computer can be a useful and indispensable tool. But if we allow it to devour our time with vain, unproductive, and sometimes destructive pursuits, it becomes an entangling net.

Many of us enjoy watching athletic contests, but if we can recite the statistics of our favorite players and at the same time fail to remember birthdays or anniversaries, neglect our families, or ignore opportunities to render acts of Christ-like service, then sports may also be an entangling net.

Since the days of Adam, man has by the sweat of his brow earned his daily bread. But when our work consumes us to the point where the spiritual dimensions of life are neglected, work can also be an entangling net.

Some have been ensnared in the net of excessive debt. The net of interest holds them fast, requiring them to sell their time and energies to meet the demands of creditors. Such persons surrender their freedom, becoming slaves to their own extravagance.

It is impossible to list the many nets that can ensnare us and keep us from following the Savior. But if we are sincere in our desire to follow Him, we must straightway leave the world's entangling nets and follow Him.

I do not know of another period in the history of the world that has been so filled with such a variety of entangling nets. Our lives are typically filled with appointments, meetings, and tasks. It is so easy to get caught in a multitude of nets that sometimes even a suggestion of breaking free can be threatening and even frightening to us.

Sometimes we feel that the busier we are, the more important we are—as though our busyness defines our worth. Brothers and sisters, we can spend a lifetime whirling about at a feverish pace, checking off list after list of things that in the end really don't matter.

That we do a lot may not be so important. The Lord has often enjoined us to invest the energy of our minds, our hearts, and our souls in those things of eternal significance—that is essential.

As the clatter and clamor of life bustle about us, we hear shouting to "come here" and to "go there." In the midst of the noise and seductive voices that compete for our time and interest, a solitary figure stands on the shore of our Sea of Galilee, calling quietly to us, "Follow me."

## Balance

We can easily get our lives out of balance. I remember a few years that were particularly challenging for me. Our family had grown to seven children. I had served as a counselor in the bishopric and was then given the sacred call as bishop of our ward. At the same time I was striving to manage our business that required long hours each day.

I pay tribute to my wonderful wife, who always made it possible for me to serve the Lord.

There was simply too much to do in the time available. Instead of sacrificing things of significance, I decided I'd get up earlier, take care of my business, then spend the time required to be a good father and husband and a faithful member of the Church. It wasn't easy. There were mornings when the alarm clock went off that I cracked open an eyelid and glared at it, daring it to keep ringing.

Nevertheless, the Lord was merciful and helped me to find the energy and time to do all I had committed to do. Although it was difficult, I have never regretted making the choice to heed the Savior's call and follow Him.

## Peace and Eternal Life

Think of the debt we owe Him. Jesus is "the resurrection, and the life: he that believeth in [Him], though he were dead, yet shall he live" (John 11:25). There are those who have great wealth, yet they would give their all to add just a few additional years, months, or even days to their mortal lives. What should we be willing to give for eternal life?

There are those who would give all they have to experience peace. "Come unto me, all ye that labour and are heavy laden," the Savior taught, "and I will give you rest" (Matthew 11:28). But it is not merely peace that the Savior promises to those who keep His commandments and endure to the end, but eternal life, "which gift is the greatest of all the gifts of God" (D&C 14:7).

Because of the Savior's promise of resurrection, we will live forever. Immortality means that we will never die. But eternal life means to live forever in exalted spheres in companionship with those we cherish, encompassed about by profound love, exquisite joy, and glory.

No amount of money can purchase this exalted state. Eternal life is a gift from a loving Heavenly Father, offered freely and liberally to all who heed the call of the Man of Galilee.

Unfortunately, many are too entangled in their nets to heed the call. The Savior explained that, "Ye believe not, because ye are not of my sheep . . . My sheep hear my voice, and I know them, and they follow me" (John 10:26–27).

## Following the Savior

How do we follow the Savior? By exercising faith. By believing in Him. By believing in our Heavenly Father. By believing God speaks to man on earth today.

We follow the Savior by repenting of our sins—by experiencing sorrow because of wrongdoings and forsaking them.

We follow the Savior by entering the waters of baptism and receiving a remission of our sins, by receiving the gift of the Holy Ghost and allowing that influence to inspire, instruct, guide, and comfort us.

How do we follow the Savior? By obeying Him. He and our Heavenly Father have given us commandments—not to punish or torment us, but to help us come to a fulness of joy, both in this life and for the eternities to come, worlds without end.

In contrast, when we cling to our sins, our pleasures, and sometimes even our perceived obligations; resist the influence of the Holy Ghost; and put aside the words of the prophets; we then stand at the shore of our *own* Galilee, nets tightly entangling us. We find ourselves unable to leave them behind and follow the living Christ.

But the Shepherd calls to each of us today. Will we recognize the voice of the Son of God? Will we follow Him?

## *Not Free From Sorrow and Pain*

May I extend a word of caution? There are those who feel that if we follow the Savior, our lives will be free from worry, pain, and fear. This is not so! The Savior Himself was described as "a man of sorrows" (Isaiah 53:3; Mosiah 14:3). Those early disciples who followed the Christ experienced great persecution and trials. Joseph Smith was no exception. Nor were the other early Saints of this, the last dispensation. And it is no different today.

I have had the opportunity to speak with a woman who heard the call of the Savior when she was eighteen. Her father, who was a high official in another church, became angry with her and forbade her from being baptized. He let her know that if she became a member of The Church of Jesus Christ of Latter-day Saints, she would be ostracized from the family.

Even though the sacrifice was great, this young woman heeded the call of the Savior and entered the waters of baptism.

Her father could not accept her decision, however, and tried to force her into abandoning her new faith. He and his wife reviled her for her decision to become a member of the Church and demanded that she recant and forsake her new religion.

Even through the rage, the bitterness, and the indignity, her faith remained strong. She endured the verbal and emotional abuse, knowing she had heard the call of the Savior and being determined to follow Him, whatever the consequence.

Eventually this young woman managed to find a safe haven, a place of refuge with a kind member family far away from the threats and unkindness of her angry father.

She met a faithful young man, and the two of them were married in the temple, receiving the choice blessings that accompany a temple marriage.

Today she stands among the multitude of those who have sacrificed so much to follow the call of the Savior.

Yes, I do not suggest that the road will be easy. But I will give you my witness that those who, in faith, leave their nets and follow the Savior will experience happiness beyond their ability to comprehend.

As I meet the wonderful members of this Church—both young and old—I am encouraged and filled with gratitude for the faithfulness of those who have heard the call of the Savior and have followed Him.

For example, a steelworker follows the Savior day after day, as over a period of more than three decades, he endures the ridicule of his co-workers as he pulls out his scriptures to read during his lunch break. The 70-year-old widow confined to her wheelchair follows the Savior as she cheers the spirits of everyone who visits and never fails to tell them of how fortunate she is. The child follows the Savior as he or she seeks through prayer to commune with the Master of the universe. The wealthy member follows the Savior as he gives so generously to the Church and his fellowmen.

## *"Follow Me"*

As Jesus the Christ stood on the shores of the Sea of Galilee 2,000 years ago, so stands He today, issuing the same call He gave to those faithful fishermen and now to all who will hear His voice: "Follow me!"

We have nets that must be tended and nets that must be mended. But when the Master of ocean, earth, and sky calls to us, "Follow me," we should leave the entangling, worldly nets behind and follow his footsteps.

I proclaim with joyful voice that the gospel is restored once again! The heavens opened to the Prophet Joseph Smith, and he saw and conversed with God the Father and His Son, Jesus Christ. Under divine

9

direction and tutelage from celestial beings, eternal truths are restored once again to man!

In our day another great prophet lives who daily adds his witness to these hallowed truths. President Gordon B. Hinckley stands in his sacred office as the mouthpiece of our Lord and Savior, Jesus Christ. At his side stand his noble counselors. In addition, he has the sustaining support of the Quorum of the Twelve Apostles, the Quorums of the Seventy, and the millions of members throughout the world who assist him, each adding his voice to proclaim the glorious restoration of the gospel that is once again restored unto man!

Jesus the Christ is "the way, the truth, and the life: no [one] cometh unto the Father, but by [Him]" (John 14:6). As a special witness of Him, I testify to you this day that the time will come when every man, woman, and child will look into the Savior's loving eyes. On that day, we will know with a surety the worth of our decision to straightway follow Him.

That each of us may hear the call of the Master and straightway leave our entangling nets and joyfully follow Him is my earnest prayer.

*(Adapted from an April 2002 general conference address)*

# 2

## CULTIVATING DIVINE ATTRIBUTES

### *Important Dates*

We often mark significant dates on our calendars, such as holidays and birthdays. Dates that come around every year help us measure progress in our lives. One annual event, New Year's Day, is a time of reflection and resolution.

Our baptism date, which commemorates our spiritual rebirth, is an annual occasion worthy of special note. We pause to recognize the date of our temple sealing as a special anniversary because that ordinance binds us together forever with our most cherished loved ones. Worthiness interviews, especially temple recommend interviews, give us another opportunity to review our progress in fulfilling the glorious stewardship our Father in Heaven has given each of us. Certainly we must watch over and care for our own souls. On these occasions, we renew covenants, reaffirm commitments, and reestablish eternal goals.

A few significant events occur only once in a lifetime. For example, in the year 2000, we experienced a New Year's Day when all four numerals in the calendar year changed at the same time. Public opinion polls at the time indicated that this singular calendar change was "looming increasingly large in the public consciousness." Surveys showed that people were also anticipating the moment with "a very positive out-look." Speaking of that singular event, one forecaster said that the millennial calendar change would "be a profound milestone in people's lives, an opportunity to stop and start anew" (*Outlook*, NFO Research, Inc., summer 1998).

## The Savior's Mortal Ministry

The birth of the Savior into mortality is an event of immeasurable significance that occurred some 2,000 years ago. In much of the world, calendar years are numbered forward and backward from the time of His birth. He taught the gospel of repentance and organized His Church, atoned for the sins of all mankind, and was crucified. He was resurrected, opening the way for all to overcome death and have our sins forgiven if we repent. His teachings established standards of human behavior that will endure eternally.

## The Second Coming of the Savior

Perhaps in an effort to escape the challenges of our times, a few voices proclaim that the second coming of the Savior is imminent. Perhaps, but the Lord could not have been more plain when He said of His triumphal return to the earth, "But of that day and hour knoweth no man, no, not the angels of heaven, but my Father only" (Matthew 24:36). He taught this truth on the Mount of Olives and repeated it in modern revelation through the Prophet Joseph Smith by saying, "the hour and the day no man knoweth, neither the angels in heaven, nor shall they know until he comes" (D&C 49:7).

Yes, the time will come when "Christ will reign personally upon the earth" (Articles of Faith 1:10). Certainly we are closer to that time now than in 1831 when the Lord admonished the elders of the Church to "labor . . . in my vineyard for the last time—for the last time call upon the inhabitants of the earth. . . . For the great Millennium, of which I have spoken by the mouth of my servants, shall come" (D&C 43:28, 30).

Though we do not know the precise time of the second coming of the Savior, we do know that we are living in the latter days and are closer to that great event than when the Savior lived his mortal life in the meridian of time. We should resolve to begin a new era of personal obedience to prepare for His return. Mortality is fleeting. We all have much to accomplish in preparation to meet Him. As Latter-day Saints, "we believe all things, we hope all things. . . . If there is anything virtuous, lovely, or of good report or praiseworthy, we seek after these things" (Articles of Faith 1:13). What do we believe that will motivate us to move forward? What do we hope for? What are the virtuous, lovely, or praiseworthy things we should seek after? I believe we should strive to develop within ourselves the traits of the character of the Savior.

## Faith, Hope, and Charity

The words of the Apostle Paul come to mind: "And now abideth faith, hope, charity, these three; but the greatest of these is charity" (1 Corinthians 13:13). These divine attributes should become fixed in our hearts and minds to guide us in all of our actions. Moroni gives us this wise counsel: "Cleave unto charity, which is the greatest of all. . . . Whoso is found possessed of it at the last day, it shall be well with him" (Moroni 7:46–47). Charity can be the outward expression of faith and hope. If sought and obtained, these three foundation elements of celestial character will abide with us in this life and beyond the veil into the next life. Remember that the "same spirit which doth possess your bodies at the time that [you] go out of this life . . . will have power to possess your body in [the] eternal world" (Alma 34:34). We should not wait a single day to intensify our personal efforts to strengthen these virtuous, lovely, and praiseworthy attributes.

When we keep the Lord's commandments, faith, hope, and charity abide with us. These virtues "distil upon [our] soul as the dews from heaven" (D&C 121:45), and we prepare ourselves to stand with confidence before our Lord and Savior, Jesus Christ, "without blemish and without spot" (1 Peter 1:19).

As I read and ponder the scriptures, I see that developing faith, hope, and charity within ourselves is a step-by-step process. Faith begets hope, and together they foster charity. We read in the Book of Mormon, "Wherefore, there must be faith; and if there must be faith there must also be hope; and if there must be hope there must also be charity" (Moroni 10:20). These three virtues may be sequential initially, but once obtained, they become interdependent. Each is incomplete without the others; they support and reinforce each other. Mormon explained, "And except ye have charity ye can in nowise be saved in the kingdom of God; neither can ye be saved in the kingdom of God if ye have not faith; neither can ye if ye have no hope" (Moroni 10:21).

These are the virtuous, lovely, praiseworthy characteristics we seek. We all are familiar with Paul's teaching that "charity never faileth" (1 Corinthians 13:8). Certainly we need unfailing spiritual strength in our lives. Moroni recorded the revelation "that faith, hope and charity bringeth [us] unto [the Lord]—the fountain of all righteousness" (Ether 12:28).

The Church of Jesus Christ of Latter-day Saints, the restored Church of the Lord on the earth today, guides us to the Savior and helps us develop, nurture, and strengthen these divine attributes. In fact, He revealed the qualifications required to labor in His service in these words: "No one can assist in this work except he shall be humble and full of love, having faith, hope, and charity" (D&C 12:8).

Mormon taught that "charity is the pure love of Christ" and exhorted us to "pray unto the Father with all the energy of heart, that [we] may be filled with this love, which he hath bestowed upon all who are true followers of his Son, Jesus Christ" (Moroni 7:47–48). Note that charity is given only to those who seek it, only to those who earnestly pray for it, only to those who are disciples of Christ. Before we can be filled with this pure love, we must start at the beginning with the first principle of the gospel. We must have "first, Faith in the Lord Jesus Christ" (Articles of Faith 1:4).

## Faith

"Now *faith* is the substance of things *hoped* for, the evidence of things not seen" (Hebrews 11:1; emphasis added). "Faith is not to have a perfect knowledge of things; therefore if [we] have faith [we] hope for things which are not seen, which are true" (Alma 32:21). Latter-day Saints can rejoice in the strength of our faith because we have the fulness of the gospel. If we study, ponder, and pray, our faith in the unseen but true things of God will grow. Even if we start with only "a particle of faith, . . . even if [we] can no more than desire to believe" (Alma 32:27. See also verses 28–43), with nurturing attention, a tiny seed of faith can grow into a vibrant, strong, fruitful tree of testimony.

Faith in the Lord, Jesus Christ, motivates us to repent. Through repentance, made possible by the Lord's atonement, we can feel the calming peace of forgiveness for our sins, weaknesses, and mistakes. With faith in a spiritual rebirth, we are baptized and receive the gift of the Holy Ghost.

We strive to keep the commandments of God, acting on our faith that obedience will help us become as He is. By virtue of the resurrection of our Savior, we have faith that death is not the end of life. We have faith that we once again will know the pleasant company and warm embrace of loved ones who have departed from mortality.

## Hope

Mormon asked the Saints of his day, "And what is it that ye shall hope for?" He gave them this answer: "Behold I say unto you that ye shall have hope through the atonement of Christ and the power of his resurrection, to be raised unto life eternal, and this because of your faith in him according to the promise" (Moroni 7:41). In Ether, we learn that "whoso believeth in God might with surety hope for a better world, yea, even a place at the right hand of God, which hope cometh of faith, [and] maketh an anchor to the souls of men" (Ether 12:4).

Even when the winds of adversity blow, our Father keeps us anchored to our hope. The Lord has promised, "I will not leave you comfortless" (John 14:18), and that He will "consecrate [our] afflictions for [our] gain" (2 Nephi 2:2). Even when our trials seem overwhelming, we can draw strength and hope from the sure promise of the Lord: "Be not afraid nor dismayed . . . for the battle [is] not yours, but God's" (2 Chronicles 20:15).

## Charity

Once faith grows into a firm, abiding testimony, giving us hope in our Heavenly Father's plan of happiness; once we see through the eye of faith that we are children of a loving Father who has given us the gift of His Son to redeem us, we experience a mighty change in our hearts (see Alma 5:14). We feel "to sing the song of redeeming love" (Alma 5:26), and our hearts overflow with charity. Knowing that the love of God "is the most desirable of all things . . . and the most joyous to the soul" (1 Nephi 11:22–23), we want to share our joy with others. We want to serve them and bless them.

## Family

"The Family: A Proclamation to the World" clearly states the sacredness of the family and declares that a "husband and wife have a solemn responsibility to love and care for each other and for their children" (*Ensign*, Nov. 1995, 102). Children should be taught at an early age of the sacredness of temples and that their ultimate goal should be to go to the temple to enjoy the blessings that our Heavenly Father has in store for them. The parents' fondest hope is that their children will come to know for themselves that receiving the sacred temple ordinances is the greatest blessing that can come to them in this life.

## Temples

The ideals of faith, hope, and charity are most evident in the holy temples. There we learn the purpose of life, strengthen our commitment as disciples of Christ by entering into sacred covenants with Him, and seal our families together for eternity across generations. Receiving our own endowment in a temple and returning frequently to perform sacred ordinances for our kindred dead increases our faith, strengthens our hope, and deepens our charity. We receive our own endowment on the basis of faith and hope in the Lord's merciful plan for His children and in the divine potential within each of us as children of our Heavenly Father. It is that same faith and hope that enables us to remain true to the end in keeping the covenants we make. Performing temple ordinances for the dead is a manifestation of charity, offering essential blessings to those who have preceded us, blessings that were not available to them during their own mortal lives. We have the privilege of doing for them what they are unable to do for themselves.

When President Gordon B. Hinckley announced the construction of an unprecedented number of new temples in April 1998, he declared that "temple ordinances become the crowning blessings the Church has to offer" ("New Temples to Provide 'Crowning Blessings' of the Gospel," *Ensign,* May 1998, 88). President Hinckley is extending these crowning blessings to more Latter-day Saints than ever before. In the house of the Lord, faithful Church members can be endowed "with power from on high" (D&C 95:8), power that will enable us to resist temptation, honor covenants, obey the Lord's commandments, and bear fervent, fearless testimony of the gospel to family, friends, and neighbors.

In July 1998, we were privileged to participate with President Hinckley in the dedication of the Monticello Utah Temple, the first of the new generation of temples that the Lord has directed our prophet to have built closer to the Saints. What a great spiritual experience that was to be among faithful Saints who never expected that a temple would be built in their town. These are people of great faith; some of them are descendants of the Hole-in-the-Rock pioneers who struggled, labored, and sacrificed through many years of toil to establish Zion on the high plateaus of southeastern Utah (see *Church News,* 1 Aug. 1998, 4).

Great things are happening in the Church! We are moving forward as never before. President Hinckley's leadership is challenging us to rise to the occasion. We will attain new levels of spirituality and place our lives in closer harmony with Jesus the Christ based on how fully faith, hope, and charity become integral components of our lives. We surely will have challenges and trials, but with more assurance than ever we will have greater peace and joy, for He has promised us His peace (see John 14:27).

*(Adapted from an October 1998 general conference address)*

# 3

# CHRISTIANS IN BELIEF
# AND ACTION

Some people erroneously believe that The Church of Jesus Christ of Latter-day Saints and its members are not Christian. We have difficulty understanding why anyone could accept and promote an idea that is so far from the truth. President Gordon B. Hinckley has described Church members as a people "bound [together] by a common love for our Master, who is the Son of God, the Redeemer of the world. We are a covenant people who have taken upon ourselves His holy name" ("This Glorious Easter Morn," *Ensign,* May 1996, 65).

Our beliefs and actions may differ from those of others, but we, as good Christians, do not criticize other religions or their adherents. "We claim the privilege of worshiping Almighty God according to the dictates of our own conscience, and allow all men the same privilege, *let them worship how, where, or what they may*" (Articles of Faith 1:11; emphasis added).

A dictionary defines a Christian as "one who professes *belief* in Jesus as the Christ or follows the religion based on [the life and teachings of Jesus]," and "one who *lives* according to the teachings of Jesus" (see *American Heritage Dictionary* [1992], 340; emphasis added). Thus two characteristics identify Christians: (1) they profess *belief* in Jesus as their Savior, and (2) they *act* in harmony with the Savior's teachings.

Faithful members of the Church, called Saints or Latter-day Saints, clearly qualify in both criteria. In our belief and our action, we demonstrate that "Jesus Christ himself [is] the chief corner stone" of our faith (Ephesians 2:20).

## Our Profession of Belief

The Church of Jesus Christ of Latter-day Saints bears the Lord's name. He stands at its head and directs it through His chosen prophets.

Members of the Church believe the *first principle of the gospel* is "Faith in the Lord Jesus Christ" (Articles of Faith 1:4). And we accept the dictum that "No [one] cometh unto the Father, but by [Him]" (John 14:6). As His disciples, we echo boldly the words of Peter's resounding testimony to our Master: "Thou art the Christ" (Mark 8:29). The burning witness of the Holy Spirit that we feel deep within our hearts prompts us to make this declaration humbly and gratefully. When we explain our regard for Jesus, we lovingly and plainly testify that He is "that Christ, the Son of the living God" (John 6:69).

Further, we rejoice in our sure knowledge that "there is none other name under heaven given among men, whereby we must be saved" (Acts 4:12). With obedient hearts and through eyes of faith, "we see that the gate of heaven is open unto all, even to those who will believe on the name of Jesus Christ, who is the Son of God" (Helaman 3:28).

We declare that Jesus is the Firstborn Son of our Heavenly Father in the spirit and the Only Begotten Son of God in mortality. He is a God, one of the three in the Godhead. He is the Savior and Redeemer of the human race. In a premortal council at which we were all present, He accepted our Father's great plan of happiness for His children and was chosen by the Father to give effect to that plan. The premortal Lord led the forces of good against those of Satan and his followers in a battle for the souls of men that began before this world was formed. That conflict continues today. We were all on the side of Jesus then. Latter-day Saints are on the side of Jesus today.

The atonement of Jesus Christ, an act of pure love, overcame the effects of the Fall and provided the way for all mankind to return to the presence of God. As part of the Atonement, the Savior overcame physical death and provided immortality, the ability to live forever as resurrected beings, for every one of God's children through the Resurrection. He also overcame spiritual death and provided the possibility of eternal life, the life that God lives and the greatest of all the gifts of God. This He did by taking upon Himself the suffering for the sins of all humankind.

Under the direction of His Father, Christ created this world and numberless others. He came to this earth as the Son of God, the Eternal Father, and the mortal virgin Mary. He lived a sinless life. Through His teachings, His example, and His divinely appointed works, He had a greater effect upon the people of this world than any other who has ever lived or will ever live upon it. He "stands first, foremost, and alone as a directing personality in the world's progression" (James E. Talmage, *Jesus the Christ,* 3rd ed. [1916], 2). He was crucified and resurrected, and He ascended to His Father in Heaven. After His resurrection, He ministered to people who lived in the Western Hemisphere.

After the great Apostasy, He initiated the restoration of the gospel on a spring day in 1820 when He and His Father visited young Joseph Smith. The Lord subsequently directed and authorized the organization of His restored Church on 6 April 1830.

He will return in glory to reign in righteousness for 1,000 years, after which He will deliver the kingdom to His Father (see Revelation 20:6; D&C 76:107–9; Articles of Faith 1:8). We base our belief and conviction of the divine nature and mission of the Lord Jesus Christ on the holy scriptures and on continuing revelation to latter-day prophets.

"We believe the Bible to be the word of God" (Articles of Faith 1:8). We delight in the knowledge of the Lord that we find recorded in the Old and New Testaments. We know that Jehovah of the Old Testament and Jesus of the New Testament are one and the same. We are grateful that this sacred record of God's dealings with the people of ancient Israel and of His mortal ministry has been preserved and passed to us to enlighten our minds and strengthen our spirits. The fragmentary nature of the biblical record and the errors in it, resulting from multiple transcriptions, translations, and interpretations, do not diminish our belief in it as the word of God "as far as it is translated correctly" (Articles of Faith 1:8). Latter-day Saints read and study the Bible; we teach and preach from it, and we strive to live according to the eternal truths it contains. We love this collection of holy writ.

"We also believe the Book of Mormon to be the word of God" (Articles of Faith 1:8). It is "Another Testament of Jesus Christ, Written by way of commandment, and also by the spirit of prophecy and of revelation . . . to the convincing of [all people] that Jesus is the Christ, the Eternal God, manifesting himself unto all nations" (title page, Book of Mormon). God brought forth the Book of Mormon as a second witness, which corroborates and strengthens the Bible's testimony of the Savior. The Book of Mormon does not supplant the Bible. It expands, extends, clarifies, and amplifies our knowledge of the Savior. Surely, this second witness should be cause for great rejoicing by all Christians.

We invite our friends who are not of our faith to read the Book of Mormon and to ponder its content prayerfully. To them we offer this scriptural promise: "And now, my beloved brethren, . . . and all ye ends of the earth, hearken unto these words and believe in Christ; and if ye believe not in these words believe in Christ. And if ye shall believe in Christ ye will believe in these words, for they are the words of Christ, and he hath given them unto me; and they teach all men that they should do good" (2 Nephi 33:10).

Latter-day Saints "believe all that God has revealed, all that He does now reveal, and we believe that He will yet reveal many great and important things pertaining to the Kingdom of God" (Articles of Faith 1:9). We feel blessed to know that God speaks to His children, as He has throughout the ages, through living prophets (see Amos 3:7; Ephesians

4:11–14). We testify that God called, prepared, and sustained Joseph Smith, the Prophet of the Restoration. Prophets have no other purpose, no other mission, except to serve God. Of his own sacred responsibility and holy calling, our living prophet, President Gordon B. Hinckley, has said: "I have no desire other than to do that which the Lord would have done. I am His servant, called to serve His people. This is His Church. We are only custodians of that which belongs to Him" ("This Glorious Easter Morn," *Ensign,* May 1996, 65).

The Explanatory Introduction to the Doctrine and Covenants explains that in this compilation of revelations, "one hears the tender but firm voice of the Lord Jesus Christ, speaking anew in the dispensation of the fulness of times . . . in fulfillment of and in concert with the words of all the holy prophets since the world began."

Furthermore, this book of latter-day revelations is "of great value to the human family and of more worth than the riches of the whole earth" because of "the testimony that is given of Jesus Christ—his divinity, his majesty, his perfection, his love, and his redeeming power."

The Pearl of Great Price is a book of additional scripture, providing the knowledge that Jesus Christ is the central figure in every dispensation from Adam down to Joseph Smith.

## How We Live Our Lives

To repeat, by definition a Christian not only professes *belief* in the Savior, but a Christian *lives and acts* according to the teachings and commandments of Jesus Christ. He taught, "Not every one that saith unto me, Lord, Lord, shall enter into the kingdom of heaven; but he that *doeth* the will of my Father" (Matthew 7:21; emphasis added). Jesus also said, "If ye love me, keep my commandments" (John 14:15). True disciples of the Lord, therefore, must be "*doers* of the word, and not hearers only." (James 1:22; emphasis added).

The Savior also commanded us to pattern our lives after His (see 3 Nephi 27:27).

Our faith in the Lord moves us to the *second principle of the gospel:* repentance (see Alma 12:32–34; D&C 130:20–21). As our faith in Christ grows, we develop a desire to purify and sanctify ourselves, that we might be worthy to return to God's presence. We learn of the great plan of happiness that our Father has designed for His children, and we seek the blessings of peace and joy that are irrevocably linked to obedience to the laws of God. Through the marvelous power of the atonement of Jesus Christ, a power activated by our obedience to His commandments, we can be cleansed of our sins. His infinite "mercy can satisfy the demands of justice" (Alma 34:16; see also Mosiah 15:9; Alma 42) for every one who will repent. One of the great truths restored to the earth through modern revelation is that the atonement of Jesus Christ is universal! The saving power of the gospel spans all generations of time and extends to all nations, kindred, tongues, and peoples. Through humble repentance, we offer the sacrifice of a broken heart and a contrite spirit that the Lord requires of us before we can enter the waters of baptism (see D&C 20:37).

Our faith in the Lord moves us also to the *third principle of the gospel,* which is "Baptism by immersion for the remission of sins," an ordinance that must be performed by one who has priesthood authority (Articles of Faith 1:4; 1:5). The Savior commanded that we all must be born again: "Except a man be born of water and of the Spirit, he cannot enter into the kingdom of God" (John 3:5). Latter-day Saints therefore accept baptism as an essential saving ordinance that is required of all people. Through baptism, we covenant to take upon us the Lord's name and commit to honor it by keeping His commandments. He, in turn, promises us the guiding and enlightening presence of His Spirit. The *fourth principle of the gospel* is the "laying on of hands [by priesthood authority] for the gift of the Holy Ghost" (Articles of Faith 1:4).

As we take His name upon us, we most certainly are Christians, for we bear the name of Christ. Each week, as we partake of the emblems of His suffering, we do it in remembrance of Him and at the same time renew our covenant that we "are willing to take upon [us] the name of [the] Son [of God], and always remember him and keep his commandments which he has given [us]" (D&C 20:77).

Through faith in the Lord, repentance, baptism, and receiving the gift of the Holy Ghost, we are born anew. We experience "a mighty change . . . in our hearts" (Mosiah 5:2; see also Alma 5:12–14) and become "quickened in the inner man" (Moses 6:65). If we are faithful and obedient, this mighty change will cause that "we have no more disposition to do evil, but to do good continually" (Mosiah 5:2).

By obeying God's commands, we deny ourselves of all ungodliness. Through obedience, motivated by a wholehearted love of God, we come fully unto Christ and allow His grace, through the Atonement, to lead us into perfection (see Moroni 10:32).

Latter-day Saints covenant to keep the Lord's commandments. Though we may fall short, our hearts are committed to striving earnestly to be obedient. We follow the teachings of the Savior. We try always to go the extra mile, to fast, to pray for our enemies, to care for the poor, and to do our acts of charity in private. We try to follow the example He gave in the parable of the good Samaritan. We avoid profanity. We avoid finding fault, we keep the Sabbath day holy, and strive to be reconciled to our brother. With patience and forgiveness, we try to turn the other cheek, knowing that we will be judged as we judge others. We are aware of the dangers of materialism and debt. We seek to put the kingdom of God and His righteousness first in our lives because we know that our hearts will follow what we treasure. We know that the gate is strait and the way is narrow, so we labor to develop self-discipline to follow in His footsteps.

We love our neighbors. We strive to treat others with courtesy and respect, to treat them as we would want to be treated, both in public settings and in our homes. We strive to show concern for others and courtesy in all that we do even as we drive in a traffic jam. We know that "out of small things proceedeth that which is great" (D&C 64:33).

Because we find joy in what we know and in how we live, we desire to share the gospel with others.

Can anyone doubt that Latter-day Saints profess a profound belief in Jesus Christ or doubt that we follow a religion based on the life and teachings of the Savior? He is, without question, "the author and finisher of our faith" (Hebrews 12:2). President Hinckley gave this powerful testimony of our Redeemer: "Towering above all mankind stands Jesus the Christ, the King of glory, the unblemished Messiah, the Lord Emmanuel. . . . He is our King, our Lord, our Master, the living Christ, who stands on the right hand of His Father. He lives! He lives, resplendent and wonderful, the living Son of the living God" ("This Glorious Easter Morn," *Ensign,* May 1996, 67).

I add my personal testimony to that borne by others: Jesus is the Christ, the Son of God, the Savior and Redeemer of all mankind, our mediator with the Father, and our perfect example. I love Him and serve Him and seek only to do His will.

*(Adapted from an October 1996 general conference address)*

# 4

# FAITH OF OUR FATHERS

It is my opinion that much of the remarkable progress of the Church is due to the faith in the Lord, Jesus Christ, held by our pioneer forefathers. I stand in awe of their resolve and tenacity in holding fast to their convictions despite the obstacles they had to overcome.

## *Faith in Christ*

The first principle of the gospel is faith in the Lord, Jesus Christ. He is the foundation principle of the gospel and the basis of all righteousness. The Prophet Joseph Smith taught that "faith is the assurance . . . of the existence of things . . . not seen" (*Lectures on Faith* 1:9). The scriptures define faith as "the substance of things hoped for, the evidence of things not seen" (Hebrews 11:1).

We delight in our faith in our Savior today. We testify to the world that "the words of Christ will tell you all things what ye should do" (2 Nephi 32:3). As members of the Lord's Church and as faithful advocates of His restored gospel, we declare soberly that God lives, that Jesus is, indeed, the Firstborn Son of our Heavenly Father, the Christ, the Savior and Redeemer of the world. The Atonement, including the Resurrection of the Savior, provides immortality and the possibility of eternal life for all of our Father's children. How grateful we should be for these blessings.

We declare gladly to all who have "ears to hear" (Matthew 11:15) that the Lord, "knowing the calamity which should come upon the inhabitants of the earth, called upon [His] servant Joseph Smith, Jun., and spake unto him from heaven, and gave him commandments" (D&C 1:17) to restore the fulness of the gospel had by the Saints of earlier days.

We testify "from the top of the mountains" (Isaiah 42:11) that President Gordon B. Hinckley is God's prophet on the earth today. Because of our faith in our prophet, Latter-day Saints echo the words of the Apostle Peter: "We have therefore a more sure knowledge of the word of prophecy, to which word of prophecy ye do well that ye take heed, as unto a light which shineth in a dark place, until the day dawn, and the day star arise in your hearts" (JST, 2 Peter 1:19; cf. KJV, 2 Peter 1:19). The light of divine revelation shines forth from a living prophet to brighten a darkened world.

## Church Growth

From the beginning of the restoration of the gospel of Jesus Christ in America, religious freedom has allowed the Church to flourish. Roots sunk deep into the rich soil of obedience and sacrifice have borne good fruit. Generations of faithful members have forged a firm foundation. From this base of strength "shall the gospel roll forth unto the ends of the earth, as the stone which is cut out of the mountain without hands shall roll forth, until it has filled the whole earth" (D&C 65:2).

President Joseph F. Smith, who came across the plains as a boy, and who knew much of adversity in his life, declared his testimony as follows: "The kingdom of God is here to grow, to spread abroad, to take root in the earth, and to abide where the Lord has planted it by His own power and by His own word, in the earth, never more to be destroyed nor to cease, but to continue until the purposes of the Almighty shall be accomplished, every whit that has been spoken of by the mouths of the holy prophets since the world began" (in Conference Report, Apr. 1902, 2).

President Hinckley noted that "the Church is growing in a marvelous and wonderful way. . . . It is spreading over the Earth in a miraculous manner." He explained that one of the reasons for this growth is that "we have a demanding religion. . . . We have great expectations concerning our people. We have standards that we expect them to live by, and that is one of the things that attracts people to this church: It stands as an anchor in a world of shifting values" (quoted in *Deseret News,* 26 Feb. 1996, A2).

The exciting global growth of the Church has focused our attention on the prophesied glorious future of the kingdom. At the same time that we look ahead with optimism, we should pause and look back on the faith of our humble pioneer forefathers. Their faith built the foundation on which the Church continues to flourish.

## *Pioneers Leaving Nauvoo*

During February of 1996, citizens in Nauvoo and communities across Iowa commemorated the 150th anniversary of the exodus of the Saints. In 1846, more than 10,000 left the thriving city that had been built on the banks of the Mississippi River. With faith in prophetic leaders, those early Church members left their "City Beautiful" and struck off into the wilderness of the American frontier. They did not know exactly where they were going, precisely how many miles lay ahead, how long the journey would take, or what the future might hold in store for them. But they *did know* they were led by the Lord and His servants. Their faith sustained them. They hoped "for things which [were] not seen, which are true" (Alma 32:21). Like Nephi of old, they were also "led by the Spirit, not knowing beforehand the things which [they] should do" (1 Nephi 4:6).

Fearing more of the mob violence that had on 27 June 1844 claimed the lives of the Prophet Joseph and his brother Hyrum, Brigham Young, leading the Church as president of the Quorum of the Twelve Apostles, announced in September 1845 that the Saints would leave Nauvoo in the spring of 1846. Most of those in Nauvoo believed fully that when Brigham Young announced that they must leave, they were hearing what the Lord wanted them to do. They responded in faith to the direction of the Lord. Throughout the fall and winter months of 1845–46, Church members set about vigorously making preparations for the journey.

When Newel Knight informed his wife, Lydia, that the Saints would have to leave Nauvoo and move yet again, she responded with tenacious faith, saying, "Well, there's nothing to discuss. Our place is with the Kingdom of God. Let us at once set about making preparations to leave" (quoted in *Church News,* 10 Feb. 1996, 3). Brother Knight had already moved his family several times as many of the Saints moved from New York to Ohio to Missouri and to Illinois. Lydia Knight's devoted submission to what she knew was God's will powerfully typifies the faith of those heroic early Saints. With their faith in mind, the words of a familiar hymn take on added meaning:

> *Faith of our fathers, living still,*
> *In spite of dungeon, fire, and sword;*
> *Oh, how our hearts beat high with joy*
> *Whene'er we hear that glorious word.*
> *Faith of our fathers, holy faith,*
> *We will be true to thee till death!*
> (Hymns, *no. 84).*

Though winter's chill was not yet past, heightened fears of mob attacks and swirling rumors of government intervention compelled President Young to set things in motion to get the Saints under way. He directed the first company of pioneer families to leave Nauvoo on 4 February 1846, a cold winter day. They drove their laden wagons and their livestock down Parley Street—a road that became known as the "Street of Tears"—to a landing where they were ferried across the river to Iowa. Chunks of ice floating in the river crunched against the sides of the flat-boats and barges that carried the wagons across the Mississippi. A few weeks later, temperatures dropped even further, and wagons were able to cross the river more easily over a bridge of ice.

Sister Wirthlin and I visited Nauvoo in early March of 1996. The weather was bitterly cold. As we stood in the chilling wind, looking out across the broad expanse of the Mississippi, we felt a deeper sense of appreciation and gratitude for those Saints as they left their beloved city. We wondered how they ever survived. What a sacrifice to leave behind so much for the uncertain future that lay ahead! No wonder so many tears were shed as the fleeing pioneers drove their wagons rumbling down Parley Street to cross the river with no hope of ever returning to their "City Beautiful."

Once across the river, they camped temporarily at Sugar Creek before starting their trek west toward the Rocky Mountains. The journey, which historian H. H. Bancroft described as a migration without "parallel in the world's history" (*History of Utah* [1964], 217) had begun.

When President Brigham Young joined the departing pioneers at their campsite in Iowa on 15 February 1846, the Lord revealed to him to begin organizing a modern "Camp of Israel." On the 1st of March, the advance company began its push westward across Iowa. Hardships caused by cold, snow, rain, mud, sickness, hunger, and death challenged the faith of those hardy pioneers. But they were determined to follow their leaders and to do, no matter the cost, what they fervently believed to be the will of God. Their faith was challenged, and for some it faltered in especially difficult times. But it did not fail them. Many were sustained by the assurances they had received in temple ordinances performed in the Nauvoo Temple prior to their departure.

## Faith of the Women Pioneers

One of the more difficult hardships endured by many of the sisters was delivering their babies under harsh, extreme conditions along the trail. Eliza R. Snow wrote that as the pioneers "journeyed onward, mothers gave birth to offspring under almost every variety of circumstances imaginable, except those to which they had been accustomed; some in tents, others in wagons—in rainstorms and in snowstorms." Sister Snow went on to record in her journal that she "heard of one birth which occurred under the rude shelter of a hut, the sides of which were formed of blankets fastened to poles stuck in the ground, with a bark roof through which the rain was dripping. Kind sisters stood holding dishes to catch the water . . . , thus protecting the [little one] and its mother from a showerbath [on its entrance to] the stage of human life" (as quoted in B. H. Roberts, *A Comprehensive History of the Church*, 3:45).

What a sacrifice these good sisters made! Some mothers lost their own lives in childbirth. Many babies did not survive. My wife's grandmother, Elizabeth Riter, was born at Winter Quarters in the back of a covered wagon during a rainstorm. Fortunately, both the mother and the newborn infant survived. With great love for the woman who gave life to her, Elizabeth often lovingly recounted how an umbrella was held over her mother throughout the ordeal to shield her from the water leaking through the wagon's cover.

Let us never forget the faith of our fathers and the selfless sacrifice of our mothers, those pioneering Saints who have left us such an inspiring example of obedience. Let us remember them as we strive to be valiant servants in our work to "invite all to come unto Christ" (D&C 20:59) and "be perfected in him" (Moroni 10:32).

## Debt of Gratitude to Pioneers

Some forty-four years ago, my father spoke from this pulpit and explained how an appreciation of our heritage can strengthen and enliven our service in the kingdom. Referring to his own pioneer grandparents, he said: "Because of the faith of these forefathers of mine, I am here, living in [these] peaceful valleys, in the shadows of great mountains, and above all, within hearing of the voice of latter-day prophets. So, I owe to them . . . a debt of gratitude, . . . a debt that can best be paid in service to this great cause" (Joseph L. Wirthlin, *A Heritage of Faith,* comp. Richard Bitner Wirthlin [1964], 47).

Now, as we see the kingdom expand throughout the world, an ever smaller percentage of Church members live in the valleys of Utah, in the shadows of our beautiful mountains. But today, modern communication technology allows Saints throughout the world to be "within hearing of the voice of latter-day prophets." As it was with my father, so it is for all of us. We who have been blessed to know the fulness of the restored gospel owe a debt of gratitude to those who have gone before us, who have given so much to build the kingdom into the worldwide miracle that it is today. Our debt of gratitude to our forebears is "a debt that can best be paid in service to this great cause."

No matter who we are—no matter our talents, abilities, financial resources, education, or experience—we all can serve in the kingdom. He who calls us will qualify us for the work if we will serve with humility, prayer, diligence, and faith. Perhaps we feel inadequate. Maybe we doubt ourselves, thinking that what we have to offer the Lord personally is too slight to even be noticed. The Lord is well aware of our mortality. He knows our weaknesses. He understands the challenges of our everyday lives. He has great empathy for the struggle required to resist the temptations of earthly appetites and passions. The Apostle Paul wrote in his epistle to the Hebrews that the Savior is "touched with the feeling of our infirmities" because he "was in all points tempted like as we are" (Hebrews 4:15).

President Thomas S. Monson taught the importance of our being willing to serve in this great cause when he asked: "Are we sufficiently in tune with the Spirit that when the Lord calls, we can hear, as did Samuel, and declare, 'Here am I'? Do we have the fortitude and the faith, whatever our callings, to serve with unflinching courage, and unshakable resolve? When we do, the Lord can work His mighty miracles through us" ("The Priesthood in Action," *Ensign,* Nov. 1992, 48; see 1 Samuel 3:4).

President James E. Faust has reassured us that whatever our abilities, faithful service not only is acceptable to the Lord but also qualifies us for great blessings bestowed by Him, blessings that enrich and expand our lives. President Faust explained "that this church does not necessarily attract great people but more often makes ordinary people great. . . .

"A major reason this church has grown from its humble beginnings to its current strength is the faithfulness and devotion of millions of humble and devoted people who have only five loaves and two small fishes to offer in the service of the Master. They have largely surrendered their own interests, and in so doing have found 'the peace of God, which passeth all understanding'" ("Five Loaves and Two Fishes," *Ensign,* May 1994, 5–6).

With the Lord to strengthen us, "we have endured many things, and hope to be able to endure all things" (Articles of Faith 1:13). He encourages us to "be not weary in well-doing, for [we] are laying the foundation of a great work. And out of small things proceedeth that which is great" (D&C 64:33). May we be faithful, brothers and sisters, in fulfilling the duties of whatever calling we have in the kingdom. Let us pay heed to the "small things" that make all the difference. Let us be faithful in keeping the commandments as we have made sacred covenants to do. As our heritage and our growth clearly show, we are, indeed, "laying the foundation of a great work."

Let us dedicate ourselves to doing the Lord's work to the best of our abilities. May we honor the faith of our fathers by giving our own faithful service to this great cause. May we "follow the prophet" (*Children's Songbook,* 110) and by so doing, "come unto Christ, and partake of the goodness of God" (Jacob 1:7).

*(Adapted from an April 1996 general conference address)*

# 5

# LIVING WATER TO QUENCH SPIRITUAL THIRST

## Samaritan Woman at the Well

Early in his mortal ministry, the Savior and his disciples passed through Samaria while traveling from Judea to Galilee. Weary, hungry, and thirsty from their journey, they stopped at Jacob's well in the city of Sychar. While the disciples went in search of food, the Savior remained at the well where he requested a drink from a Samaritan woman who had come to draw water. Because the Jews and Samaritans were divided by rancor and did not often speak to one another, the woman responded to the Savior's request with a question: "How is it that thou, being a Jew, askest drink of me, which am a woman of Samaria?" (John 4:9).

The Savior used this simple encounter at the well to teach powerful, eternal truths. Though weary and thirsty, the Master Teacher took this opportunity to testify of His divine role as the Redeemer of the world and to proclaim authoritatively His true identity as the long-promised Messiah. He patiently, yet thoughtfully, answered the woman: "If thou knewest the gift of God, and who it is that saith to thee, Give me to drink; thou wouldest have asked of him, and he would have given thee living water" (John 4:10).

Intrigued but skeptical, and seeing that Jesus had no container with which to draw water, the woman queried further: "From whence then hast thou that living water?" (John 4:11). In a powerful promise, Jesus then declared Himself to be the source of living water, the wellspring of life everlasting. He said: "Whosoever drinketh of this water shall thirst again:

"But whosoever drinketh of the water that I shall give him shall never thirst; but the water that I shall give him shall be in him a well of water springing up into everlasting life" (John 4:13–14).

Missing entirely the spiritual meaning in the Lord's message, the woman, thinking only of satisfying her physical thirst and of her convenience, demanded: "Sir, give me this water, that I thirst not, neither come hither to draw" (John 4:15).

In commenting on the conversation between the Savior and the woman, Elder Robert L. Simpson taught:

> Throughout history men have always been looking for the easy way. [Some] have devoted their lives to finding the 'fountain of youth,' a miracle water which would bring everlasting life. Today [many] are still seeking . . . some magic 'fountain' that [will] bring forth success, fulfillment, and happiness. But most of this searching is in vain. . . . It is only this 'living water,' the gospel of Jesus Christ, that can and will bring a happy, a successful, and an everlasting life to the children of men (in Conference Report, Oct. 1968, 96).

The Savior's promise to that woman extends to all of our Heavenly Father's children. By living the gospel of Jesus Christ, we develop within ourselves a living spring that will quench eternally our thirst for happiness, peace, and everlasting life. The Lord explains clearly in latter-day scripture that only faithful obedience can tap the well of living water that refreshes and enlivens our souls: "But unto him that *keepeth my commandments* I will give the mysteries of my kingdom, and the same shall be in him a well of living water, springing up unto everlasting life" (D&C 63:23; emphasis added).

When the woman said she knew the Messiah would come, Jesus said, "I that speak unto thee am he" (John 4:25–26). He demonstrated his power of prophetic discernment by telling the woman personal details about her life that only one with divine insight could have known. Astonished, the Samaritan woman left her water pot and hurried off to tell others of her interview with the Lord, saying, "Come, see a man, which told me all things that ever I did: is not this the Christ?" (John 4:29). While she gathered those of her city who would listen, Jesus taught his now-returned disciples that he already had "meat to eat that ye know not of" (John 4:32). To his puzzled disciples who were carrying the food they had acquired, he explained, "My meat is to do the will of him that sent me, and to finish his work" (John 4:34).

When the crowd of curious Samaritans arrived to see and hear the man who had proclaimed himself to be the Messiah "they besought him that he would tarry with them: and he abode there two days" (John 4:40). The scriptures tell us that many believed the Savior's teachings. As they listened, their initial curiosity matured into testimony. They declared, "We have heard him ourselves, and know that this is indeed the Christ, the Saviour of the world" (John 4:42).

## Spiritual Thirst

These latter days are a time of great spiritual thirst. Many in the world are searching, often intensely, for a source of refreshment that will quench their yearning for meaning and direction in their lives. They crave a cool, satisfying drink of insight and knowledge that will soothe their parched souls. Their spirits cry out for life-sustaining experiences of peace and calm to nourish and enliven their withering hearts.

Indeed, "there are many yet upon the earth among all sects, parties, and denominations, who are blinded by the subtle craftiness of men, whereby they lie in wait to deceive, and who are only kept from the truth because they know not where to find it" (D&C 123:12). Let us work with all our heart, might, mind, and strength to show our thirsty brothers and sisters where they may find the living water of the gospel, that they may come to drink of the water that springs "up unto everlasting life."

The Lord provides the living water that can quench the burning thirst of those whose lives are parched by a drought of truth. He expects us to supply to them the fulness of the gospel by giving them the scriptures and the words of the prophets to bear testimony as to the truth of the restored gospel to alleviate their thirst. When they drink from the cup of gospel knowledge, their thirst is satisfied as they come to understand our Heavenly Father's great plan of happiness.

## Jesus Is the Source of Living Water

As at Jacob's well, so today the Lord Jesus Christ is the only source of living water. That water will quench the thirst of those suffering from the drought of divine truth that so afflicts the world. The words of the Lord to ancient Israel spoken by the prophet Jeremiah describe the condition of many of God's children in our own day: "My people . . . have forsaken me the fountain of living waters, and hewed them out . . . broken cisterns, that can hold no water" (Jeremiah 2:13). Too many of our Heavenly Father's children spend their precious lives carving out broken cisterns of worldly gain that cannot hold the living water that would fully satisfy their natural thirst for everlasting truth.

On the last day of the feast of tabernacles, the Savior, now returned to Jerusalem, extended this timeless, universal invitation: "If any man thirst, let him come unto me, and drink" (John 7:37).

Elder Bruce R. McConkie defined living water as "the words of eternal life, the message of salvation, the truths about God and his kingdom; it is the doctrines of the gospel." He went on to explain, "Where there are prophets of God, there will be found rivers of living water, wells filled with eternal truths, springs bubbling forth their life-giving draughts that save from spiritual death" (*Doctrinal New Testament Commentary,* 1:151–52).

## Prophets and Apostles

The Lord has declared that "whether by mine own voice or by the voice of my servants, it is the same" (D&C 1:38). We are blessed to live in a day when prophets and apostles live upon the earth. Through them, we are refreshed continually by an abundant stream of eternal truth that, if obeyed, brings the living water of the Lord into our lives. Echoing those Samaritans who listened to the Savior at Jacob's well, we, too, can say with faith and with firm conviction, "We have heard him ourselves, and know that this is indeed the Christ, the Saviour of the world" (John 4:42).

### President Howard W. Hunter

We miss hearing the voice of President Howard W. Hunter. Surely, it was the love, hope, and compassion of Jesus Christ that we heard in President Hunter's simple eloquence. He raised us to new heights of understanding and urged us to renew our commitment to keep sacred covenants. He reminded us that "Christ's supreme sacrifice can find full fruition in our lives only as we accept the invitation to follow him" ("First Presidency Message: He Invites Us to Follow," *Ensign,* Sept. 1994, 2). When President Hunter asked us to "treat each other with more kindness, more courtesy, more humility and patience and forgiveness" ("President Howard W. Hunter: Fourteenth President of the Church," *Ensign,* July 1994, 4) his personal example of these Christlike virtues taught us with a persuasive power that even transcended his unforgettable spoken words. He encouraged us to bring spiritual enrichment into our lives by drinking more often and more deeply of the living water.

In his clarion statement, President Hunter said: "It would be the deepest desire of my heart to have every member of the Church be temple worthy. I would hope that every adult member would be worthy of—and carry—a current temple recommend, even if proximity to a temple does not allow immediate or frequent use of it." He wanted every one of us to be strengthened by the "sanctity and safety which is provided within [the] hallowed and consecrated walls" (Ibid., p. 5) of the house of the Lord. What better way to become more closely acquainted with the Savior and to strengthen our commitment to be more like Him than to visit frequently His holy house and drink deeply of the living waters that flow there. President Hunter wanted us to qualify ourselves through righteous living for the blessings of beauty, revelation, and peace that can be enjoyed in our temples. Hence, his oft-repeated invitation "to establish the temple . . . as the great symbol of [our] membership" (Ibid.) in the Lord's church.

## President Gordon B. Hinckley

Today, we sustain President Hunter's successor, President Gordon B. Hinckley, as prophet, seer, and revelator and as spokesman for our Lord Jesus Christ here upon the earth. I testify that he is the Lord's anointed. He holds all priesthood keys and is authorized to exercise them in leading and directing the kingdom of God. President Hinckley is a faithful servant of the Lord whose heart and voice we know well. We have come to love him through his nearly 50-year ministry as a General Authority of the Church. In 1961, he was ordained an Apostle, a special witness of the Lord Jesus Christ, and he is the longest-serving General Authority now living. When President Hinckley was called to the Twelve, the Church had 1,900,000 members and 336 stakes, compared with 13,000,000 members and nearly 3,000 stakes today.

Born of a noble father and a saintly mother, President Hinckley learned as a young boy the truths of the restored gospel from his faithful parents. He came to respect deeply and value highly his pioneer heritage. He served valiantly as a young missionary in England. Throughout his adult life, he has worked tirelessly to build the kingdom. He has served under eight presidents of the Church, including fourteen years as a counselor to the last three: presidents Spencer W. Kimball, Ezra Taft Benson, and Howard W. Hunter.

President Hinckley's preparation for his current service has been life-long. As President Boyd K. Packer reminded us recently, "No man comes to be President of this church except he has been apprenticed for a lifetime" ("President Howard W. Hunter—He Endured to the End," Funeral Address, 8 March 1995). From the scriptures we learn that those who serve as prophets were "prepared from the foundation of the world according to the foreknowledge of God" (Alma 13:3).

I bear my witness that President Hinckley was foreordained and has been duly raised up, prepared, and called of God "to declare his word among his people, that they might have everlasting life" (3 Nephi 5:13). I have been well-acquainted with him since my early youth and have observed firsthand that the fabric of his noble character contains not a single shoddy thread. From the living water of the Lord and his restored gospel, President Hinckley has drunk deeply throughout his entire life-time. Because of his righteous obedience, streams of living water have flowed and will continue to flow from him (see John 7:38 and D&C 63:23) to quench the thirst of a spiritually parched world.

I am grateful today to sustain President Thomas S. Monson and President James E. Faust as counselors in the First Presidency. They, too, have been tried and tested in the service of God and all humankind over many years. They are valiant and faithful. These three presiding high priests of the First Presidency merit our loyalty and devotion. We can sustain and follow them with absolute trust and confidence.

As one who also stands as a special witness, I join my testimony with those believing Samaritans of long ago. To you and to all the world, I testify in all soberness that this same Jesus of Nazareth who spoke with the woman at Jacob's well "is indeed the Christ, the Saviour of the world" (John 4:42). He lives today. He is our Redeemer and our

Advocate with the Father. He stands at the head of this church, which bears His name. I testify that the First Presidency and the Quorum of the Twelve Apostles stand as His duly authorized and ordained servants, charged with the sacred and solemn responsibility to guide His Church in these latter days. Our responsibility "is to do the will of Him that sent [us]" (John 4:34) and bring that living water to all who thirst for it.

*(Adapted from an April 1995 general conference address)*

# 6

# THE ABUNDANT LIFE

Harry de Leyer was late to the auction on that snowy day in 1956, and all of the good horses had already been sold. The few that remained were old and spent and had been bought by a company that would turn them into dog food.

Harry, the riding master at a girl's school in Pennsylvania, was about to leave when one of the horses that had been marked for slaughter caught his eye. The horse was a dirty, gray gelding with ugly-looking sores on its legs. The marks left by a heavy work harness gave evidence to the hard life it had led. But something about him captured Harry's attention and so he offered $80 for it.

It was snowing when Harry's children saw the horse for the first time and, because of the coat of snow on the horse's back, the children named it "Snowman."

Harry took good care of the horse. He was a gentle and reliable animal—a horse the girls liked to ride because he was steady and didn't startle like some of the others. In fact, Snowman made such rapid improvement that a neighbor purchased him for twice what Harry had originally paid.

But Snowman kept disappearing from the neighbor's pasture—sometimes ending up in adjoining potato fields, other times back at

Harry's place. How Snowman got out of the pasture was something of a mystery. It appeared that the horse must have jumped over the fences between the properties, but that seemed impossible—Harry had never seen Snowman jump over anything much higher than a fallen log.

But eventually, the neighbor's patience came to an end, and he insisted Harry buy the horse back.

For years, Harry's great dream had been to produce a champion jumping horse. He had had moderate success in the past, but in order to compete at the highest levels, he knew he would have to buy a pedigreed horse that had been specifically bred to jump. And that kind of pedigree would cost far more than what he could afford.

Snowman was already getting old—he was eight when Harry had purchased him—and he had been badly treated. But, apparently, Snowman wanted to jump and so Harry decided to see what the horse could do. What Harry saw made him think that maybe his horse had a chance to compete.

In 1958, Harry entered Snowman in his first jumping competition. Snowman stood among the beautifully bred, champion horses, looking very much out of place. Other horse breeders called Snowman a "flea-bitten gray."

But a wonderful, unbelievable thing happened that day.

Snowman won!

Harry continued to enter Snowman in other competitions, and Snowman continued to win.

Audiences cheered madly every time Snowman made a jump. He became a symbol of how extraordinary an ordinary horse could be. He appeared on television. Stories and books were written about him.

As Snowman continued to win, one buyer offered $100,000 for the old plow horse, but Harry would not sell. In 1958 and 1959, Snowman was named "Horse of the Year." Eventually, the gray gelding—who had once been marked for slaughter—was inducted into the show jumping hall of fame.

For millions of people, Snowman was much more than a horse. He was a symbol of the hidden, untapped potential that lies within each of us.

I have had the opportunity to meet and become acquainted with many wonderful people from many different walks of life. I have known rich and poor, famous and modest, wise and not so wise.

Some were burdened with heavy sorrows, others radiated a confident inner peace. Some smoldered with unquenchable bitterness, while others glowed with irrepressible joy. Some appeared defeated while others—in spite of adversity—overcame discouragement and despair.

I have heard some claim that the only happy people are those who simply don't have a firm grasp of what is happening around them.

But I believe otherwise.

I have known many who walk in joy and radiate happiness.

I have known many who live abundant lives.

And I believe I know why.

I want to list a few of the characteristics that the happiest people I know have in common. They are qualities that can transform ordinary existence into a life of abundance.

## First, They Drink Deeply from Living Waters

The Savior taught that, "Whosoever drinketh of the water that I shall give him shall never thirst; [for it] shall be in him a well of water springing up into everlasting life" (John 4:13, 14).

Fully understood and embraced, the gospel of Jesus Christ heals broken hearts, infuses meaning into lives, binds loved ones together with ties that transcend mortality, and brings to life a sublime joy.

President Lorenzo Snow said, "The Lord has not given us the gospel that we may go around mourning all the days of our lives" (*Teachings of Lorenzo Snow*, 61–62).

The gospel of Jesus Christ is not a religion of mourning and gloom.

The faith of our fathers is one of morning, hope, and joy. It is not a gospel of chains but of wings.

To embrace it fully is to be filled with wonder and to walk with an inner fire. Our Savior proclaimed, "I am come that they might have life, and that they might have it more abundantly" (John 10:10).

Do you seek peace of mind?

Drink deeply of living waters.

Do you seek forgiveness? Peace? Understanding? Joy?

Drink deeply of living waters.

The evil one offers many counterfeits of the abundant life. His marketing team goes to great lengths to suggest that those seeking happiness need not approach heaven to find it. Instead, he claims it can be found within the pages of his own catalog of wealth, comfort, culture, excitement, power, and pleasure.

There are millions upon millions who have devoted their lives in search of these things who now mournfully testify that these promises of happiness were merely vapors.

The abundant life is a spiritual life.

To find it, drink deeply of living waters.

Too many sit at the banquet table of the gospel of Jesus Christ and merely nibble at the feast placed before them. They go through the motions—attending their meetings, glancing at scriptures, repeating familiar prayers—but their hearts are far away. If they are honest, they would admit to being more interested in the latest neighborhood gossip, stock market trends, and the plot line of their favorite TV show than they are about the supernal wonders and sweet ministerings of the Holy Spirit.

Do you wish to partake of this living water and experience that divine well springing up within you to everlasting life?

Then be not afraid. Believe with all your hearts. Develop an unshakeable faith in the Son of God, and let your hearts reach out in earnest prayer. Fill your minds with knowledge of Him. Lay your sins on the altar of sacrifice and forsake them. Joyously walk in holiness and in harmony with the commandments.

Drink deeply of the living waters of the gospel of Jesus Christ.

## *Second, They Fill Their Hearts with Love*

Love is at the core of the gospel. The Savior taught that all the commandments and prophetic teachings hang on love (see Matthew 22:40). Paul wrote that, "all the law is fulfilled in one word, even in this; Thou shalt love thy neighbor as thyself" (Galatians 5:14).

We often never know the reach of a simple act of kindness. The Prophet Joseph Smith was a model of compassion and love. One day, a group of eight African-Americans arrived at the prophet's home in Nauvoo. They had traveled from their home in Buffalo, New York, some eight hundred miles away so that they could be with the Saints and with the prophet of God. Although they were free, they were forced to hide from those who might mistake them for runaway slaves. In their journey, they had endured cold and hardship, wearing out shoes and then socks, arriving barefoot in the City of Joseph. When they reached Nauvoo, the Prophet welcomed them into his home and helped each of them find a place to stay.

But there was one, a young girl named Jane, who had no place to go, and she wept, not knowing what to do.

"We won't have tears here," Joseph said to her. He turned to Emma and said, "Here's a girl who says she's got no home. Don't you think she has a home here?"

Emma agreed.

From that day on, Jane lived as a member of the family.

Years after the Prophet's martyrdom and after she had joined the pioneers and made the long trek to Utah, Jane said that sometimes she would still "wake up in the middle of the night and just think about Brother Joseph and Sister Emma and how good they was to me. Joseph Smith," Jane said, "was the finest man I ever saw on earth" (Neil K.

Newell, "Joseph Smith Moments: Stranger in Nauvoo," *Church News,*
31 Dec. 31, 2005, 16).

President Gordon B. Hinckley has said that those who reach out to
lift and serve others "will come to know a happiness . . . never known
before. Heaven knows there are so very, very, very many people in this
world who need help. Oh, so very, very many. Let's get the cankering,
selfish attitude out of our lives, my brothers and sisters, and stand a
little taller and reach a little higher in the service of others" (Liverpool
England Fireside, 31 August 1995).

We are all busy. It's easy to find excuses for not reaching out to others, but I imagine they will sound as hollow to our Heavenly Father as
the elementary schoolboy who gave his teacher a note asking that he be
excused from school, March 30th through the 34th.

Those who devote their lives to selfishly pursuing their own desires
at the exclusion of others will discover, in the end, that their joy is
shallow and their lives have little meaning.

On a tombstone of one such person was carved the following
epitaph:

> *Here lies a miser who lived for himself,*
> *And cared for nothing but gathering pelf,*
> *Now, where he is, or how he fares,*
> *Nobody knows and nobody cares.*
> *(Quoted in Obert C. Tanner,*
> Christ's Ideals for Living, *253).*

We are happiest when our lives are connected to others through
unselfish love and service. President J. Reuben Clark Jr. taught that,
"There is no greater blessing, no greater joy and happiness than comes
to us from relieving the distress of others" (*Church News,* 2 March
1946).

## *Third, They Create a Masterpiece of Their Lives*

No matter our age, circumstances, or abilities, each of us can create something remarkable of our life.

David saw himself as a shepherd, but the Lord saw him as a king. Joseph of Egypt served as a slave, but the Lord saw him as a seer. Mormon wore the armor of a soldier, but the Lord saw him as a prophet.

We are sons and daughters of an immortal, loving, and all-powerful Father in Heaven. We are created as much from the dust of eternity as we are from the dust of the earth. Every one of us has potential we can scarcely imagine.

The Apostle Paul wrote, "Eye hath not seen, nor ear heard, neither have entered into the heart of man, the things which God hath prepared for them that love him" (1 Cor. 2:9).

How is it possible, then, that so many see themselves merely as an old, gray gelding that isn't good for much more than scrap? There is a spark of greatness within every one of us—a gift from our loving and eternal Heavenly Father. What we do with that gift is up to us.

Henry David Thoreau wrote, "It is something to be able to paint a particular picture, or to carve a statue, and so to make a few objects beautiful; but it is far more glorious to carve and paint the very atmosphere and medium through which we look, which morally we can do. To affect the quality of the day, that is the highest of arts" (*Walden*, 38).

We may not be gifted artists, sculptors, or musicians, but the greatest art of all is the art of living. We can take the clay of time and create from it a masterpiece of an abundant life.

Love the Lord with all your heart, might, mind, and strength. Enlist in great and noble causes. Create of your homes sanctuaries of holiness and strength. Magnify your callings in the Church. Fill your minds with learning. Strengthen your testimonies. Reach out to others.

Create of your life a masterpiece.

The abundant life does not come to us packaged and ready-made.

It's not something we can order and expect to find delivered with the afternoon mail. It does not come without hardship or sorrow.

It comes through faith, hope, charity, and perseverance. It comes to those who, in spite of hardship and sorrow, understand the words of one writer who said, "In the depth of winter, I finally learned that there was in me an invincible summer" (Albert Camus, L' Été, 1954, 155–56).

The abundant life isn't something we arrive at. Rather, it is a magnificent journey that began long, long ages ago, and will never, never end.

One of the great comforts of the gospel of Jesus Christ is our knowledge that this earthly existence is merely a blink in the eye of eternity. Whether we are at the beginning of our mortal journey or at the end, this life is merely one step—one small step.

Our search for the abundant life is cloaked not only in the robes of this mortal clay; its true end can only be comprehended from the perspective of the eternity that stretches infinitely before us.

I testify that it is in the quest of the abundant life that we realize our destinies.

The story of an old, discarded horse sold at auction for scrap is not so different from the story of our own lives. There is within each of us a divine spark of greatness. Who knows of what we are capable if we only try? The abundant life is within our reach if we will drink deeply of living water, fill our hearts with love, and create of our lives a masterpiece.

*(Adapted from an April 2006 general conference address)*

# 7

## THE UNSPEAKABLE GIFT

### *The Light of Christ*

Have you ever thought about the amount of light and energy generated by our sun? The quantity is almost beyond comprehension. Yet the heat and light that we receive come as a free gift from God. This is another proof of the goodness of our Heavenly Father. (Experts at the National Aeronautics and Space Administration estimate that "the total energy radiated by the Sun adverages 383 billion trillion kilowatts, [which is] equivalent [to] the energy generated by 100 billion tons of TNT exploding each . . . second" [NASA Office of Space Science, "Solar Superstorm," Internet, http://science.nasa.gov/headlines/y2003/23Oct_superstorm.htm].)

The light from the sun breaks through space, bathing our planet as it encircles the sun, with life-giving warmth and light. Without the sun there could be no life on this planet; it would be forever barren, cold, and dark.

As the sun gives life and light to the earth, a spiritual light gives nourishment to our spirits. We call this the Light of Christ, and the scriptures teach that it "lighteth every man that cometh into the world" (John 1:9; see also Moroni 7:16; D&C 84:46).

Thus, all mankind can enjoy its blessings. The Light of Christ is the divine influence that allows every man, woman, and child to distinguish between good and evil. It encourages all to choose the right, to seek eternal truth, and to learn again the truths that we knew in our premortal existence but have forgotten in mortality.

The Light of Christ should not be confused with the personage of the Holy Ghost, for the Light of Christ is not a personage at all. Its influence is preliminary to and preparatory to one's receiving the Holy Ghost. The Light of Christ will lead the honest soul to "[hearken] to the voice of the Spirit" (D&C 84:46) and to find the true gospel and the true Church and thereby receive the Holy Ghost.

## The Holy Ghost

The Holy Ghost is a personage of spirit, a separate and distinct third member of the Godhead (see D&C 130:22).

He is a witness or testifier of the power of God, the divinity of Christ, and the truth of the restored gospel. Many throughout history in all nations have sought diligently to commune with the heavens and gain the light of gospel truth. They have felt the influence of the Holy Ghost confirm the truth of the gospel.

## The Gift of the Holy Ghost

The Prophet Joseph Smith explained: "There is a difference between the Holy Ghost and the gift of the Holy Ghost. Cornelius received the Holy Ghost before he was baptized, which was the convincing power of God unto him of the truth of the Gospel, but he could not receive the gift of the Holy Ghost until after he was baptized. Had he not taken this . . . ordinance upon him, the Holy Ghost which convinced him of the truth of God, would have left him" (*History of the Church*, 4:555).

The gift of the Holy Ghost, which is the right to receive the Holy Ghost as a constant companion, is obtained only upon condition of faith in Christ, repentance, baptism by immersion, and the laying on of hands by authorized servants endowed with the Melchizedek Priesthood. It is a most precious gift available only to worthy members of the Lord's Church.

In the Doctrine and Covenants, the Lord calls the gift of the Holy Ghost "the unspeakable gift" (see D&C 121:26).

It is the source of testimony and spiritual gifts. It enlightens minds, fills our souls with joy (see D&C 11:13), teaches us all things, and brings forgotten knowledge to our remembrance (see John 14:26). The Holy Ghost also "will show unto [us] all things what [we] should do" (2 Nephi 32:5).

President James E. Faust added that the gift "of the Holy Ghost is the greatest guarantor of inward peace in our unstable world" ("The Gift of the Holy Ghost—A Sure Compass," *Ensign,* May 1989, 32).

President Gordon B. Hinckley taught, "How great a blessing it is to have the ministering influence of a member of the Godhead" (*Teachings of Gordon B. Hinckley* [1997], 259). Think of what this means, the ability and the right to receive the ministrations of a member of the Godhead, to commune with infinite wisdom, infinite knowledge, and infinite power!

## *Gift Received*

As with all gifts, this gift must be received and accepted to be enjoyed. When priesthood hands were laid upon your head to confirm you a member of the Church, you heard the words, "Receive the Holy Ghost." This did not mean that the Holy Ghost unconditionally became your constant companion. Scriptures warn us that the Spirit of the Lord will "not always strive with man" (Genesis 6:3; see also 2 Nephi 26:11; D&C 1:33; Moses 8:17). When we are confirmed, we are given the *right* to the companionship of the Holy Ghost, but it is a right that we must continue to earn through obedience and worthiness. We cannot take this gift for granted.

The Holy Ghost will warn us of danger, and it will inspire us to help others in need. President Thomas S. Monson counseled us: "We watch. We wait. We listen for that still, small voice. When it speaks, wise men and women obey. Promptings of the Spirit are not to be postponed" (*Live the Good Life*, 1988, 59).

I once had the opportunity to tour a large cave. While there, the guide turned off the lights for a moment to demonstrate what it was like to be in total darkness. It was an amazing experience. I put my hand an inch from my eyes and could not see it. It was frightening in a way. I was relieved when the lights were turned back on.

As light penetrates the darkness and makes physical things visible, so does the Holy Ghost penetrate the spiritual darkness that surrounds us and make plainly visible spiritual things that once were hidden. The Apostle Paul taught that "the natural man receiveth not the things of the Spirit of God: for they are foolishness unto him: neither can he know them, because they are spiritually discerned" (1 Corinthians 2:14).

## *We Live Far beneath Our Privileges*

I fear that some members of the Lord's Church live far beneath our privileges with regard to the gift of the Holy Ghost. Some are distracted by the things of the world that block out the influence of the Holy Ghost, preventing them from recognizing spiritual promptings. This is a noisy and busy world that we live in. Remember that being busy is not necessarily being spiritual. If we are not careful, the things of this world can crowd out the things of the Spirit.

Some are spiritually deadened and past feeling because of their choices to commit sin. Others simply hover in spiritual complacency with no desire to rise above themselves and commune with the Infinite.

If such persons would open their hearts to the refining influence of this unspeakable gift of the Holy Ghost, a glorious new spiritual dimension would come to light. Their eyes would gaze upon a vista scarcely imaginable. They could know for themselves things of the Spirit, which are choice, precious, and capable of enlarging the soul, expanding the mind, and filling the heart with inexpressible joy.

President Brigham Young spoke of a sacred experience when the martyred Prophet Joseph Smith came in vision to President Young, bringing the Saints one more message. It is a message that Saints need today more than ever before: "[Be sure to] tell the people to . . . keep the spirit of the Lord," Joseph said, "and it will lead them right. Be careful and not turn away the small still voice; it will teach you what to do and where to go; it will yield the fruits of the kingdom. Tell the brethren to keep their hearts open to conviction, so that when the Holy Ghost comes to them, their hearts will be ready to receive it" (*Manuscript History of Brigham Young* 1846–1847, comp. Elden J. Watson [1971], 529).

We must ask ourselves, do we turn away the still, small voice? Do we do things that offend the Holy Ghost? Do we allow influences into our homes that drive the Spirit from our homes? The type of entertainment that we permit into our homes will certainly have an impact on our ability to enjoy power of the Holy Ghost. Much of the entertainment of the world is offensive to the Holy Ghost. Surely we should not watch movies or television shows that are filled with violence, vulgar language, and immorality.

## Do I Have the Spirit in My Life?

I invite you to ponder individually in a humble and prayerful manner these questions: "Do I have the Spirit in my life? Am I happy? Am I doing anything in my life that is offensive to the Spirit and preventing the Holy Ghost from being my constant companion?" Have the courage to repent, if needed, and again enjoy the companionship of the Holy Ghost.

Do we enjoy the influence of the Holy Ghost in our homes? Are we doing anything as a family that is offensive to the Spirit? Can we more effectively invite the Holy Ghost into our homes?

Our homes need to be more Christ-centered. We should spend

more time at the temple and less time in the pursuit of pleasure. We should lower the noise level in our homes so that the noise of the world will not drown out the still, small voice of the Holy Ghost. One of our greatest goals as parents should be to enjoy the power and influence of the Holy Ghost in our homes. We should pray and study the scriptures. We could sing the hymns of the Restoration to invite the Holy Ghost into our home. Regular family home evening will also help.

In these perilous times, we need this unspeakable gift in our lives. President Boyd K. Packer reminds us: "We need not live in fear of the future. We have every reason to rejoice and little reason to fear. If we follow the promptings of the Spirit, we will be safe, whatever the future holds. We will be shown what to do" ("The Cloven Tongues of Fire," *Ensign,* May 2000, 8).

The Prophet Joseph Smith taught that the Saints could distinguish the gift of the Holy Ghost from all other spirits, for "it will whisper peace and joy to their souls; it will take malice, hatred, strife and all evil from their hearts; and their whole desire will be to do good, bring forth righteousness and build up the kingdom of God" (*Manuscript History of Brigham Young,* 529).

## Feeling the Power of the Holy Ghost

A friend of mine once told me about his experience in coming to know and understand the gift of the Holy Ghost. He had prayed often and longed to know the truth of the gospel. Although he felt at peace with his beliefs, he had never received the certain knowledge for which he hungered. He had reconciled himself to the fact that he might be one of those who would have to walk through this life relying upon the faith of others.

One morning, while pondering the scriptures, he felt something surge through his body from the top of his head to the bottom of his feet. "I was immersed in a feeling of such intense love and pure joy," he explained. "I cannot describe the measure of what I felt at that time other than to say I was enveloped in joy so profound there was no room in me for any other sensation."

Even as he felt this outpouring of the Holy Ghost, he wondered if possibly he was just imagining what was happening. "The more I wondered," he said, "the more intense the feelings became, until it was all I could do to tearfully say, 'It is enough.'"

As a boy, my father had a similar experience on the day he was baptized. He related, "When the bishop laid his hands upon my head and . . . said, 'Receive the Holy Ghost,' . . . I had a peculiar feeling . . . something that I had never experienced before . . . [that] came to my soul [and] gave me . . . a feeling of happiness, a feeling that filled my soul."

From that moment on and throughout his life, he always knew that Jesus Christ lived and directed His Church through a living prophet (Joseph L. Wirthlin, in Conference Report, Apr. 1956, 12).

There are many today who have felt promptings from the Holy Ghost as they have studied the Book of Mormon or listened to the testimonies of missionaries and friends. Unto these I say, as an Apostle of the Lord Jesus Christ, the gospel in its fulness is restored to the earth once again! Joseph Smith was a true prophet who translated the Book of Mormon through the gift and power of God. I urge all to read the Book of Mormon and apply its promise: "When ye shall receive these things, I would exhort you that ye would ask God, the Eternal Father, in the name of Christ, if these things are not true; and if ye shall ask with a sincere heart, with real intent, having faith in Christ, he will manifest the truth of it unto you, by the power of the Holy Ghost" (Moroni 10:4).

To you who are not members of the Church, I urge you with all the tenderness of my heart—do not resist the truth any longer. Give place in your hearts to this heavenly light. Have faith, repent, and be baptized in the name of Jesus Christ for the remission of your sins, and you too shall receive this unspeakable gift of the Holy Ghost.

*(Adapted from an April 2003 general conference address)*

8

# SHALL HE FIND FAITH ON THE EARTH?

I invite you to think about this question the Savior asked nearly 2,000 years ago: "When the Son of man cometh, shall he find faith on the earth?" (Luke 18:8).

## *First Principle of the Gospel*

What is true faith? Faith is defined as "belief and trust in and loyalty to God; . . . firm belief in something for which there is no proof" (*Webster's Ninth New Collegiate Dictionary*, 446). We believe that "faith is to hope for things which are not seen, but which are true . . . , and must be centered in Jesus Christ." In fact, we believe that "faith in Jesus Christ is the first principle of the gospel" (Bible Dictionary, 669–70).

## *A Widow's Faith*

There are those who can teach us regarding faith if we will but open our hearts and our minds. One such person is a woman whose husband had died. Left alone to raise her son, she had tried to find ways of supporting herself, but she lived in a time of terrible famine. Food was scarce and many were perishing because of hunger.

As available food diminished, so did the woman's hope of surviving.

Every day, she watched helplessly as her meager supply of food decreased.

Hoping for relief but finding none, the woman finally realized the day had come when she had only enough food for one last meal.

It was then that a stranger approached and asked the unthinkable. "Bring me, I pray thee," he said to her, "a morsel of bread."

The woman turned to the man and said, "As the Lord thy God liveth, I have not a cake, but an handful of meal in a barrel, and a little oil in a cruse." She told him she was about to prepare it as a last meal for herself and her son, "that we may eat it, and die."

She did not know that the man before her was the prophet Elijah, sent to her by the Lord. What this prophet told her next may seem surprising to those today who do not understand the principle of faith.

"Fear not," he said to her, "but make me thereof a little cake first, and bring it unto me, and after make for thee and for thy son."

Can you imagine what she must have thought? What she must have felt? She hardly had time to reply when the man continued, "For thus saith the Lord God of Israel, The barrel of meal shall not waste, neither shall the cruse of oil fail, until the day that the Lord sendeth rain upon the earth."

The woman, after hearing this prophetic promise, went in faith and did as Elijah had directed. "And she, and he, and her house, did eat many days. And the barrel of meal wasted not, neither did the cruse of oil fail, according to the word of the Lord, which he spake by Elijah" (1 Kings 17:11–16).

In the wisdom of our day, the prophet's request may seem unfair and selfish. In the wisdom of our day, the widow's response may appear foolish and unwise. That is largely because we often learn to make decisions based upon what we see. We make decisions based on the evidence before us and what appears to be in our immediate, best interest.

"Faith," on the other hand, "is the substance of things hoped for, the evidence of things not seen" (Hebrews 11:1–40; Ether 12:7–22). Faith has eyes that penetrate the darkness, seeing into the light beyond. "Your faith should not stand in the wisdom of men, but in the power of God" (1 Corinthians 2:5).

## Failure to Exercise Faith

Too often today, we do not rely on faith so much as on our own ability to reason and solve problems. If we become ill, we trust that modern medicine can work healing miracles. We can travel great distances in a short time. We have at our fingertips information that five hundred years ago would have made the poorest man a prince.

## True Faith

"The just shall live by faith" (Romans 1:17), we are told in holy writ. I ask again, what is faith?

Faith exists when absolute confidence in that which we cannot see combines with action that is in absolute conformity to the will of our Heavenly Father. Without all three—first, absolute confidence; second, action; and third, absolute conformity—all we have is a counterfeit, a weak and watered-down faith. Let me discuss each of these three imperatives of faith.

### Confidence

First, we must have confidence in that which we cannot see. When Thomas finally felt the prints of the nails and thrust his hand into the side of the resurrected Savior, he confessed that he, at last, believed.

"Jesus saith unto him, Thomas, because thou hast seen me, thou hast believed: blessed are they that have not seen, and yet have believed" (John 20:29).

Peter echoed those words when he praised early followers for their faith in Jesus the Christ. He said: "Whom having not seen, ye love; in whom, though now ye see him not, yet believing, ye rejoice with joy unspeakable and full of glory: Receiving the end of your faith, even the salvation of your souls" (1 Peter 1:8–9).

## Action

Second, for our faith to make a difference, we must act. We must do all that is in our power to change passive belief into active faith, for truly, "faith, if it hath not works, is dead" (James 2:17).

In 1998, President Gordon B. Hinckley raised a voice of warning to the Church as well as to the world at large. He said: "I am suggesting that the time has come to get our houses in order. So many of our people are living on the very edge of their incomes. In fact, some are living on borrowings. . . . I am troubled by the huge consumer installment debt which hangs over the people of the nation, including our own people" ("To the Boys and to the Men," *Ensign*, Nov. 1998, 53).

When these prophetic words were uttered, some faithful members of the Church mustered their faith and heeded the counsel of the prophet. They are profoundly grateful today that they did. Others perhaps believed that what the prophet said was true but lacked faith, even as small as a grain of mustard seed. Consequently, some have suffered financial, personal, and family distress.

## Conformity with the Will of God

Third, one's faith should be in conformity with the will of our Heavenly Father, including His laws of nature. The sparrow flying into a hurricane may believe that he can successfully navigate the storm, but in the end, the unforgiving natural law will convince him otherwise.

Are we wiser than the sparrow? Often what passes for faith in this world is little more than gullibility. It is distressing to see how eager some people are to embrace fads and theories while rejecting or giving less credence and attention to the everlasting principles of the gospel of Jesus Christ. It is distressing also how eagerly some rush into foolish or unethical behavior, believing that God will somehow deliver them from the inevitable tragic consequences of their actions. They even go so far as to ask for the blessings of heaven, knowing in their hearts that what they do is contrary to the will of our Father in Heaven.

How do we know when our faith conforms to the will of our Heavenly Father and that He approves of that which we seek? We must know the word of God. One of the reasons we immerse ourselves in the scriptures is to know of Heavenly Father's dealings with man from the beginning. If the desires of our heart are contrary to scripture, then we should not pursue them further.

Next, we must heed the counsel of latter-day prophets as they give inspired instruction.

Additionally, we must ponder and pray and seek the guidance of the Spirit. If we do so, the Lord has promised, "I will tell you in your mind and in your heart, by the Holy Ghost, which shall come upon you and which shall dwell in your heart" (D&C 8:2).

Only when our faith is aligned with the will of our Heavenly Father will we be empowered to receive the blessings we seek.

## Principle of Power

Truly understood and properly practiced, faith is one of the grand and glorious powers of eternity. It is a force powerful beyond our comprehension. "Through faith . . . the worlds were framed by the word of God" (Hebrews 11:3). Through faith, waters are parted, the sick healed, the wicked silenced, and salvation made possible.

Our faith is the foundation upon which all our spiritual lives rest. It should be the most important resource of our lives. Faith is not so much something we believe; faith is something we live.

Remember the words of the Savior: "If thou canst believe, all things are possible to him that believeth" (Mark 9:23). "He that believeth on me, the works that I do shall he do also; and greater works than these shall he do" (John 14:12).

## *Teaching the Principle*

Those who walk in faith will feel their lives encompassed with the light and blessings of heaven. They will understand and know things that others cannot. Those who do not walk in faith esteem the things of the Spirit as foolishness, for the things of the Spirit can only be discerned by the Spirit (see 1 Corinthians 2:14).

The manifestations of heaven are sealed from the understanding of those who do not believe. "For if there be no faith among the children of men," Moroni tells us, "God can do no miracle among them; wherefore, he showed not himself until after their faith" (Ether 12:12).

Yet throughout history, even in times of great spiritual darkness, there were those who, through eyes of faith, pierced the darkness and beheld things as they truly are. Moroni reveals that "there were many whose faith was so exceedingly strong . . . [they] could not be kept from within the veil, but truly saw with their eyes the things which they had beheld with an eye of faith, and they were glad" (Ether 12:19).

Our homes should be havens of faith. Mothers and fathers should teach the principles of faith to their children. Grandparents, too, can help. When I'm at a family gathering, I try to spend time, when appropriate, in one-on-one discussions with some of our grandchildren. I sit with them and ask them a few questions: "How are you doing?" "How is school?"

Then I ask them how they feel about the true Church, which means so much to me. I try to discover the depth of their faith and testimony. If I perceive areas of uncertainty, I'll ask them, "Would you accept a goal from your granddad?"

Then I'll suggest they read the scriptures daily and recommend they kneel down every morning and night in family prayer and also pray individually. I admonish them to always go to their sacrament meetings. I admonish them to keep themselves pure and clean, always attend their meetings, and finally, among other things, always strive to be sensitive to the whisperings of the Lord.

One time after such a talk with Joseph, our eight-year-old grandson, he looked into my eyes and asked this pointed question, "May I go now, Granddad?" He ran from my arms, and I've often thought, "Did I do any good?" Apparently I did because the next day he said, "Thanks for the little talk we had."

I promise that if we approach our children and grandchildren with love rather than reproach, we will find that their faith will increase as a result of the influence and testimony of someone who loves the Savior and His divine Church.

## Trials

Sometimes the world appears dark. Sometimes our faith is tried. Sometimes we feel that the heavens are closed against us. Yet we should not despair. We should never abandon our faith. We should not lose hope.

A few years ago, I began to notice that things around me were beginning to darken. It troubled me because simple things such as reading the print in my scriptures were becoming more difficult. I wondered what had happened to the quality of the light bulbs and wondered why manufacturers today couldn't make things as they had in years past.

I replaced the bulbs with brighter ones. They, too, were dim. I blamed the poor design of the lamps and bulbs. I even questioned whether the brightness of the sun was fading before the thought occurred to me that the problem might not be with the amount of light in the room—the problem might be with my own eyes.

Shortly thereafter I went to an ophthalmologist who assured me that the world was not going dark at all. A cataract on my eye was the reason the light seemed to be fading. I placed my faith in the capable hands of this trained specialist, the cataract was removed, and behold, light again flooded my life! The light had never diminished; only my capacity to see the light had been lessened.

This taught me a profound truth. Often when the world seems dark, when the heavens seem distant, we seek to blame everything around us, when the real cause of the darkness may be a lack of faith within ourselves.

Be of good cheer. Have faith and confidence. The Lord will not forsake you.

The Lord has promised: "Search diligently, pray always, and be believing, and all things shall work together for your good, if ye walk uprightly" (D&C 90:24).

I know, as did Alma of old, that "whosoever shall put their trust in God shall be supported in their trials, and their troubles, and their afflictions, and shall be lifted up at the last day" (Alma 36:3).

Our Heavenly Father is a powerful, moving, directing being. Though we may, at times, bear burdens of sorrow, pain, and grief; though we may struggle to understand trials of faith we are called to pass through; though life may seem dark and dreary—through faith we can have absolute confidence that a loving Heavenly Father is at our side.

As the Apostle Paul promised, "Therefore being justified by faith, we have peace with God through our Lord Jesus Christ" (Romans 5:1).

And one day, we will fully see through the darkness into the light. We will understand His eternal plan, His mercy, and His love.

"When the Son of man cometh, shall he find faith on the earth?"

Perhaps as members of the Church trust with all their hearts, transform their hopes and beliefs into action, and seek to align themselves with the will of the Lord, the answer to the question the Savior asked 2,000 years ago will be a resounding "Yes! He will find faith. He will find faith among those who take upon themselves His name. He will find it among those who are living His divine principles."

*(Adapted from an October 2002 general conference address)*

# 9

## TRUE TO THE TRUTH

In our day, great things are happening in the Kingdom!

The Church is moving forward throughout the world as never before. It is a privilege for us to witness in our lifetime such exciting progress toward fulfillment of the great prophecy that "the kingdom . . . may become a great mountain and fill the whole earth" (D&C 109:72; see also Daniel 2:31–45).

Great things are happening because so many Latter-day Saints faithfully "act upon the points of [God's] law and commandments." As one of the leaders of the Lord's Church, I am thrilled to see so much good being done by many righteous and faithful members of the Church. Please know that the General Authorities pray often that our Heavenly Father will help you to be true to the covenants that you have made with Him.

### "Walk the Path of Faith"

In a powerful message, President Gordon B. Hinckley issued both an invitation and a challenge to the members of the Church: "I invite you," he said, "to walk the path of faith with me. I challenge you to stand for that which is right and true and good" ("'True to the Faith,'" *Ensign*, June 1996, 4). Our prophet exemplifies an unwavering commitment and example of walking in this path of faith and diligence. In our everyday lives, are we following his inspired example? As members of The Church of Jesus Christ of Latter-day Saints, are we rising to his challenge "to stand for that which is right and true and good"? Citing a favorite hymn, President Hinckley went on to admonish, "Let us be [true], 'true to the faith that our parents have cherished, *true to the truth* for which martyrs have perished'" (Gordon B. Hinckley, "'True to the Faith,'" *Ensign*, June 1996, 8; emphasis added).

I ask, are you "true to the truth"?

The thirteenth article of faith states that "we believe in being . . . true." The truth of the restored gospel, as this hymn highlights, is "the fairest gem, . . . the brightest prize to which mortals or Gods can aspire. . . . Truth, the sum of existence, will weather the worst, eternal, unchanged, evermore" ("Oh Say, What Is Truth?" *Hymns*, no. 272).

Yes, the fulness of the gospel is a pearl of great price, worth any effort to obtain it. Though we are taught to develop our talents and provide for our families, nevertheless we must be careful not to let the pursuit of our career path divert us from the gospel path.

We must be "true to the truth" and stay on the "strait and narrow path which leads to eternal life" (2 Nephi 31:18). Remember Alma's counsel to his son, Corianton: "Suffer not yourself to be led away by any vain or foolish thing" (Alma 39:11).

"Keep the commandments. In this there is safety and peace" (*Hymns*, no. 303). Nothing this world has to offer can surpass the joy of living the gospel! No worldly wealth or possession, no degree of fame or recognition, can supplant the satisfaction of feeling the warmth and peace of the Spirit of the Lord in our hearts and in our homes.

Little wonder that we sing:

> *Sweet is the peace the gospel brings*
> *To seeking minds and true.*
> *With light refulgent on its wings*
> *It clears the human view.*
>
> (Hymns, *no. 14*)

As we strive for success, we cannot allow "any vain or foolish thing" to divert us from the path of faith and lead us away from being *true* to our covenants.

## "*True to the Faith*"

I like the word *true*. It powerfully explains basic gospel principles with insightful clarity.

*True* means: "steadfast, loyal . . . honest, just" (definitions in this and the following paragraph are from *Merriam-Webster's Collegiate Dictionary*, 10th ed., "true")—all virtues that we should cultivate in our lives.

## "*No Hypocrisy and No Deception*"

Truth can also describe "that which is [actually] the case rather than what is manifest or assumed," as in the true dimensions of a problem or the true nature of an individual.

Do we, indeed, actually live the gospel, or do we just *manifest* the appearance of righteousness so that those around us *assume* we are faithful when, in reality, our hearts and unseen actions are *not* true to the Lord's teachings?

Do we take on ourselves only the "form of godliness" while denying the "power thereof"? (see JS–H 1:19).

Are we righteous in fact, or do we feign obedience only when we think others are watching?

The Lord has made it clear that He will not be fooled by appearances, and He has warned us not to be false to Him or to others. He has cautioned us to be wary of those who project a false front, who put on a bright pretense that hides a darker reality. We will be well advised to remember that the Lord "looketh on the heart" and *not* on the "outward appearance" (see 1 Samuel 16:7).

The Savior taught us to "judge not according to the appearance"

(John 7:24) and warned us against ravening wolves who "come to [us] in sheep's clothing" and whose deception can only be discovered "by [examining] their fruits" (Matthew 7:15–16).

Nephi taught that we must walk the path of faith "with full purpose of heart, acting no hypocrisy and no deception before God" (2 Nephi 31:13; see also Jacob 6:5; Mosiah 7:33; 3 Nephi 10:6; D&C 18:27–28).

We know that "a double minded man is unstable in all his ways" (James 1:8) and that we cannot "serve two masters" (Matthew 6:24; see also Luke 16:13; 3 Nephi 13:24). President Marion G. Romney wisely observed that there are too many of us "who try to serve the Lord without offending the devil" ("The Price of Peace," *Ensign,* Oct. 1983, 6).

We are also counseled, "The Lord requireth the heart and a willing mind" (D&C 64:34). Hence, the first of the Ten Commandments is "Thou shalt have no other gods before me" (Exodus 20:3), and the Savior confirmed that the first and great commandment is "Thou shalt love the Lord thy God with *all* thy heart, and with *all* thy soul, and with *all* thy mind" (Matthew 22:37–38; emphasis added; see also verses 36–40). Only when we give our all and overcome our pride and walk the path of faith without deviation can we honestly sing, "Lord, accept our *true* devotion" (*Hymns,* no. 107; emphasis added).

## Faith in Every Footstep

The valiant pioneer Saints who sacrificed so much "to bring forth and establish the cause of Zion" (D&C 6:6) walked a path of faith through great physical hardship that forged and tempered their souls. With genuine commitment to the cause of truth, they held fast to the iron rod in spite of opposition or challenge. They were "true to the truth" and gave their all in establishing and living the restored gospel.

## Be True to Your Covenants

One of the great blessings of the restored gospel is the privilege of entering into sacred covenants with our Father in Heaven—covenants made binding by virtue of the holy priesthood. When we are baptized and confirmed, when brethren are ordained in the offices of the priesthood, when we go to the temple and receive our endowments, when we enter into the new and everlasting covenant of eternal marriage—in all these sacred ordinances, we make solemn commitments to keep God's commandments.

We covenant that we will show our love for our Heavenly Father through humble service and diligent obedience and thereby prove ourselves to be "good and faithful servant[s]" (Matthew 25:21, 23).

If we are obedient to the commandments and true to our covenants, our Father in Heaven will grant us the blessing of "eternal life, which gift is the greatest of all the gifts of God" (D&C 14:7). "All that [the] Father hath" (D&C 84:38) is promised to those who walk the path of faith and remain true to their covenants. Those "who [do] the works of righteousness shall receive [their] reward, even peace in this world, and eternal life in the world to come" (D&C 59:23).

## An Eternal Stewardship

Each of you has an eternal calling from which no Church officer has authority to release you. This is a calling given you by our Heavenly Father himself. In this eternal calling, as with all other callings, you have a stewardship, and "it is required of the Lord, at the hand of every steward, to render an account of his stewardship, both in time and in eternity" (D&C 72:3). This most important stewardship is the glorious responsibility your Father in Heaven has given you to watch over and care for your own soul.

At some future day, you and I will each hear the voice of the Lord calling us forward to render an account of our mortal stewardship. This accounting will occur when we are called up to "stand before [the Lord] at the great and judgment day" (2 Nephi 9:22).

Each day on this earth is but a small part of eternity. The day of resurrection and final judgment will surely come for each one of us.

Then our Father in Heaven's great and noble heart will be saddened for those of His children who, because they chose evil, will be cast out, unworthy to return to His presence. But He will welcome with loving arms and with indescribable joy those who have succeeded in being "*true to the truth.*" Righteous living, combined with the grace of the Atonement, will qualify us to stand before Him with clean hearts and clear consciences.

As leaders of the Church, as servants of a compassionate Father in Heaven, we likewise want each of you to return to His presence. We love you and desire with all our hearts to see you rejoice with your Father in Heaven and with your parents, your children, and other loved ones in that great day of judgment and accountability. So we ask, "Are you true?" And, therefore, we admonish you, as did Jacob, to "prepare your souls for that glorious day when justice shall be administered unto the righteous, even the day of judgment, that ye may not shrink with awful fear; that ye may not remember your awful guilt in perfectness" (2 Nephi 9:46).

What can help us to strengthen our resolve to keep on the narrow path of righteousness and truth so our souls will welcome our day of judgment as a glorious day? May I offer five suggestions.

First, the fundamental reason why the Lord has instructed us to conduct worthiness interviews in His Church is to teach us to keep the commitments we make. In short, we are to be trained during this season of mortal probation to master ourselves (see Alma 34:33–37) to live with integrity and be true to our covenants. Worthiness interviews are conducted in a spirit of loving concern for each son and daughter of a loving God. These interviews represent a rehearsal for final judgment. Such interviews are a blessing, a choice opportunity to account to the

Lord through His authorized servants for the sacred stewardship we all have to "watch [ourselves], and [our] thoughts, and [our] words, and [our] deeds" (Mosiah 4:30).

Second, in the Lord's Church, we are reminded of our sacred covenants every time we partake of the sacrament.

Third, each time we return to the temple, we are reminded of the covenants we made when we received our endowments.

Fourth, in our home teaching and visiting teaching we demonstrate our determination to keep our promise to serve others (see Mosiah 18:8–10).

Fifth, the Savior Himself knew as we also should know that He was accountable to His Father. He taught that His sacred stewardship was "to do the will of him who sent me" (John 4:34). In His great intercessory prayer, the Lord reported to the Father, "I have finished the work which thou gavest me to do" (John 17:4).

When we are living righteously, we rejoice that we can report positively our worthiness and our preparation for continued blessings, whether they be the honor of receiving the priesthood, the blessings of temple attendance, the satisfaction of the Young Women Personal Progress achievements, or the blessings of service in whatever our calling might be.

Such mortal experiences give us the opportunity to assess what we are doing with our lives. All help us school our souls and strengthen our characters in preparation for that final interview.

Should the prospect of that interview frighten us? Not if we are faithful because "if [we] are prepared [we] shall not fear" (D&C 38:30).

When we have need to repent, interviews are not always easy. Thank goodness the Lord has called wonderful bishops, stake presidents, and other priesthood leaders, who can provide loving guidance to help us repent and cleanse ourselves "that [we] may stand blameless before God at the last day" (D&C 4:2).

Worthiness interviews, sacrament meetings, temple attendance, and other Church meetings are all part of the plan that the Lord provides to educate our souls, to help us develop the healthy habit of constantly checking our bearings in order to stay on the path of faith. Regular spiritual "checkups" help us successfully navigate life's highways and byways.

In my own quiet moments of personal reflection, I have benefited from humbly asking myself the simple question, "Am I true?"

May I suggest that we can all benefit by looking deep inside our hearts during reverent moments of worship and prayer and asking ourselves this simple question, "Am I true?"

The question becomes more powerfully useful if we are completely honest in our answers and if we are motivated by them to make necessary repentant course corrections that will keep us on the path of faith.

I testify that our Father in Heaven loves each of us and that if we are true to the truth, accept the invitation to walk with President Gordon B. Hinckley in the path of faith, and keep our covenants, we *will* find "peace in this world, and eternal life in the world to come" (D&C 59:23). I testify also that our Heavenly Father lives, that His Beloved Son is our Redeemer, and that President Gordon B. Hinckley is, indeed, our prophet, seer, and revelator during this inspiring time of our mortal lives. May we be blessed in our efforts to prepare for that great day when, with our loved ones, we can return rejoicing into the presence of our Father in Heaven.

*(Adapted from an April 1997 general conference address)*

# 10

# THE BOOK OF MORMON: FOUNDATION OF OUR FAITH

I love the Book of Mormon. I know that it's true. I have studied it; I have prayed about it. And I will continue to study it. It is another testament of our Lord and Savior, Jesus Christ. The events and people described in the book are real. The Book of Mormon can teach us powerful, eternal truths if we will simply open its pages to search, ponder, and pray about this priceless treasure that the Lord has given us.

I want very much for you to come to love the Book of Mormon as I do. Studying the Book of Mormon will bless your life. Obeying its teachings will bring you peace and happiness. Your Father in Heaven loves you. Your church leaders love and respect you. "I have no greater joy than to hear that my children [and this pertains to all of you, also] walk in truth" (3 John 1:4). I promise you as a special witness of the Lord Jesus Christ, that if you will live according to the teachings of the gospel found in the Book of Mormon, your life will be full and rewarding.

## Teaching about the Book of Mormon

In my lifelong study of the Book of Mormon, I have been struck by Nephi's approach to scripture study and teaching. Nephi always wanted to "more fully persuade [his people] to believe in the Lord their Redeemer" (1 Nephi 19:23). He was anxious to bear testimony of the

Savior and teach future generations about the saving power of Christ's atonement. Nephi wrote, "we are made alive in Christ because of our faith . . . we prophesy of Christ, and we write according to our prophecies that our children may know to what source they may look for a remission of their sins" (2 Nephi 25:25–26). In teaching his people, Nephi sought to "liken all scriptures unto [them], that it might be for [their] profit and learning" (1 Nephi 19:23).

In this chapter, I would like to follow Nephi's good example in teaching you about the Book of Mormon.

In November of 1841, on a Sabbath Day in Nauvoo, Illinois, Joseph Smith "spent the day in . . . council with the Twelve Apostles at the house of President [Brigham] Young, conversing with them upon a variety of subjects." On that occasion, the Prophet "told the brethren that the Book of Mormon was the most correct of any book on earth, and the keystone of our religion, and a man would get nearer to God by abiding by its precepts, than by any other book" (*Teachings of the Prophet Joseph Smith*, 194).

## Nearer to God

As members of the Savior's church, we struggle with the challenges of living in "a world set on a course which we cannot follow" (Boyd K. Packer, "The Father and the Family," *Ensign,* May 1994, 21). Satan is working overtime to lead us astray. Swirling all around us are the whirlwinds of temptation. As the world moves further away from our Heavenly Father, we have the promise of the Prophet Joseph Smith that abiding by the precepts of the Book of Mormon will draw us nearer to God than the teachings of any other book.

Though the Internet now gives us access to a worldwide web of vast data banks, too many people find themselves "ever learning, and never able to come to the knowledge of the truth" (2 Timothy 3:7). Too many are "tossed to and fro, and carried about with every wind of doctrine"; they are deceived "by the sleight of men, and cunning craftiness whereby they lie in wait to deceive" (Ephesians 4:14). But, for us, the Book of Mormon is an iron rod that we can hang on to, to guide us through the mists of darkness and confusion. We need not desperately search for meaning in our lives among the many philosophies of men. We know where we can find God, where we can learn His truths and gain strength to be like Him.

The Book of Mormon teaches that we get nearer to God when we follow the example of the Savior and do what He did. In that book, the Lord invites us: "Follow me, and do the things which ye have seen me do" (2 Nephi 31:12). He also directs us: "Behold I am the light which ye shall hold up—that which ye have seen me do" (3 Nephi 18:24). Finally, the Lord poses and answers this sobering question: "Therefore, what manner of men ought ye to be? Verily I say unto you, even as I am" (3 Nephi 27:27).

Why should we seek to be closer to God? Because "the love of God . . . is the most desirable above all things . . . and the most joyous to the soul" (1 Nephi 11:22–23). President Ezra Taft Benson, who taught powerfully about the Book of Mormon, explained that there is "something deep in our hearts that longs to draw nearer to God, to be more like Him in our daily walk, to feel His presence with us constantly" ("The Book of Mormon—Keystone of Our Religion," *Ensign*, Nov. 1986, 7). President Benson further explained that the Book of Mormon helps us draw nearer to God because: "There is a power in the book which will begin to flow into your lives the moment you begin a serious study of the book. You will find greater power to resist temptation. You will find the power to avoid deception. . . . These are not idle promises, but exactly what the Prophet Joseph Smith meant when he said the Book of Mormon will help us draw nearer to God" (*Teachings of Ezra Taft Benson*, Bookcraft, 1988, 54).

## Testifies of Christ

In the October 1982 General Conference, Elder Boyd K. Packer announced the decision of the General Authorities to include in the title of the Book of Mormon the subtitle, "Another Testament of Jesus Christ" ("Scriptures," *Ensign,* Nov. 1982, 53). Though significant for many reasons, this decision did not represent a radical new direction. This action simply emphasized what has always been true of the Book of Mormon. Its purpose is to testify of Jesus Christ. The title page states clearly that the book was "written by way of commandment, and also by the spirit of prophecy and of revelation . . . to the convincing of the Jew and the Gentile that Jesus is the Christ, the Eternal God, manifesting himself unto all nations."

President Benson pointed out that "over one-half of all the verses in the Book of Mormon refer to our Lord. Some form of Christ's name is mentioned more frequently per verse in the Book of Mormon than even in the New Testament" ("Come unto Christ," *Ensign,* Nov. 1987, 83). President Gordon B. Hinckley has told us that "the great and stirring . . . [message of the Book of Mormon] is a testimony, vibrant and true, that Jesus is the Christ, the promised Messiah." (*Teachings of Gordon B. Hinckley,* 1997, 37). President Hinckley also makes this suggestion for studying the Book of Mormon: "I suggest that you read it . . . and take a pencil, a red one if you have one, and put a little check mark every time there is a reference to Jesus Christ in that book. And there will come to you a very real conviction as you do so that this [book] is in very deed another witness for the Lord Jesus Christ" (Ibid., 44).

## Contains the Fulness of the Gospel

In the twentieth section of the Doctrine and Covenants, in verse nine, the Lord declares that the Book of Mormon contains "the fulness of the gospel of Jesus Christ." This is another reason why we can get nearer to God by abiding by its precepts, than by any other book because the full gospel of the Savior is presented in clarity and plainness. Nephi twice repeats that his "soul delighteth in plainness," (2 Nephi 25:4; 2 Nephi 31:3) and explains that communicating in plainness is how "the Lord God work[s] among the children of men. . . . for he speaketh unto men according to their language, unto their understanding" (2 Nephi 31:3).

The Book of Mormon speaks plainly in our language to help us clearly understand sublime gospel concepts. President Benson put it this way: "The Book of Mormon contains the clearest, most concise, and complete explanation [of the gospel]. There is no other record to compare with it. . . . The Book of Mormon contains the most comprehensive account of . . . fundamental doctrines" (*Teachings of Ezra Taft Benson,* 56).

"We believe the Bible to be the word of God" (Articles of Faith 1:8). But the fragmentary nature of the biblical record and the errors in it, resulting from multiple transcriptions, translations, and misinterpretations, means that some "plain and most precious" (1 Nephi 13:26) truths were lost. God brought forth the Book of Mormon as a second witness that corroborates and strengthens the Bible's testimony of the Savior. The Book of Mormon does not replace the Bible. Rather, it expands, extends, clarifies, and amplifies our knowledge of the Savior. It restores "the plain and precious things taken away from the [Bible]" (1 Nephi 13:28). For example, the Book of Mormon clarifies the mode of baptism and clearly explains it is done by immersion (see Mosiah 18:13–15).

## Keystone of Our Religion

Joseph Smith said that the Book of Mormon is "the keystone of our religion." The keystone is the crown of an arch, the center stone that holds both sides in place. The whole structure of the arch is dependent on the keystone. If it is removed, the arch crumbles. And so it is with The Church of Jesus Christ of Latter-day Saints. If the keystone Book of Mormon were not true, then Joseph Smith would not be a prophet of God, and the whole structure of the Restoration would collapse in a heap of rubble. In this regard, President Ezra Taft Benson taught that the Book of Mormon "is the keystone in our witness of Christ. It is the keystone of our doctrine It is the keystone of our testimony" ("The Book of Mormon—Keystone of Our Religion," *Ensign*, Nov. 1986, 5).

Significantly, the only major event of the Restoration preceding the coming forth of the Book of Mormon was the First Vision. After Joseph's humble prayer was answered in the Sacred Grove in the spring of 1820, the Prophet was carefully prepared by the Lord and by the angel Moroni over the next seven years to become the instrument through which the Book of Mormon was translated by the gift and power of God and then published to the world. Joseph received the plates at the age of twenty-one in September 1827. Before priesthood authority could be restored, before the Church could be organized, before the revelations that eventually became the Doctrine and Covenants, the work of bringing forth the Book of Mormon took priority.

Because of the Book of Mormon's preeminence in "the restoration of all things" (D&C 27:6), the Lord has warned us not to take lightly the book and its resounding testimony of His gospel. In the twentieth section of the Doctrine and Covenants, the Lord warns that for "those who harden their hearts in unbelief, and reject [the Book of Mormon], it shall turn to their own condemnation" (D&C 20:15), while promising that "those who receive it in faith, and work righteousness, shall receive a crown of eternal life" (D&C 20:14).

The Book of Mormon is also the keystone of our missionary labors throughout the world. It is tangible evidence of the divine calling of the Prophet Joseph Smith. It can be read, studied, pondered, and discussed. Individual sons and daughters of our Father in Heaven can ask God if it is true. When the Holy Ghost bears witness of its truthfulness, people's hearts are changed. They gain an increased faith in Christ, they desire the blessings of repentance and baptism, and they join the Church.

Today [2007], the Book of Mormon is available in 90 languages: 72 languages with complete translations of the entire book and an additional 32 with translated selections. Since its first printing in 1830, the

Church has published nearly 90 million copies. But there is still much to be done.

As you young people prepare to serve missions and to become parents, I invite you to study the Book of Mormon and pray to gain a strong testimony of its truthfulness. Nothing will be of greater value to you as you prepare for the responsibilities and trials of adulthood. A heartfelt testimony of the Book of Mormon will make you great missionaries and loving, patient parents.

And so I repeat, I love the Book of Mormon. I know that it is true. I bear fervent testimony that it will bless your life if you will prayerfully, humbly study its message. I testify also that God is our Father and loves us very much. Jesus Christ is our Savior. He lives today and leads this Church. "Knowing the calamity which should come upon the inhabitants of the earth" (D&C 1:17) in our time, He raised up the Prophet Joseph Smith to restore His true Church to the earth. We are led today by a living prophet.

If you don't have your own testimony of these glorious truths, please take out your Book of Mormon, find a quiet place, say a prayer to invite the Holy Ghost to help you understand, and begin to read. I promise you that your prayer will be answered and that a testimony will come.

*(Adapted from a talk to the youth of the*
*Bonneville First Ward, Salt Lake Bonneville*
*Stake, on 9 January 1998)*

# PRESS
# ON
## WITH HOPE

# 11

# Press On

## Why Me?

I have lived long enough to experience firsthand many of the challenges of life. I have known exceptional people who have endured severe trials while others, at least on the surface, seem to have lived charmed lives.

Often those who struggle with adversity ask the question "Why did this happen to me?" They spend sleepless nights wondering why they feel so lonely, sick, discouraged, oppressed, or brokenhearted.

The question "Why me?" can be a difficult one to answer and often leads to frustration and despair. There is a better question to ask ourselves. That question is "What can I learn from this experience?"

The way we answer that question may determine the quality of our lives not only on this earth but also in the eternities to come. Though our trials are diverse, there is one thing the Lord expects of us no matter our difficulties and sorrows: He expects us to press on.

## The Doctrine of Enduring to the End

The gospel of Jesus Christ includes enduring unto the end as one of its bedrock doctrines. Jesus taught, "He that shall endure to the end, the same shall be saved" (Matthew 24:13) and, "If ye continue in my word, then are ye my disciples indeed" (John 8:31). Some think of enduring to the end as simply patiently suffering through challenges. It is so much more than that—it is part of the process of coming unto Christ and being perfected in Him.

Nephi, the Book of Mormon prophet, taught: "Wherefore, ye must press forward with a steadfastness in Christ, having a perfect brightness of hope, and a love of God and of all men. Wherefore, if ye shall press forward, feasting upon the word of Christ, and endure to the end, behold, thus saith the Father: Ye shall have eternal life" (2 Nephi 31:20).

Enduring to the end is the doctrine of continuing on the path leading to eternal life after one has entered into the path through faith, repentance, baptism, and receiving the Holy Ghost. Enduring to the end requires our whole heart or, as the Book of Mormon prophet Amaleki teaches, we must "come unto him, and offer [our] whole souls as an offering unto him, and continue in fasting and praying, and endure to the end; and as the Lord liveth [we] will be saved" (Omni 1:26).

Enduring to the end means that we have our lives firmly planted on gospel soil, remaining in the mainstream of the Church, humbly serving our fellowmen, living Christ-like lives, and keeping our covenants. Those who endure are balanced, consistent, humble, constantly improving, and without guile. Their testimony is not based on worldly reasons—it is based on truth, knowledge, experience, and the Spirit.

## The Parable of the Sower

The Lord Jesus Christ uses the simple parable of the sower to teach the doctrine of enduring to the end.

The sower soweth the word.
And these are they by the way side, where the word is sown;

but when they have heard, Satan cometh immediately, and taketh away the word that was sown in their hearts.

And these are they likewise which are sown on stony ground; who, when they have heard the word, immediately receive it with gladness;

And have no root in themselves, and so endure but for a time: afterward, when affliction or persecution ariseth for the word's sake, immediately they are offended.

And these are they which are sown among thorns; such as hear the word,

And the cares of this world, and the deceitfulness of riches, and the lusts of other things entering in, choke the word, and it becometh unfruitful.

And these are they which are sown on good ground; such as hear the word, and receive it, and bring forth fruit, some thirtyfold, some sixty, and some an hundred. (Mark 4:14–20.)

This parable describes the types of soil onto which seeds of truth are sown and nourished. Each type of soil represents our degree of commitment and ability to endure.

The first type of soil, that of the "way side," represents those who hear the gospel but never give the truth a chance to take root.

The second type of soil, "stony ground," represents those in the Church who, at the first sign of sacrifice or trial, run away offended, not willing to pay the price.

The third type of soil, "sown among thorns," represents some members of the Church who are distracted and obsessed by the cares, riches, and enticements of the world.

Finally, those on "good ground" are those members of the Church whose lives reflect their discipleship to the Master, whose roots go deep into gospel soil, and thereby produce abundant fruit.

## *Obstacles to Endurance*

In the parable of the sower, the Savior identifies three obstacles to endurance, obstacles that can canker our souls and stop our eternal progress.

The first obstacle of endurance, "the cares of the world," is essentially pride (see Ezra Taft Benson, "Beware of Pride," in Conference Report, Apr. 1989). Pride rears its ugly head in so many ways that are destructive. For example, intellectual pride is very prevalent in our day. Some people presume to exalt themselves above God and His anointed servants because of their learning and scholarly achievements. We must never allow our intellect to take priority over our spirit. Our intellect can feed our spirit, and our spirit can feed our intellect, but if we allow our intellect to take precedence over our spirit, we will stumble, find fault, and may even lose our testimonies.

Knowledge is very important and one of the few things that accompanies us into the next life (see D&C 130:18–19). We should always be learning; however, we must be careful not to set aside our faith in the process, because faith actually enhances our ability to learn.

The second obstacle to endurance is "the deceitfulness of riches." We should end our fixation on wealth. It is only a means to an end, which end should ultimately be the building up of the kingdom of God. I feel that some are so concerned about the type of car they drive, the expensive clothes they wear, or the size of their house in comparison to others that they lose sight of the weightier matters (see Matthew 23:23). We must be careful in our daily lives that we do not allow the things of this world to take precedence over spiritual things.

The third obstacle to endurance mentioned by the Savior is "the lusts of other things." The plague of pornography is swirling about us as never before. Pornography brings a vicious wake of immorality, broken homes, and broken lives. Pornography will sap spiritual strength to endure. Pornography is much like quicksand. Not recognizing the danger it represents, users are quickly entrapped and easily overcome as soon as they step into it. Most likely you will need assistance to escape the quicksand of pornography. But how much better it is never to step into it! It is not enough to be careful and cautious. I plead with you to resist with all your might getting involved in the least degree, lest you be caught in its insidious clutches.

## Enduring to the End Is a Principle for All

A few weeks before President Heber J. Grant passed away, one of the Brethren went to visit him in his home. Before the man left, President Grant prayed, "O God, bless me that I shall not lose my testimony and keep faithful to the end!" (cited by Elder John Longden, in Conference Report, Oct. 1958, 70). Can you imagine President Grant, one of the great prophets of the Restoration, the President of the Church for nearly twenty-seven years, praying that he would remain faithful to the end?

No one is immune from Satan's influence and temptations. Do not be so proud to think that you are beyond the adversary's influence. Be watchful that you do not fall prey to his deceptions. Stay close to the Lord through daily scripture study and daily prayer. We cannot afford to sit back and take our salvation for granted. We must be anxiously engaged our whole lives (see D&C 58:27). These words of President Brigham Young motivate and remind us that we can never give up the fight to endure: "The men and women, who desire to obtain seats in the celestial kingdom, will find that they must battle every day [for this sacred goal]" (*Discourses of Brigham Young*, selected and arranged by John A. Widtsoe [Salt Lake City: Deseret Book Co., 1954], 392).

## Strength to Endure

I know there are many who suffer from heartbreak, loneliness, pain, and setback. These difficult trials are a necessary part of the human experience. However, please do not lose hope in the Savior and His love for you. That love is constant. For He has promised that He will not leave us comfortless (see John 14:18).

When we face challenges in our lives, we are comforted by the words of the Lord in section 58 of the Doctrine and Covenants: "Ye cannot behold with your natural eyes, for the present time, the design of your God concerning those things which shall come hereafter, and the glory which shall follow after much tribulation. *For after much tribulation come the blessings.* Wherefore the day cometh that ye shall be crowned with much glory; the hour is not yet, but is nigh at hand" (D&C 58:3–4; emphasis added).

## Warren M. Johnson

Therefore, we must press on and progressively become more like the Lord in the process. We all know those who have faced great trials in life and have endured faithfully. One inspiring example is from an early Saint of the nineteenth century, Warren M. Johnson. He was assigned by Church leaders to operate Lee's Ferry, an important crossing over the Colorado River in the desert of Northern Arizona. Brother Johnson endured great challenges yet remained faithful his entire life. Listen to Brother Johnson explain his family tragedy in a letter to President Wilford Woodruff:

> In May 1891 a family . . . came here [to Lee's Ferry] from Richfield Utah, where they . . . spent the winter visiting friends. At Panguitch they buried a child, . . . without disinfecting the wagon or themselves. . . . They came to our house, and remained overnight, mingling with my little children.
>
> We knew nothing of the nature of the disease [diphtheria], but had faith in God, as we were here on a very hard mission, and had tried as hard as we knew how to obey the [commandments] . . . that our children would be spared. But alas, in four

and a half days [the oldest boy died] in my arms. Two more
were taken down with the disease and we fasted and prayed as
much as we thought it wisdom as we had many duties to perform here. We fasted [for] twenty-four hours and once I fasted
[for] forty hours, but to no avail, for both my little girls died
also. About a week after their death my fifteen year old daughter Melinda was [also] stricken down and we did all we could for
her but she [soon] followed the others. . . . Three of my dear
girls and one boy [have] been taken from us, and the end is not
yet. My oldest girl nineteen years old is now prostrate [from]
the disease, and we are fasting and praying in her behalf today
. . . I would ask for your faith and prayers in our behalf however.
What have we done that the Lord has left us, and what can we
do to gain his favor again[?]

A short time later, Brother Johnson wrote a local leader and friend,
expressing his faith to press on:

It is the hardest trial of my life, but I set out for salvation
and am determined that . . . through the help of Heavenly
Father that I [would] hold fast to the iron rod no matter what
troubles [came] upon me. I have not slackened in the performance of my duties, and hope and trust that I shall have the faith
and prayers of my brethren, that I can live so as to receive the
blessings.

(as quoted in *Best Loved Stories of the LDS People,* vol. 3,
107–08.)

Though heavy trials such as those endured by Brother Johnson can
help us face our own challenges, may I suggest three attributes to foster
endurance in our day.

## Suggestions for Endurance

First, testimony. Testimony gives us the eternal perspective necessary to see beyond the trials or challenges we will inevitably face. Remember what Heber C. Kimball prophesied:

> The time will come when no man nor woman will be able to endure on borrowed light. Each will have to be guided by the light within himself. . . .
>
> . . . If you don't have it you will not stand; therefore seek for the testimony of Jesus and cleave to it, that when the trying time comes you may not stumble and fall.
>
> (Orson F. Whitney, *Life of Heber C. Kimball,* 1945, 450.)

Second, humility. Humility is the recognition and attitude that one must rely on the Lord's assistance to make it through this life. We cannot endure to the end on our own strength. Without Him, we are nothing (see John 15:5).

Third, repentance. The glorious gift of repentance allows us to return to the journey refreshed, with a new heart, giving us the strength to endure on the path leading to eternal life. The sacrament thus becomes a key component of our endurance in this life. The sacrament provides a precious weekly opportunity to renew our baptismal covenants and repent and evaluate our progress toward exaltation.

We are sons and daughters of the Eternal God, with the potential to be joint-heirs with Christ (see Romans 8:17). Knowing who we are, we should never give up the goal of achieving our eternal destiny.

I testify that in the eternities, as we look back upon our little span of existence here on this earth, we will lift our voices and rejoice that, in spite of the difficulties we encountered, we had the wisdom, the faith, and the courage to endure and press on.

*(Adapted from an October 2004 general conference address)*

# 12

## FINDING A SAFE HARBOR

More than sixty years ago, I served as a missionary in Austria and Switzerland. It was a challenging but wonderful time in my life. I grew to love the people of that area of the world and was reluctant to leave them. But my term of service ended in late August of 1939, and I made preparations to sail home.

After a long journey across the Atlantic Ocean, which was a hazardous passage at that time because of the war, I rejoiced when I saw that wonderful beacon of freedom and democracy, the Statue of Liberty. I cannot express to you my relief when we finally reached that safe harbor.

I imagine I felt something of what the disciples of Jesus Christ felt on a certain day when they had set sail with the Savior upon the Sea of Galilee. The scriptures tell us that Jesus was weary, and He went to the back of the ship and fell asleep on a pillow (see Mark 4:38). Soon the skies darkened and "there arose a great tempest in the sea, insomuch that the ship was covered with the waves" (Matthew 8:24). The storm raged. The disciples panicked. It seemed as though the boat would capsize, yet the Savior still slept. At last, they could wait no longer and they awakened Jesus. You can almost hear the anguish and despair in their voices as they pled with their Master, "Carest thou not that we perish?" (Mark 4:38).

Many today feel troubled and distressed; many feel that, at any moment, the ships of their lives could capsize or sink. It is to you who are looking for a safe harbor that I wish to address this chapter, you whose hearts are breaking, you who are worried or afraid, you who bear grief or the burdens of sin, you who feel no one is listening to your cries, you whose hearts are pleading, "Master, carest thou not that I perish?" To you I offer a few words of comfort and of counsel.

## Peace amidst the Storms

Be assured that there is a safe harbor. You can find peace amidst the storms that threaten you. Your Heavenly Father—who knows when even a sparrow falls—knows of your heartache and suffering. He loves you and wants the best for you. Never doubt this. Though He allows all of us to make choices that may not always be for our own or even others' well-being, and though He does not always intervene in the course of events, He has promised the faithful peace even in our trials and tribulations.

How is this possible? The prophet Alma tells us, "And [Christ] shall go forth, suffering pains and afflictions and temptations of every kind; and this that the word might be fulfilled which saith he will take upon him the pains and the sicknesses of his people" (Alma 7:11).

Jesus offered us comfort when He said, "Peace I leave with you, my peace I give unto you: not as the world giveth, give I unto you. Let not your heart be troubled, neither let it be afraid" (John 14:27).

Draw close to the Lord Jesus Christ. He is the Son of God, an eternal king, and He bears a special love for those who suffer. In His mortal ministry He sought such out and blessed them.

To the meek and discouraged, His every word was one of compassion and encouragement. To the sick, He brought a healing balm. Those who yearned for hope, who yearned for a caring touch, received it from the tender hand of this King of kings, this Creator of ocean, earth, and sky.

Today Jesus the Christ stands at the right hand of our Heavenly Father. Do you suppose that today He is any less inclined to aid those who suffer, who are sick, or who appeal to the Father in prayer for succor?

## Suffering—Why?

Be of good cheer. The Man of Galilee, the Creator, the Son of the Living God will not forget nor forsake those whose hearts are drawn to Him. I testify that the Man who suffered for mankind, who committed His life to healing the sick and comforting the disconsolate, is mindful of your sufferings, doubts, and heartaches.

"Then," the world would ask, "why does He sleep when the tempest rages all around me? Why does He not still this storm, or Why would He let me suffer?"

Your answer may be found in considering a butterfly. Wrapped tightly in its cocoon, the developing chrysalis must struggle with all its might to break its confinement. The butterfly might think, *Why must I suffer so? Why cannot I simply, in the twinkling of an eye, become a butterfly?*

Such thoughts would be contrary to the Creator's design. The struggle to break out of the cocoon develops the butterfly so it can fly. Without that adversity, the butterfly would never develop the strength to achieve its destiny. It would never develop the strength to become something extraordinary.

President James E. Faust has observed that "into every life there come the painful, despairing days of adversity and buffeting. There seems to be a full measure of anguish, sorrow, and often heartbreak for everyone, including those who earnestly seek to do right and be faithful" ("The Refiner's Fire," *Ensign*, May 1979, 53). But, President Faust explains, the adversity we experience allows our souls to become like clay in the hands of the Master. "Trials and adversity can be preparatory to becoming born anew" (Ibid., 54).

When we are called to sail through troubled waters, we need to know the place of adversity in shaping our divine potential. For one thing, adversity can strengthen and refine us. As with the butterfly, adversity is necessary to build character in people. If only we would look beyond our present suffering and see our struggles as a temporary chrysalis. If only we would have the faith and trust in our Heavenly Father to see how, after a little season, we can emerge from our trials more refined and glorious.

What parent would say to a child, "Learning to walk is such a painful and difficult experience; you will stumble, you will most likely hurt yourself, you will cry many times when you fall. I will protect you from the struggle"? I watched our youngest grandson, Seth, as he was learning to walk. Through this process of gaining experience, he now walks with confidence. Should I have said to him, "Out of my love for you, I will save you from this"? If so, because I could not bear to see him take a tumble at times, he may have never learned to walk. But those who loved Seth knew that the necessity and joy of walking would outweigh any temporary pain or adversity. That we would deprive him of that learning experience was unthinkable for a loving parent or grandparent.

## Faith and Hard Work

What is mortality if not a long process similar to learning to walk? We must learn to walk in the ways of the Lord.

You are stronger than you think. Your Heavenly Father, the Lord and Master of the universe, is your Creator. When I think of it, it makes my heart leap for joy. Our spirits are eternal, and eternal spirits have immeasurable capacity!

Our Father in Heaven does not wish us to cower. He does not want us to wallow in our misery. He expects us to get back on our feet, square our shoulders, and overcome our challenges.

That kind of spirit—that blend of faith and hard work—is the spirit we should emulate as we seek to reach a safe harbor in our own lives.

## You Are Not Alone

You are not alone in The Church of Jesus Christ of Latter-day Saints today; millions of fellow Saints stand beside you. Those who follow the teachings and example of the Savior are "willing to bear one another's burdens, that they may be light; yea, and are willing to mourn with those that mourn; yea, and comfort those that stand in need of comfort" (Mosiah 18:8–9).

The question Cain asked of the Lord, "Am I my brother's keeper?" (Moses 5:34) has been answered by prophets in these latter days. "Yes, we are our brothers' keepers," President Thomas S. Monson has said. When we work together to benefit those in need, "we eliminate the weakness of one person standing alone and substitute the strength of many serving together. While we may not be able to do everything, we can and must do something" ("Our Brothers' Keeper," *Ensign,* June 1998, 33–38).

Bishops, home teachers, visiting teachers, and members of priest-hood quorums and of Relief Societies and other auxiliary organizations all stand ready to help. The Savior's teachings and the Church constitute our best safe harbor—yes, our most secure "refuge from the storm" (D&C 115:6).

Of course, your brothers and sisters in the Church are not to solve your problems for you. It has been my experience that when we do for others what they can and ought to do for themselves, we often weaken rather than strengthen them. But your brothers and sisters will be at your side to strengthen you, encourage you, and lend you a hand.

## Strength through Adversity

As you overcome adversity in your life, you will become stronger. Then you will be better able to help others—those who are working, in their turn, to find a safe harbor from the storms that rage about them.

When you feel tossed by the storms of life and when the waves rise and the winds howl, on those occasions it would be natural for you to cry in your heart, "Master, carest thou not that I perish?" When these times come, think back upon that day when the Savior awakened in the stern of the ship, rose up, and rebuked the storm. "Peace, be still," (Mark 4:39) He commanded, and it was so.

At times we may be tempted to think the Savior is oblivious to our trials. In fact, the reverse is true; it is we who need to be awakened in our hearts to His teachings.

Use your ingenuity, your strength, your might to resolve your challenges. Do all you can do and then leave the rest to the Lord. President Howard W. Hunter said: "If our lives and our faith are centered on Jesus Christ and his restored gospel, nothing can ever go permanently wrong. On the other hand, if our lives are not centered on the Savior and his teachings, no other success can ever be permanently right" (*The Teachings of Howard W. Hunter,* ed. Clyde J. Williams, [1997], 40).

Living the gospel does not mean the storms of life will pass us by, but we will be better prepared to face them with serenity and peace. "Search diligently, pray always, and be believing," the Lord admonished, "and all things shall work together for your good, if ye walk uprightly" (D&C 90:24).

## The Savior Is Our Solace in the Storms

Draw close to the Lord Jesus Christ. Be of good cheer. Keep the faith. Doubt not. The storms will one day be stilled. Our beloved prophet, President Gordon B. Hinckley, has said: "We have nothing to fear. God is at the helm . . . [and] He will shower down blessings upon those who walk in obedience to His commandments" ("This Is the Work of the Master," *Ensign,* May 1995, 71).

In our own storms in life the Savior is our solace and our sanctuary. If we seek peace, we must come unto Him. He Himself spoke this eternal truth when He said, "My yoke is easy, and my burden is light" (Matthew 11:30). When our souls are anchored in the safe harbor of the Savior, we can proclaim as did Paul: "We are troubled on every side, yet not distressed; we are perplexed, but not in despair; persecuted, but not forsaken; cast down, but not destroyed" (2 Corinthians 4:8–9).

The Prophet Joseph Smith, who knew much about the storms of life, during one of his darkest moments, cried in anguish: "[My] God, where art thou? And where is the pavilion that covereth thy hiding place?" (D&C 121:1). Even as he lifted up his tormented voice, Joseph heard the serene comfort of the Lord: "My son, peace be unto thy soul; thine adversity and thine afflictions shall be but a small moment; and then, if thou endure it well, God shall exalt thee on high; thou shalt triumph over all thy foes" (D&C 121:7–8).

The gospel gives us that harbor of enduring safety and security. The living prophet and the apostles today are as lighthouses in the storm. Steer toward the light of the restored gospel and the inspired teachings of those who represent the Lord on earth.

I bear solemn testimony that Jesus is the living Christ, our Savior and Redeemer. He leads and directs His Church through our prophet, President Gordon B. Hinckley. If we live by the Savior's teachings, we will with surety find a safe harbor in this life and in the eternities to come.

*(Adapted from an April 2000 general conference address)*

# 13

# "A More Excellent Way"

Over the span of my lifetime, I have had the remarkable opportunity to know and work closely with many men and women who exemplify excellence. I have learned from each one of them. They have served as guiding lights during my life and provided direction that has been an immense help to me.

## Polynesian Pilots

Hundreds of years ago, Polynesian sailors traveled vast distances using only the stars to navigate. To be able to launch a craft not much larger than a canoe, travel thousands of miles through often treacherous waters, and find a tiny pinprick of an island in the midst of a vast ocean is a remarkable feat to say the least.

That such a thing is possible was demonstrated by a group from Hawaii in the 1970s. Having enlisted the help of one of the last remaining Polynesian pilots they set out from Hawaii. Thirty days and 2,500 miles later, they arrived at their destination—a group of islands near Tahiti (http://pvs.kcc.hawaii.edu/nainoa80tahiti.html).

How did they accomplish this remarkable feat?

These navigators spent their lives learning about the stars and their paths through the heavens. They had memorized them so carefully, that they were able to use them as reference points throughout their voyage. Whenever they drifted off course, they looked to the stars and adjusted their sails. As long as they followed the stars, they knew they would reach their destination.

History is filled with examples of righteous men and women who can serve as guiding stars for us. Although they may have lived in different times and faced different trials, fundamentally, their challenges are ours; the problems we face were theirs. The more we learn of them—the more we use them as a guide for us—the more certain it is that we will reach a final destination worthy of sons and daughters of our Heavenly Father.

There have been many such guiding lights in my life. The examples and words of my mother and father remain with me to this day. Many of the great men and women of my youth, in a similar way, still are with me. I honor and revere them and thank them for the positive influences they had on me as a young boy.

Although I never knew him, my great-grandfather is another example to me. As a teenager in Berne, Switzerland, he heard the elders preach the restored gospel. The power of testimony was so strong that he accepted the message immediately and was baptized that very Sunday. Because of this decision, his parents disowned him, and he was left without a home. Eventually, he took passage on a ship and ended up in Nauvoo in time to secure a handcart and make the long journey with the Saints coming to the Salt Lake Valley.

There are other great individuals whose lives and example have served as a guiding light to millions. I would like to write about three such individuals—people who are already familiar to you.

Their stars shine brightly in the annals of history. Clear, bright, and ever true, their light is radiant and never-failing. Their examples of excellence, like the stars that guided the Polynesian pilots, can guide us in our own journeys through life.

## President Gordon B. Hinckley

President Gordon B. Hinckley is a man whom I have revered and loved for a very long time. I was a teenager when he returned from serving a mission to England. I remember the day he spoke in sacrament meeting about his mission experiences and described his love and admiration of the British people. Many of my friends were present, and both they and I felt inspired to serve missions as a result of this talk. After the meeting, I spoke with Elder Hinckley and he said to me: "One of the most important things you can do is go on a mission. The privilege of serving the Lord full-time is a gift beyond measure."

His words had such an influence on me that it strengthened my resolve to serve a mission.

When my father passed away in 1963, Elder Hinckley, who was then serving as a member of the Council of the Twelve, came to our home. I'll never forget his kindness. He gave my mother a blessing and, among other things, promised that she had much to look forward to and that life would yet be sweet to her. These words gave comfort and encouragement to my mother and were an inspiration to me.

President Hinckley is a visionary man. In his patriarchal blessing, it was promised that "the nations of the earth shall hear thy voice and be brought to a knowledge of the truth by the wonderful testimony which thou shalt bear" (Sheri L. Dew, *Go Forward with Faith*, Deseret Book, 1996, 60). When President Hinckley finished his mission, he felt that this portion of his blessing had been fulfilled as he had testified of the truth in more than one nation. Since that time he has visited nearly every nation on earth.

Of course those early experiences were only the first of thousands he has had since that time to bear his testimony throughout the world to millions of people. That experience has taught President Hinckley never to underestimate the promises and power of the Lord.

I can tell you from personal experience that he is a man of faith who believes that when the Lord speaks, the Lord provides. Like Nephi of old, he knows that no matter how impossible the divinely appointed task may seem, our Heavenly Father will provide a way for it to be accomplished.

One of the great challenges the Church faced not long ago was that its membership was expanding throughout the world and yet there were so few temples. Often Church members went to great lengths and immense sacrifice and expense to travel to a temple to receive the holy ordinances that are available there.

President Hinckley struggled with this. How could the eternal blessings of the temple be made available to the many faithful members who did not live near a temple? As he wrestled with this problem, an idea came to him. *Why couldn't we build smaller temples? We could build them on smaller plots of ground, it would take fewer people to serve as temple workers, we could open them only as demand required. Why couldn't the blessings of the temple be extended to millions of faithful members of the Church that otherwise would be without the opportunity?*

During the April 1998 general conference, President Hinckley announced "a program to construct some 30 smaller temples immediately" ("New Temples to Provide 'Crowning Blessings' of the Gospel," *Ensign,* May 1998, 88). At that time, there were just fifty-one temples in operation, and it had taken roughly one hundred fifty years to reach that number. In the seven years since that announcement, sixty-eight new temples have been dedicated, bringing the total to one hundred nineteen Deseret Morning News, 2007 *Church Almanac,* 493–95). In addition, eleven more of these sacred buildings have been announced and are in the process of being constructed.

You will never find a man as kind and considerate as President Gordon B. Hinckley. When it comes to doctrine, he never deviates. And he is one of the hardest working General Authorities I have known.

In one of his interviews with Larry King, President Hinckley was asked how he was doing since his beloved wife, Marjorie, passed away. He said that he felt pretty lonely at times.

Mr. King asked, "How do you get over that?"

President Hinckley's response was as touching as it was profound: "You never get over it . . . the best thing you can do is just keep busy," he said. "Keep working hard, so you're not dwelling on it all the time. Work is the best antidote for sorrow" (http://www.cesnur.org/2004/lds.htm).

I have watched President Hinckley throw his every effort into accomplishing the work the Lord has set for him. I testify to you that he is a prophet of God and that he is authorized by the Lord to lead The Church of Jesus Christ of Latter-day Saints today.

I am honored to call President Gordon B. Hinckley my prophet and my friend.

## The Prophet Joseph Smith

In 2005, we celebrated the 200th anniversary of the birth of the Prophet Joseph Smith. He is the second guiding light I would like to recommend to you. Sometimes, the more familiar we are with someone, the less we appreciate them. But when it comes to the Prophet Joseph, the more I learn of him, the more I love and revere him. We believe that in the history of the world, he has done more for the salvation of mankind than any other person save Jesus only (D&C 135:3).

He was a man for whom the heavens parted. He witnessed the reality of a loving Heavenly Father and His Son, Jesus Christ. He saw and spoke with angels, received priesthood keys from heavenly messengers, and had discourse with many of the great souls who had previously lived on earth.

When the Prophet spoke, he could hold the interest of people for hours at a time. One who heard him speak said, "The testimony of Joseph struck through the heart, and, like the thunder of the cataract, declared at once the dignity and matchless supremacy of the Creator" (Lyman O. Littlefield, quoted in Mark L. McConkie, *Remembering Joseph*, 2003, 98).

Those who met the Prophet, even those who did not believe what he taught, often described him as "extraordinary," "noble," and "God-like."

Missourian General Moses Wilson was a bitter enemy of the Church. At one point Joseph was delivered into General Wilson's hands as a prisoner. General Wilson later said of him, "He was a very remarkable man. I carried him into my house, a prisoner in chains and in less than two hours my wife loved him better than she did me" (George A. Smith, *Journal of Discourses,* 17:92).

On another occasion, a large group of men approached, stating they had come to "kill Joe Smith and all the Mormons." Joseph smiled and shook their hands. He sat down with them and explained to them many of the difficulties the Saints had suffered and described their claim against the injustices that had been heaped upon them. After talking to them for some time he turned and said, "I believe I will go home now—Emma will be expecting me."

At this, two of the officers who had come to kill him suggested that he should not go home alone and insisted that they would provide an escort to ensure his safety.

As they left, Joseph's mother heard one say, "Did you not feel strangely when Smith took you by the hand?"

Another said, "I could not move. I would not harm a hair of that man's head for the whole world" (Lucy Mack Smith, *History of Joseph Smith by His Mother,* 255–56).

Joseph Smith was the man who, before he had reached the age of twenty-five, had translated the Book of Mormon. He did this in a period of less than three months.

Our translators at Church headquarters can translate the Book of Mormon at the rate of roughly a page a day. Joseph Smith translated the original at a rate of ten manuscript pages per day.

Could you imagine being given that task as an assignment in one of your classes? Your goal would be to write a book of more than 500 single-spaced pages that recounts the history of a nation over a period of a thousand years? The book you write must be consistent with historical evidence of the period. It must stand under the strictest scrutiny and have no contradictions in date, personalities, or events. It must contain revelations from God to man and have the power of testimony such that millions upon millions who read it can testify of its truth.

When you take into consideration that Joseph had logged less time in school than our average third grader, it makes what he did seem more impossible by human standards. Consider Joseph Smith carefully and you are left with only one conclusion: Joseph Smith saw what he said he saw. He heard what he said he heard. And he translated The Book of Mormon through the power of God.

Joseph Smith was a man who had been granted the privilege of transcending space and time. He not only had seen the past, but he knew the future. I have read one account where Joseph was waiting in Dimick Huntington's boot shop and, to pass the time, he began speaking about events in earth's history, explaining many events Brother Huntington was not familiar with. But, "when he came to present times, he didn't stop, but went on and related the principal events that will transpire in the history of the world down to the time when the angel will declare that time shall be no longer" (Hyrum L. Andrus and Helen Mae Andrus, *They Knew the Prophet,* Bookcraft, 1974, 66).

But even though the Prophet Joseph was a man who had conversed with angels, he was a humble man of a compassionate and kind heart.

When Joseph was serving as mayor of Nauvoo, a man was brought to him and accused of selling liquor on Sunday. The man explained that he had a dear child who was being held as a slave in a Southern state and that he was trying to get enough money to buy the child's freedom. He pled with the prophet not to punish him.

"I am sorry, Anthony," Joseph said to the man, "but the law must be observed, and we will have to impose a fine."

The next day, the Prophet gave the man one of his fine horses, telling him to sell it and use the money to purchase the freedom of the child (see Mark L. McConkie, *Remembering Joseph,* Deseret Book, 2003, 54–55).

Like millions of others, my life is richer, sweeter, and transformed because of the life and words of the Prophet of the Restoration, Joseph Smith.

## Jesus, the Christ

The third guiding light I wish to call to your mind is our Lord and Savior, Jesus Christ.

Oh, that I had the voice of an angel, that I could convey the depth of the feelings of my heart for this man among men, who is my Savior.

He lived that we may live forever. He lived that we may experience a fulness of joy. He lived that our sojourn—not only through these few years we pass in mortality, but through the infinite reaches of limitless eternity—may be glorious and our hearts and minds filled with a fulness of love, joy, and peace.

He rebuked death and raised those whose spirits had departed this life. He commanded the sick, the lame, and the afflicted to be healed, and they were healed. He commanded the earth and the skies, and they obeyed. He stood in majesty before those who would destroy him and bore solemn testimony of the truth. He took a few morsels of food and fed thousands. He rebuked Satan, and the evil one departed.

Though Jesus could command legions of angels—though the ocean, earth, and sky obeyed his word—the man from Galilee was meek and humble and mild. Often he knelt in prayer and supplication as He communed with His Father in Heaven.

Because of the sublime words of Jesus Christ, we understand what it means to love our neighbor, become holy, and we understand the true power of faith.

Once, when traveling through Samaria, the Savior asked a woman to draw water and give Him to drink. Because of the animosity between the Jews and the Samaritans, the woman marveled at His request.

Jesus then spoke to her and said, "Whosoever drinketh of this water shall thirst again: But whosoever drinketh of the water that I shall give him shall never thirst; but the water that I shall give him shall be in him a well of water springing up into everlasting life" (John 4:13–14).

As with the woman of Samaria, this living water is available to us if only we will partake of it.

The Savior calls to us today as he has done in ages past: "Follow Me."

When we follow the Savior in spirit and in truth, we leave behind us the mundane enticements of this tired earth and take upon us the life of adventure in the Spirit. As we covenant to remember the Lord and drink of living water, we step into the threshold of a new day; we enter a world of faith, wonder, and light.

## The Pursuit of Perfection

Our Lord and Savior, Jesus Christ; the Prophet Joseph Smith; and President Gordon B. Hinckley are three great examples worthy of emulation. Although each of them lived in different times and faced different challenges, each is a beacon of excellence that can provide light for our own journey.

Now, there are some who, instead of being inspired by the examples of great men and women, instead become discouraged.

If you have ever felt inadequate, if you have ever felt that you don't have the inherent capacity of others, if you have ever felt that no matter how hard you try, you are never good enough, I have a word of advice for you.

Your life is not a race.

You are not competing against anyone else for entrance into the presence of our Heavenly Father.

The plan of salvation is not a reality show where you have to beat out other contestants to win.

I have more good news. As long as you seek to grow closer to your Heavenly Father and your heart and spirit are contrite—as long as you repent and strive in faith to overcome weaknesses—you will be rewarded by our Heavenly Father.

Our purpose in this life is to fill our minds with all truth and our hearts with the Spirit of the Lord that we may become more holy and more like those great souls who preceded us.

As we learn and apply the principles of the gospel in our lives, the atonement of the Savior will cleanse us of iniquity, enabling us to live in peace and righteousness in this world and in glory throughout the worlds to come.

Our task is not in one day to become perfect but to grow a little more perfect every day. Even if it's only a small step, the important thing is that we keep walking forward, each day getting a little closer to our glorious destination.

Do you think perfection is too high of a standard?

I know people who are perfect in paying their tithing.

I know many who are perfect in sacrament meeting attendance, going to the temple often, reading the scriptures daily.

They didn't start out being perfect perhaps, but they made a commitment, and they followed through.

I encourage you to do the same. We all know the things we need to work on. We don't need well-intentioned people to reveal our shortcomings—although at times it appears there is never a scarcity of them.

On every side we have before us the examples of many great souls. Their lives can inspire us. Their actions can encourage us. Their faithfulness can give us hope and confidence that we can do the same.

Never be satisfied with less than your best. And don't allow yourself to get discouraged when your actions don't measure up to your thoughts and feelings.

Work every day to become a little more perfect, a little more righteous, and a little more holy.

Remember, your destiny as sons and daughters of the Most High God is to overcome challenges and stand triumphant and victorious at the final day.

That is your destiny.

It is your birthright as sons and daughters of our Heavenly Father.

I have learned to do something that may be of use to you. Each evening, I take inventory of my day. I review the events of the day and give thanks for the things that went well and consider the things I could have done better.

Instead of getting discouraged when I make mistakes, I try to learn from them.

I write down the things I need to accomplish the next day and make a plan as to how I can accomplish them.

Finally, I go before the Lord with my report. I ask for His forgiveness for my shortcomings and plead for strength and wisdom to improve. I invite the Spirit of the Lord into our home and our family. And I ask for the Lord's guiding hand to help me become more like Him.

Don't fret when your thoughts or actions fail to measure up to your potential. Instead, rejoice that through the atonement of our Savior, you can repent. Regardless of our shortcomings, through the refining influence of the Holy Ghost, we can improve our lives daily.

Be of good cheer. This journey we are taking is not one of drudgery or discouragement, but one of delight and destiny.

Learn from your mistakes. Seek forgiveness from those you have wronged. Forgive those who have wronged you. Have faith that your loving Heavenly Father knows you. He will bless you as you pursue righteous desires. And you will come to know that "all things work together for good to them who walk uprightly" (D&C 90:24).

Like the ancient Polynesian pilots who followed the stars toward their destination, you can study the lives of righteous souls of every generation and follow their examples. As you do so, you will find your way through the vast and dark oceans of the trials of this life and come at last to the land promised by the Father.

I bear witness that we lived before this life in the company of great and noble souls. After we depart this existence, we will once again have the opportunity to renew our acquaintances with them.

I testify that we are children of the infinite Heavenly Father. He exists. He hears us as we pray. He loves us with a love beyond our comprehension.

I testify that He sent his Son, Jesus Christ, to this earth to put in place the glorious blessings of the Atonement. Because of Him, we will live forever. Because of Him, our faults and weaknesses can be cleansed and we can become perfect.

I testify that Joseph Smith was called of God to restore the gospel to the earth. With help from beyond the veil, Joseph Smith brought about the work of restoring The Church of Jesus Christ. Joseph was authorized to act in these matters by virtue of the keys of the priesthood, which he received from heavenly messengers, and the church thus organized is recognized by God as the custodian of the revealed ordinances essential to salvation.

I further testify that today, The Church of Jesus Christ of Latter-day Saints is led by a man of God, a prophet, a choice servant of our Heavenly Father and that President Gordon B. Hinckley presides over and leads the Lord's Church in accordance with the will of heaven.

I testify the Church is true; that God lives; and that as we embrace and live the principles of the gospel, we will find peace in this life and immeasurable joy in the hereafter.

The great Book of Mormon prophet, Ether, wrote, "In the gift of his Son, hath God prepared a more excellent way" (Ether 12:11).

My earnest desire is that we may all rejoice in that gift and that we may find that excellent way.

*(Based on an address given at a BYU–Idaho Devotional, 13 February 2005)*

# 14

# ONE STEP AFTER ANOTHER

## Different Life Experiences

We all are going through different life experiences. While some are filled with joy today, others feel as though their hearts could burst with sorrow. Some feel as though the world is their oyster; others feel as though they were the oyster itself—plucked from the ocean, cracked open, and robbed of all that is precious to them.

No matter your station, no matter your emotional or spiritual state of mind, I would like to offer counsel to you that may be of use, regardless of where you are in your sojourn through this mortal life.

Certainly we have much to be grateful for. And I think if we will consider the blessings we have, we will be able to forget some of our worries and experience a measure of serenity and joy.

## Blind Mountain Climber

Recently, I read about Erik Weihenmayer, a 33-year-old man who dreamed of climbing Mount Everest, a feat that defies many of the world's most expert climbers. In fact, nearly ninety percent of those who attempt the climb never reach the summit. Temperatures sink lower than 30 degrees below zero. Besides extreme cold, 100-mile-per-hour winds, deadly crevasses, and avalanches, the climber must overcome the challenges of high altitude, lack of oxygen, and perhaps unsanitary food and water. Since 1953, at least 165 climbers have died in the attempt to scale the 29,000-foot-high summit.

In spite of the risks, hundreds line up each year to attempt the ascent, Erik among them. But there is an important difference between Erik and every other climber who had attempted to ascend before: Erik is totally blind.

When Erik was thirteen years of age, he lost his sight as a result of a hereditary disease of the retina. Although he could no longer do many of the things he wanted to, he was determined not to waste his life feeling depressed and useless. He then began to stretch his limits.

At age sixteen he discovered rock climbing. By feeling the face of the rock, he found handholds and footholds that allowed him to climb. Sixteen years later, he began his ascent up Mount Everest. The story of his climb, as you might imagine, was filled with many harrowing and life-threatening challenges. But Erik eventually scaled the south summit and took his place with those who had gone before him, one of the few to stand on top of the highest mountain on the face of the earth.

When asked how he did it, Erik said, "I just kept thinking, . . . keep your mind focused. Don't let all that doubt and fear and frustration sort of get in the way." Then, most importantly, he said, "Just take each day step by step" ("Everest Grueling for Blind Man," *Deseret News,* 5 June 2001, A12; see also Karl Taro Greenfeld, "Blind to Failure," *Time,* 18 June 2001).

Yes, Erik conquered Everest by simply putting one foot in front of the other. And he continued to do this until he reached the top.

## Step by Step

Like Erik, we may have obstacles that would hold us back in our own journeys. We may even make excuses for why we can't do what we want to do. Perhaps when we are tempted to justify our own lack of achievement, we can remember Erik, who, in spite of having lost his sight, accomplished what many thought was impossible simply by continuing to put one foot in front of the other.

An old proverb states that a journey of a thousand miles begins with a single step. Sometimes we make the process more complicated than we need to. We will never make a journey of a thousand miles by fretting about how long it will take or how hard it will be. We make the journey by taking each day step by step and then repeating it again and again until we reach our destination.

## Climbing to Higher Spirituality

The same principle applies to how you and I can climb to higher spirituality.

Our Heavenly Father knows that we must begin our climb from where we are. "When you climb up a ladder," the Prophet Joseph Smith taught, "you must begin at the bottom, and ascend step by step, until you arrive at the top; and so it is with the principles of the gospel—you must begin with the first, and go on until you learn all the principles of exaltation. But it will be a great while after you have passed through the veil before you will have learned them" (*Encyclopedia of Joseph Smith's Teachings,* Larry E. Dahl and Donald Q. Cannon [1997], 519).

Our Heavenly Father loves each one of us and understands that this process of climbing higher takes preparation, time, and commitment. He understands that we will make mistakes at times, that we will stumble, that we will become discouraged and perhaps even wish to give up and say to ourselves it is not worth the struggle.

We know it is worth the effort, for the prize, which is eternal life, is "the greatest of all the gifts of God" (D&C 14:7). And to qualify, to gain the spiritual heights we aspire to reach, we must take one step after another and keep going.

## Do the Best You Can

An eternal principle is revealed in holy writ: "It is not requisite that a man should run faster than he has strength. And again, it is expedient that he should be diligent, that thereby he might win the prize; therefore, all things must be done in order" (Mosiah 4:27).

We don't have to be fast, we simply have to be steady and move in the right direction. We have to do the best we can, one step after another.

In my younger days, I loved to run. Although it may be hard for you to believe it, I did win a few races. I'm not so fast anymore. In fact, I'm not sure how well I would do in a race if the only contestants were the members of the Quorum of the Twelve.

My ability to run is not so swift now. While I am looking forward to that future time when, with a resurrected body, I can once again sprint over a field and feel the wind blowing through my hair, I do not dwell on the fact that I cannot do it now.

That would be unwise. Instead, I take the steps that I can take. Even with the limitations of age, I can still take one step at a time. To do what I can is all my Heavenly Father now requires of me. And it is all He requires of you, regardless of your disabilities, limitations, or insecurities.

## Competition

John Wooden was perhaps the greatest college basketball coach in the history of the game. He had four full undefeated seasons. His teams won ten national championships. At one point, he had a streak of eighty-eight consecutive wins (http://www.coachjohnwooden.com).

One of the first things Coach Wooden drilled into his players was something his father had taught him when he was a boy growing up on a farm. "Don't worry much about trying to be better than someone else," his father said. "Learn from others, yes. But don't just try to be better than they are. You have no control over that. Instead try, and try very hard, to be the best that you can be. That you have control over" (*Wooden*, Contemporary Books, 1997, 169).

Let me cite a hypothetical example of a dear sister in any ward, the one who has perfect children who never cause a disturbance in church. She is the one working on the 20th generation in her family history, keeps an immaculate home, has memorized the book of Mark, and makes wool sweaters for the orphaned children in Romania. No disrespect, of course, intended for any of these worthy goals. Now, when you are tempted to throw your hands in the air and give up because of this dear sister, please remember you're not competing with her any more than I'm competing with the members of the Quorum of the Twelve in winning a 50-yard dash.

## Press Forward

The only thing you need to worry about is striving to be the best you can be. And how do you do that? You keep your eye on the goals that matter most in life, and you move toward them step by step.

I know many feel that the path is hard and the way is dark. But like Erik, the courageous mountain climber, we are not left without a guide.

We have the scriptures, which contain the revealed word of God to mankind through the ages. When we feast upon the word of God, we open our minds to eternal truths and our hearts to the gentle whisperings of the Holy Ghost. Truly God's word, accessed through scriptures and modern-day prophets, is a "lamp unto [our] feet, and a light unto [our] path" (Psalm 119:105).

As we read about the great souls who have preceded us, we learn that they, too, had times of discouragement and sorrow. We learn that they persevered in spite of hardship, in spite of adversity, sometimes even in spite of their own weaknesses. We learn that they too continued to press forward, one step after another. We can be like those righteous souls of whom Lehi spoke—those who "caught hold of the end of the rod of iron; and they did press forward through the mist of darkness, . . .

even until they did come forth and partake of the fruit of the tree" (1 Nephi 8:24).

We also have a living prophet, President Gordon B. Hinckley. He provides counsel and prophetic direction for us in our day. By following his counsel and through our prayers, we can reach into the heavens and personally commune with the Infinite. Through faith, heaven itself can be moved in our behalf. I testify that doors will be opened and answers received.

## Joseph Smith

Think of Joseph Smith as a young boy, hearing confusing and contradictory voices, yearning to know which of all the churches were right and true. He too felt blind—surrounded by the darkness of his day. After reading the book of James in the New Testament, he believed the words of the ancient apostle, who said, "If any of you lack wisdom, let him ask of God, that giveth to all men liberally, and upbraideth not; and it shall be given him" (James 1:5). Joseph believed these words, and on a spring morning in 1820, he retired to a grove of trees to lift up his soul in prayer and ask his Heavenly Father for wisdom.

The answer to his prayer filled him with light and direction. Our Heavenly Father and His beloved Son appeared to him. Their direction swept away the thick darkness that had seized Joseph and threatened to destroy him. Their direction also forever swept away his confusion.

From that moment until his martyrdom nearly a quarter of a century later, Joseph Smith committed himself to the path shown him by the Father and the Son. Consider how painful his days were. Consider the suffering and the persecution he had to endure. Yet he continued, step by step, never giving up, never doubting that if he only did what he could, his Heavenly Father would make up the rest.

## *Does the Journey Seem Long?*

Our time here on earth is so precious and so short. How well I understand the prophet Jacob when he said, "Our lives passed away like as it were unto us a dream" (Jacob 7:26).

All too soon, our time is finished. While we can—while we have the time to complete our work—let us walk in the right direction, taking one step after another.

That is easy enough. We don't have to be perfect today. We don't have to be better than someone else. All we have to do is to be the very best we can.

Though you may feel weary, though you sometimes may not be able to see the way, know that your Father in Heaven will never forsake His righteous followers. He will not leave you comfortless. He will be at your side, yes, guiding you every step of the way.

Listen to these beautiful words written by President Joseph Fielding Smith as he describes this life:

> *Does the journey seem long,*
> *The path rugged and steep?*
> *Are there briars and thorns on the way?*
> *Do sharp stones cut your feet*
> *As you struggle to rise*
> *To the heights thru the heat of the day?*
> *Is your heart faint and sad,*
> *Your soul weary within,*
> *As you toil 'neath your burden of care?*
> *Does the load heavy seem*
> *You are forced now to lift?*
> *Is there no one your burden to share?*
> *Let your heart be not faint*
> *Now the journey's begun;*
> *There is One who still beckons to you.*

*So look upward in joy*
*And take hold of his hand;*
*He will lead you to heights that are new—*
*A land holy and pure,*
*Where all trouble doth end,*
*And your life shall be free from all sin,*
*Where no tears shall be shed,*
*For no sorrows remain.*
*Take his hand and with him enter in.*
(Hymns, *no. 127*)

## Testimony

It is my prayer that we will have the courage to continue climbing our own Mount Everest, that we may progress in life's journey step by step until we reach the best that is within us.

Our Heavenly Father lives and knows and loves each one of us. Jesus is the Christ, the Son of God, the Savior and Redeemer of all, and yes, the Prince of Peace. Joseph Smith is the Prophet of the Restoration and President Gordon B. Hinckley is our prophet, seer, and revelator on the earth today. I bear this testimony, and it is my testimony to you that you will be happy and content if you only do your best.

*(Adapted from an October 2001 general conference address)*

# 15

## DILIGENCE

I am always humbled by the opportunity to address full-time missionaries. You represent goodness, sacrifice, and the desire to succeed. I express my admiration to you, and I commend you especially for your diligence in the service of the Lord.

I bring the greetings and love of President Gordon B. Hinckley, his counselors—President Thomas S. Monson and President James E. Faust—and the Quorum of the Twelve. They wish each of you great success and happiness in your new ministry as servants and handmaidens of the Lord.

### Set Lofty Goals for Your Mission

The Millennial year will soon be with us. It is bearing down on us at the rate of 3,600 seconds per hour. It is the most important time mark in a thousand years, that magic moment when the cosmic odometer rolls to three zeros, a new year, a new decade, a new century, a new millennium. Who knows what this new century will bring? Surely the words we find in 2 Nephi 15:26–27 will foretell, in a measure, this new millennium:

And he will lift up an ensign to the nations from far, . . . and behold, they shall come with speed swiftly; none shall be weary nor stumble among them.

None shall slumber nor sleep; neither shall the girdle of their loins be loosed, nor the latchet of their shoes be broken.

With this coming millennial season, and being young in life as most of you are, begin your missions with great enthusiasm. This is the time for you to set lofty goals for your mission, as well as for the rest of your life.

The purpose and goal of your mission and your divine commission as missionaries is to give every nation, kindred, tongue, and people the opportunity to hear and accept the fulness of the gospel of Jesus Christ.

And he said unto them, Go ye into all the world, and preach the gospel to every creature.

He that believeth and is baptized shall be saved; but he that believeth not shall be damned. (Mark 16:15–16)

Go ye therefore, and teach all nations, baptizing them in the name of the Father, and the Son, and of the Holy Ghost:

Teaching them to observe all things whatsoever I have commanded you: and, lo, I am with you alway, even unto the end of the world. (Matthew 28:11)

And it came to pass that thus they did go forth among all the people of Nephi, and did preach the gospel of Christ unto all people upon the face of the land; and they were converted unto the Lord, and were united unto the church of Christ, and thus the people of that generation were blessed, according to the word of Jesus. (3 Nephi 28:23)

And this gospel shall be preached unto every nation, and kindred, and tongue, and people. (D&C 132:37)

## Suggestions for Success in the Mission Field

We must also think of obedience, which is sometimes called the first law of heaven. As you combine obedience, diligence, and righteousness you will enjoy success during your mission.

What is diligence? Diligence is one of those spiritual, unique virtues that must be experienced before it can fully be understood. We can try to describe it, but to truly understand it, you must achieve it. I am confident that most of you missionaries have experienced the thrill of diligent service. Like any virtue, however, you must nurture it daily or it will fade.

Diligence is mentioned repeatedly in the scriptures. It is included specifically with other godly attributes in the 4th section of the Doctrine and Covenants, which describes the type of person the Lord calls to do His work.

How can you serve God with all your "heart, might, mind and strength," without being diligent?

How can you thrust in your sickle with your might, without being diligent?

How can you serve with an eye single to the glory of God, without being diligent?

Diligence is essential to your success. It is the fundamental characteristic of the very work that God requires of you. If you are not diligent, you will surely fall short of the Lord's expectations. On the other hand, if you are diligent, I can promise you will be abundantly rewarded.

## Missionaries and Diligence—A Story

To illustrate diligence, let me tell you a missionary story.

Two missionaries had spent a long day visiting people, tracting, going to appointments, and contacting referrals. They had been rejected at numerous doors, their appointments had fallen through, and no one seemed interested. Now they are tired, hungry, hot, thirsty, and a little discouraged. Finally, their dinner hour approaches, and they have the chance for some refreshment and rest. But as they are about to return to their apartment, they look far down the street. Standing on a hill, the last house was isolated at the end of the lane. The task of simply visiting the home seems almost too much to expect of them. The missionaries look at each other. Do they walk all that way to knock on that door—the last one of the afternoon, or do they go home for dinner? After all, no one has accepted their message all day long. Why should they expect the reception in this house to be any different?

These missionaries, fortunately, followed the promptings of the Spirit and made that final effort to visit this last house. Their knock was answered by a man and his wife, who looked at them with amazement and gratitude. The missionaries were invited in and learned that the couple had been praying that the Lord would send someone to teach them the truth. They had been watching the missionaries through their front window, wondering if these young men were the messengers for whom they had prayed.

The setting varies, the situation changes, but this story captures the spirit of diligent missionary work. Inspirational stories often portray second-mile efforts. Now suppose this story had a different ending, something like this:

The missionaries looked to the end of the lane, but it was so far away. They were hungry, and they returned to their apartment and enjoyed a nice dinner. If this were the story's ending, it would not be a story at all.

How often would we repeat a story that ended with the missionaries turning away from their duty? The story is worth repeating precisely because the missionaries made the effort, they persevered, and, yes, they were diligent. And, so it will be throughout our lives and, even, into the eternities.

Our own stories, the ones we create for ourselves, will be those we experience after we have gone the extra mile, after we have persevered, after we have finished the task, after we have brought forth fruits of righteousness.

## Diligence Defined

*Diligence* has several interesting definitions. Some definitions relate to attitude. For example, *diligence* means "careful attention to," or "to interest one's self most earnestly." Seen in that light, we begin to sense why the Lord used this word in reference to missionary work. Remember he said to work with "an eye single" to God's glory. If we have a proper missionary attitude, we will interest ourselves most earnestly in the eternal welfare of others.

The sons of Mosiah were the model: "Now they were desirous that salvation should be declared to every creature, for they could not bear that any human soul should perish; yea, even the very thoughts, that any soul should endure endless torment did cause them to quake and tremble" (Mosiah 28:3). Given this attitude, they were able to pay careful attention to their work.

A diligent attitude is not sufficient; however, it is a beginning, not the end. Attitudes, feelings, and beliefs must lead to action, or nothing will be accomplished.

*Diligence* has a second set of definitions that include the idea of action. It means "constant, careful effort; perseverance; industry, done with careful steady effort; painstaking." One Greek word translated as *diligence* in the New Testament means "active and zealous." Another one means "with haste; earnestness in accomplishing, promoting, or striving after anything."

The story I related earlier illustrated missionaries who applied constant, careful effort and perseverance.

Sometimes your work will be painstaking. It requires having patience and fortitude. It requires courage. Ask yourselves these questions:

Do I work hard, even when I'm not under pressure or close supervision?

Am I distracted by things that are not relevant to my calling?

Do I continue working hard until the job is successfully completed?

Do I find joy and satisfaction in my work?

You become diligent through determined effort. Set goals; make plans; follow through on your plans. Diligence provides its own reward, and it will be answered with blessings on your heads. If for some reason you have been less than diligent, remember the assurance given by President Spencer W. Kimball: "The slothful or inadequate servant can repent, exchange apathy for diligence, and receive God's forgiveness" (*The Miracle of Forgiveness*, 101).

## Suggestions for Diligence in Missionary Work

Here are my suggestions for what you should do to be diligent in this sacred work:

- Rise and retire early
- Pray often
- Feast regularly upon the scriptures
- Set goals
- Plan
- Exercise daily
- Work hard and consistently
- Keep the commandments
- Follow the guidance of your wonderful mission presidents
- Keep your granary of investigators filled and reap converts
- Demonstrate to the members your ability to teach the gospel. They will have confidence in you and provide you with referrals.

Time is very precious to you and me. I often heard my college physics professor, Dr. Thomas J. Parmley, a spiritual giant, so forcefully say: "Do not waste your life! Life is such a precious gift, it should be guarded from needless dilution. Each day is not just another day, but more like a falling drop of water, a golden moment of life's span, added to an increasingly rich pool of living. Make the most of it, and you will never regret your decision."

## Promises from the Lord—Examples of Diligence

Consider these promises from the Lord.

Peter the Apostle admonished the Saints of his day to give "all diligence" to the development of virtues such as faith, knowledge, temperance, and charity. He promised, "If these things be in you, and abound, they make you that ye shall neither be barren nor unfruitful in the knowledge of our Lord Jesus Christ" (2 Peter 1:5–8).

In the Book of Mormon, Ammon was rewarded for his diligent labors. "He did exhort [the people of king Lamoni] daily, with all diligence; and they gave heed unto his word, and they were zealous for keeping the commandments of God" (Alma 21:23).

Do you desire the same for the investigators, converts, and less-active members who you work with? One of President Hinckley's major concerns of missionary work is convert retention, and as missionaries you carry important responsibilities in this regard. Do you inspire your investigators "daily, with all diligence" so that they will give heed unto God's word?

These are just some of the rewards of diligence. Again, diligence is its own reward, satisfying in and of itself because you know that you have done all you could and you have realized the blessings that come from being persistent.

I have tried to describe diligence. Some examples may help you envision this quality as it becomes more and more a part of your personality.

The Father and the Son are themselves models of diligence. In creating this beautiful planet, they pursued a carefully designed plan. There are some interesting phrases in the book of Abraham. For example, verses 10 and 12, in chapter 4 note that "the Gods saw that they were obeyed." One meaning of this phrase is that they watched over their work, to make certain it turned out exactly as they had planned. Verse 18 of chapter 4 says, "And the Gods watched those things which they had ordered, until they obeyed." This was exemplary and diligent watch care over their work. This was necessary to bring to pass the immortality and eternal life of man. Think what it could mean to your investigators and converts if you were to exercise this same determined care for their souls until they obey because they grow and experience the blessings of a testimony of the gospel, a pure heart, and faith.

The Prophet Joseph Smith not only exhorted the Saints to diligence, but he wonderfully exemplified this principle. His accomplishments during his brief life are remarkable.

President Gordon B. Hinckley expressed his admiration for the Prophet Joseph Smith in this way, "I am now growing old, and I know that in the natural course of events before many years, I will step across the threshold to stand before my Maker . . . my Lord and give an accounting of my life. And I hope that I shall have the opportunity of embracing the Prophet Joseph Smith and of thanking him, and of speaking of my love for him" ("As One Who Loves the Prophet," as quoted in Susan Easton Black and Charles Tate, ed., *Joseph Smith: The Prophet, the Man,* BYU Religious Studies Center, 11–12).

I am also inspired by President Heber J. Grant's perseverance. He often quoted this statement from memory: "That which we persist in doing becomes easier for us to do, not that the nature of the thing itself is changed, but that our power to do is increased" (see *Gospel Standards,* 355).

As a young boy I listened to a radio broadcast of general conference and could hear President Grant singing. He was standing directly behind the microphone, and his voice could be heard above the congregation. He had a loud voice, but whether it was great, I questioned. But, regardless, President Grant practiced what he preached. It was through his dogged determination that he learned how to play baseball, to develop a penmanship that overcame his hen scratchings, and to sing well enough that he could bless others. He described one effort he made to polish his singing skills: "Upon my recent trip to Arizona, I asked elders Rudger Clawson and J. Golden Kimball if they had any objections to my singing one hundred hymns that day. They took it as a joke and assured me that they would be delighted [to hear them]. We were on the way from Holbrook to St. Johns, a distance of about sixty miles. After I had sang about forty tunes, they assured me that if I sung the remaining sixty they would be sure to have nervous prostration" (*Gospel Standards*, 354). Such diligence shows the character that qualified him for the prophetic mantle.

## Example of President Hinckley

To me personally, President Gordon B. Hinckley has become a most notable example of diligence. I wrote these thoughts when Sister Wirthlin and I accompanied him and Sister Hinckley on a trip to Asia.

This experience was similar to running a marathon. But it has been an unusual privilege to recognize in President Hinckley something special, and unusual. He is superb in every way—spiritually, intellectually, and physically. He is a polished stone, who has been groomed through his years as a General Authority. Everywhere we went, President Hinckley savored the experience. But then he would be anxious to move on. "Let's go" became his rallying cry. And go we did. President Hinckley's enthusiasm, optimism, and above all else his diligence, was evident in every step of our journey. He loves people everywhere. That's why he keeps such a busy schedule and extends himself as much as he can, for the best good of the members and friends of the Church. To him, poor and rich look the same. I have known President Hinckley since boyhood, and I always knew he was remarkable, but I never knew how remarkable until we spent eighteen days at his side in the Orient. I returned home a better person.

During our whirlwind eighteen-day-trip, President Hinckley addressed nearly 60,000 members of the Church. He presided over seven dedicatory sessions at the Hong Kong Temple, plus the cornerstone laying ceremony. He visited multiple cities in Japan, Korea, and the Philippines, plus Hong Kong and Saipan. He made stops in Taiwan, Okinawa, Cambodia, Vietnam, and mainland China.

When asked how he maintains such a pace, he joked, "I go to bed every night and make sure I get up the next morning. I just keep going." Then he admitted, "The climate in this part of the world is enervating. But you get your lift from the people. They give me the energy to keep going. I love being among the Saints."

To you elder and sister missionaries, including couples, President Hinckley provides a marvelous model. You may not visit eight countries in two weeks. No, you may not bear witness and teach the gospel to 60,000 people in a single trip, but within your sphere of influence, you can follow President Hinckley's example of diligence.

## Perseverance

Prepare yourselves diligently through gospel study. Then talk to as many people as you can, with the intent of teaching them the gospel and inviting them to accept its saving ordinances. This formula has been proven: the greater number of contacts, the larger number of conversions. In other words, no contacts, no conversions.

After the baptism and confirmation of converts, in cooperation with local leaders, you should watch over these new members diligently, until they can stand independently on their own.

Improve your performance each day with perseverance. Emulate our beloved prophet. Say to one another, "Let's go," then go to work with vigor, determination, and diligence. Go with fervent faith among the people. His contact with the people energizes President Hinckley. Your contact with the people will energize you.

In this context, I will paraphrase what the Prophet Joseph Smith said about building the Nauvoo Temple: "Let the [missionary] work . . . be continued on and not cease; and let your diligence and your perseverance and patience and your works be redoubled, and you shall in no wise lose your reward" (*Personal Writings of Joseph Smith*, 544).

I have tried to be diligent in my own life. I learned from my father and mother the importance of this principle in approaching any assignment. I would hope that each one of us will be diligent and magnify our callings. Endure to the end, which requires diligence that consists of pure, dogged determination, application to duty, and obedience to counsel. This should be your promise to the Lord. If we are diligent in this sacred work, the Lord will say to us, "Well done, thou good and faithful servant."

I testify to you, my beloved missionaries, that if we are to be successful, we must follow with exactness the great quality of diligence so evident in the ministries of our Lord and Savior, Jesus Christ, the Prophet Joseph Smith, and the prophets who followed him, which includes our living prophet, President Gordon B. Hinckley. I testify to you with the authority I bear that we do have a loving Heavenly Father, the creator of our spirits, and that His only begotten son, Jesus Christ, gave us the great atonement and resurrection. I bless each of you with that great quality of diligence as one of the attributes you should acquire, not only in the mission field, but continue this divine attribute throughout your lives as members of the true and living Church.

*(Adapted from an address to missionaries*
*at the Missionary Training Center in Provo,*
*Utah, 18 August 1998)*

# 16

# CARRY ON

## *Storms Will Come*

In recent years, we have witnessed floods, famines, hurricanes, earth-quakes, and fires destroying villages and tormenting cities, bringing untold distress into the lives of millions throughout the world.

No matter how beautiful and serene a place is, no matter how peace-ful it may appear—sooner or later, there will come a time of sorrow.

As with places, so it is with people. None can sail the seas of life expecting them to be ever calm and tranquil.

Storms will come.

Sorrow will come.

Grief will come.

I have a personal and intimate knowledge of this.

This topic has been on my mind a great deal of late. And I have spent many hours in solitude, asking the questions we all ask when grief enters our lives.

I suspect that some reading this book are currently experiencing some kind of sadness or trial. And I'd like to leave with you a few words of counsel and encouragement.

I will tell you at the start what my message will be—it is to carry on.

Through sorrow and hardship and fear; through pain, uncertainty, and discouragement: carry on.

## Pioneers

I often reflect on those early members of the restored Church who left their beloved homes and set out upon their long and difficult journeys to the valley of the Great Salt Lake. The descendents of those pioneers now live throughout the world. Many of you who are reading this are likely descended from those remarkable men, women, and children who walked across sand and rock and ice. They carried a few of their earthly possessions in handcarts, wagons, and on their backs. Most of them, too, carried deep personal sorrow. They bore with them the scars of emotional and physical suffering unthinkable to many in our day.

I marvel at the strength of character they must have had to leave their possessions behind. I marvel at their faith as they buried on the trail loved ones who had perished during the journey.

How did they do it? How did they muster the strength to carry on?

In our day, many who struggle with hardship and trial wonder "Why?" Why must *they* feel so lonely, sick, discouraged, oppressed, or brokenhearted?

The answer to the question, "Why me?" can be difficult to answer, and pondering it can lead to frustration, despair, and emotional and physical paralysis.

There is a better question; one that leads from the deepest night to the light of dawn. That question is, "What now?"

Those who endure, who persevere in spite of trials and burdens, often become our heroes. They are the ones who demonstrate the courage of the human heart and the nobility of the divine spirit.

## Ammon

Do you remember the story of Ammon in the Book of Mormon?

He and his brothers—the sons of King Mosiah—traveled deep into the heart of enemy territory to preach the gospel to the Lamanites.

While Ammon experienced great success, his brothers were not so fortunate. The Book of Mormon tells us that it was their lot to have fallen into the hands of a more hardened and more stiff-necked people. They were beaten and ridiculed, hungry and thirsty, and they suffered all manner of afflictions.

Why did Ammon experience success in his labors while his brothers experienced such hardship? Was it because he was more righteous or a better missionary or because God loved him more than his brothers?

That seems doubtful to me.

Before the little band began their missions, the Lord promised if they would, "bear with patience thine afflictions . . . I will give unto you success" (Alma 26:27).

And that is what they did. In spite of being cast out and mocked and spit upon, and stoned (see Alma 26:29), in spite of their discomfort, fears, and distress, they were "patient in all their sufferings" (Alma 20:29).

They carried on. And, ultimately, they experienced the promised success.

Like the brothers of Ammon, we are sometimes afflicted with the thorns of life. Sometimes, it seems the burden we bear is heavier than that of others around us.

President Ezra Taft Benson taught, "It is not on the pinnacle of success and ease where men and women grow most. It is often down in the valley of heartache and disappointment and reverses where men and women grow into strong characters" (in Conference Report, Stockholm Sweden Area Conference, 1974, 70; quoted by Julio E. Dávila, "The Conversion Process," *Ensign*, Nov. 1991, 24).

## Joseph Smith

To me, the Prophet Joseph Smith has always been a great example of perseverance. From the time he was a young man, he was persecuted, mocked, and reviled. And yet he carried on.

One night, a mob of forty men stormed the Prophet's house and pulled him and Sidney Rigdon outside. Joseph's wife, Emma, screamed and pleaded with the men to stop, but they did not listen. His assailants tried unsuccessfully to force nitric acid down the Prophet's throat, chipping his tooth in the process. They stripped him and covered his body with tar and feathers.

Joseph survived the assault and managed to stumble back to his house. It took his friends the entire night to scrape the tar from his skin.

The following day, the Prophet rose and spoke to those who had assembled for the Sunday meeting. Ironically, among those present in the congregation were some members of the mob who had assaulted him the night before.

Joseph Smith never looked back. From the day he was called of the Father and the Son—from the moment he understood what the Lord required of him—he carried on.

## The Savior

The Savior devoted his mortal life to accomplishing the infinite work of the Atonement and ministering to those in darkness and distress. One reason he was so effective was because He Himself knew what it was like to suffer, to be alone, to be betrayed.

Through all His trials, the Savior carried on.

Though He was the son of God, He bore His sufferings patiently. Although He had created the world and could have commanded untold worldly wealth, He lived humbly, having no place to lay his head (see Matthew 8:20). He suffered betrayal, mockery, and pain such as we cannot imagine, and yet, He freely forgave His tormentors and asked His Father to do the same.

He carried on.

## Endurance

A fundamental quality of heroes is that they endure to the end. Our literature, films, and lives are filled with stories of heroes who persevered in spite of adversity. Those who give up are often forgotten. But we remember, respect, and revere those who never give up and who never surrender.

The Apostle Paul taught that "Our light affliction, which is but for a moment, worketh for us a far more exceeding and eternal weight of glory" (2 Corinthians 4:17).

In other words, our afflictions don't merely precede the glory, they help produce it.

One of the things I learned by playing sports was that no matter how many times champions were knocked down, champions picked themselves up and carried on. Especially when they felt beaten, they carried on. The harder they were hit, the quicker they got up. The more hopeless things looked, the harder they worked.

Champions never give up.

Henry Ward Beecher once wrote, "Affliction comes to us all, not to make us sad, but sober; not to make us sorry, but wise. . . . It is trial that proves one thing weak and another strong. . . . A cobweb is as good as the mightiest cable when there is no strain upon it" (*Richard Evans' Quote Book* [Salt Lake City: Publishers Press, 1971], 56).

We must never lose faith in the face of trial. Peter wrote that "After that ye have suffered a while, [God will] make you perfect, stablish [sic], strengthen, [and] settle you" (1 Peter 5:10).

In our day, the Lord promises us the same: "Search diligently, pray always, and be believing," we are told, "and all things shall work together for your good, if ye walk uprightly" (D&C 90:24).

The Lord has not promised freedom from distress. But He has promised that if we are faithful, blessings will follow.

If we carry on, in God's own time, they will follow.

## *Example of Carrying On*

A friend of mine started having headaches when he was seventeen years old. He is eighty-eight years old now. For more than seventy years, nearly every day of his life, he has suffered with pain. Sometimes it hurts so severely, it nearly paralyzes him.

What does he do? Does he spend his days wondering "Why me?"?

No. Instead, he focuses on another question, "What now?"

His formula for success is quite simple. "I get up in the morning," he explains, "I get dressed and go to work. And sometimes, when I lose myself in my work, the pain subsides."

So many people use their trials as an excuse for failure or for giving up. I have known many successful people in my lifetime, and I can tell you that most of the work done in this world is done by people who don't feel well.

Heroes carry on.

## *Wait upon the Lord*

How long should we persevere? The answer is simple: just as long as we want the Lord to persevere with us—forever. To do so is possible, for Isaiah reassures us "that the everlasting God . . . giveth power to the faint; and to them that have no might he increaseth strength" (Isaiah 40:28, 29).

And then the prophet offers this magnificent promise to those who carry on: "But they that wait upon the Lord shall renew their strength; they shall mount up with wings as eagles; they shall run, and not be weary; and they shall walk, and not faint" (Isaiah 40:31).

Your life's journey may be a particularly difficult one; however, as we shift our thoughts from the difficulty of the path and think instead on the glory of the destination, the journey will become a little easier, our step a little surer, and the dawn a little closer.

We are sons and daughters of the Eternal God, joint-heirs with

Christ of all that the Father has (Romans 8:17; D&C 84:38). We are to be kings and queens, princes and princesses.

We stand as witnesses of God the Father and His Son. We are the heralds of the glorious second coming of our Lord and Savior Jesus Christ. We work tirelessly to bring about the blessed and prophesied Zion. We are citizens, ambassadors, and soldiers of the Lord God of Israel.

Knowing who we are, shall we slumber while the trumpet sounds? Shall we be among those foolish servants who awaited the coming of the bridegroom with lamps empty of oil? Or will we carry on in spite of our fears, in spite of our years, in spite of our tears? Will we not overcome our challenges? Will we not stand triumphant as faithful, loyal, and joyful servants of the Most High God?

I trust that, in spite of our sorrows, our burdens, our fears, we will take courage from the words of our beloved hymn:

> *Firm as the mountains around us,*
> *Stalwart and brave we stand*
> *On the rock our fathers planted*
> *For us in this goodly land—* . . .
> *O [saints] of the noble birthright,*
> *Carry on, carry on, carry on!*
> (Hymns, *no. 255)*

I witness before you, that the God of this universe loves and is mindful of His children. He will not forget nor forsake you.

I testify that His Son, Jesus the Christ, through an infinite atonement, provided a way for all mankind to participate in the incomprehensible blessings of eternal life. The Prophet Joseph Smith stands at the head of the Dispensation of the Fulness of Times, and as God's authorized servant, he ushered in an era of restoration and rebirth. A prophet of God, President Gordon B. Hinckley, lives and guides the Lord's Church in our day.

Many hands today are weary. Many hearts are heavy.

My promise to you is that one day, as we look back upon our little span of existence here on this earth, we will lift our voices and rejoice that, in spite of the difficulties we encountered, we had the wisdom, the foresight, and the courage to remain faithful and carry on.

*(Based on an address given in a stake conference broadcast to 33 stakes in Australia, 28 January 2007)*

# 17

# WINDOWS OF LIGHT AND TRUTH

This is an age of digital information. Our computers have become windows through which we can gaze upon a world that is virtually without horizons or boundaries. Literally at the click of a button, we can browse through the digitized libraries of universities, museums, government agencies, and research institutions located throughout the world. A worldwide web of electronic connections now moves data at ever-increasing speed and volume along what we call the information superhighway. Through the windows of personal computer monitors in homes and offices, we can access this network of interconnected data banks to see texts, art, photos, maps, and charts and to hear music and speech that are stored in widely dispersed locations.

Likewise, instruments of many types give us insight that we would not have without them. Telescopes and microscopes bring to our view the otherwise unseen and unknown. Modern medicine uses imaging "windows" such as magnetic resonance imaging scanners to bring into view otherwise unseen vital information that skilled physicians can use for the benefit of their patients. The air traffic controller's radar scope is another example of a window that provides lifesaving vision of faraway objects that are invisible without this crucial instrument. A skilled controller can use the information on his radar scope to guide a pilot to safety.

## *Windows of Revelation*

The Church of Jesus Christ of Latter-day Saints declares boldly that through another type of window, the windows of heaven, we can access spiritual information from the Source of light and truth. "We believe all that God has revealed, all that He does now reveal, and we believe that He will yet reveal many great and important things pertaining to the Kingdom of God" (Articles of Faith 1:9). In this, the dispensation of the fulness of times, the *revelation* superhighway has been carrying heavy traffic of eternal truth ever since that day in the spring of 1820 when the Lord answered a farm boy's fervent prayer in the Sacred Grove and ushered in the restoration of the gospel of Jesus Christ.

We are blessed to live in these, the latter days, when a loving Heavenly Father has called a great leader, President Gordon B. Hinckley, as prophet, seer, and revelator. Through him, the Lord opens windows of revelation to guide and bless all of our Father's children who will heed the words of the prophet. Today, as in ancient times, God opens windows of gospel light and truth by revealing "his secret unto his servants the prophets" (Amos 3:7). Those who have "eyes to see, and ears to hear" (Deuteronomy 29:4) can learn eternal principles; view majestic vistas of knowledge, foresight, and wisdom; and receive direction on how to live their lives.

If we configure our hearts and minds properly with faith, disciplined obedience, prayer, and scripture study, we can access the network of divine and eternal truths. We can receive the teachings and counsel of God's prophet, opening to us knowledge and revelation from our Heavenly Father and his Beloved Son, Jesus Christ.

The Lord counsels us to become skilled in using these spiritual windows so we can seek and receive personal revelation for ourselves and our families. When the storms of life leave us disoriented, the windows of revelation can guide us safely home to our Heavenly Father. If we should yield to temptations of the adversary and find ourselves weakened spiritually, inspired bishops and other caring leaders can open the windows of revelation to provide spiritual direction. Well-prepared and inspired missionaries can open the windows of heaven to enlighten those "who are only kept from the truth because they know not where to find it" (D&C 123:12).

## Obedience Opens the Windows of Heaven

The windows of heaven are open wide to the faithful and righteous; but nothing closes them faster than disobedience. The unworthy cannot fully access the network of revealed truth, for "the powers of heaven cannot be controlled nor handled only upon the principles of righteousness" (D&C 121:36). "Obedience is the first law of heaven" (*Teachings of Ezra Taft Benson,* Bookcraft, 1988, 26). That is why Alma exhorted us to "be humble, . . . submissive and . . . diligent in keeping the commandments of God at *all* times" (Alma 7:23; emphasis added). To open the windows of heaven, we must conform our will to God's will. Diligent, enduring obedience to God's laws is the key. Obedience enables us to be receptive to the mind and will of the Lord. "The Lord requireth the heart and a willing mind; and the willing and obedient" (D&C 64:34) are those who are eligible to receive the blessings of revelation.

## Missionary Service

The Lord has commanded Church members to "proclaim . . . unto the world" (D&C 1:18) the restoration of the fulness of the gospel, open the windows of light and truth to all of our brothers and sisters and to do so "with all [our] heart, might, mind and strength" (D&C 4:2). Our Savior has told us that "the voice of warning shall be unto all people, by the mouths of [His] disciples" who "shall go forth and none shall stay them" (D&C 1:4–5).

Members of the Lord's church can joyfully echo these words of the prophet Mormon: "Behold, I am a disciple of Jesus Christ, the Son of

God. I have been called of him to declare his word among his people, that they might have everlasting life" (3 Nephi 5:13).

We are the Savior's disciples who "shall go forth." All of us are "called of him to [be missionaries to] declare his word among his people." We may serve as full-time missionaries in young adulthood and later on as older couples. These windows of opportunity are open for a relatively short period of time. We should therefore follow the counsel of President Spencer W. Kimball and "Do it," and he added, "Do it right now." Ward missionaries and loving neighbors also have the opportunity to perform this divine service. We all have the sacred obligation and joyful opportunity to throw open the windows of light and truth by proclaiming the blessings of everlasting life to a darkened world. If we shy away from this responsibility, we should remember that the Lord has promised that "*none shall stay [us]*" and that "there is no eye that shall not see, neither ear that shall not hear, neither heart that shall not be penetrated" (D&C 1:5, 2; emphasis added). We can experience no greater joy than to see the light of the gospel shine in the eyes and face of a newly baptized brother or sister who has "spiritually been born of God," who has "experienced [a] mighty change in [heart]," and who has "the image of God engraven upon [his or her countenance]!" (Alma 5:14, 19).

If we are to obey the Lord's command to open the windows of heaven to all of our brothers and sisters, we must prepare to teach the gospel. With study of the scriptures, fasting, and prayer, we fortify our testimonies. We cultivate the Christ-like attributes of "faith, virtue, knowledge, temperance, patience, brotherly kindness, godliness, charity, humility, [and] diligence" (D&C 4:6). Through exemplary obedience, we can "let [our] light so shine before men, that they may see [our] good works, and glorify [our] Father which is in heaven" (Matthew 5:16). By keeping the commandments, we light our gospel candle and put it "on a candlestick; and it giveth light unto *all* that are in the house" (Matthew 5:15; emphasis added).

## The Law of Tithing

These words from Malachi have a familiar ring for faithful Latter-day Saints: "Bring ye all the tithes into the storehouse, that there may be meat in mine house, and prove me now herewith, saith the Lord of hosts, if I will not open you the windows of heaven, and pour you out a blessing, that there shall not be room enough to receive it" (Malachi 3:10; emphasis added). Perhaps we tend to think of the law of tithing as a temporal commandment only and to see it from a material perspective. We would be shortsighted and ungrateful if we failed to see and acknowledge the great spiritual blessings that result from obedience to this divine law. When we are obedient, the windows of heaven are opened not just to pour out blessings of earthly abundance but also blessings of spiritual abundance—blessings of infinite and eternal worth.

President Gordon B. Hinckley has declared that the blessings from paying tithing "may not be always in the form of financial or material benefit." He explained that "there are many ways in which the Lord can bless us beyond the riches of the world. There is the great boon of health. The Lord has promised [in Malachi 3:11] that he will rebuke the devourer for our sakes. Malachi speaks of the fruits of our ground. May not that rebuke of the devourer apply to *various* of our personal efforts and concerns?" ("Tithing: An Opportunity to Prove Our Faithfulness," *Ensign*, May 1982, 40; emphasis added).

## The Word of Wisdom

Beginning in 1833, the Prophet Joseph Smith taught the blessings of avoiding tobacco and other addictive substances when the Lord opened the windows of heaven and revealed "a word of wisdom." This revelation, given for the benefit of the "saints in Zion," warns against the "evils and designs which do and will exist in the hearts of conspiring men in the last days" (D&C 89:1, 4).

One of the first articles to document a link between smoking and lung cancer appeared in the *Journal of the American Medical Association* in 1950 (see *Time,* 24 July 1995, 19), one hundred seventeen years after the Lord opened this window to his prophet.

The physical blessings of health and strength that are promised (See D&C 89:18–21) through obedience to the Word of Wisdom are now well-known and well-documented (see Russell M. Nelson, "Joy Cometh in the Morning," *Ensign,* Nov. 1986, 69. See also James A. Enstrom, "Health Practices and Cancer Mortality among Active California Mormons," *Journal of the National Cancer Institute,* vol. 81, no. 23, 6 Dec. 1989; Edward Norden, "How to Live as Long As They Do," *Longevity,* Sept. 1990). In addition, the spiritual blessings of "wisdom and great treasures of knowledge, even hidden treasures" (D&C 89:19) are promised to those who keep their bodies free from addictive substances. When we obey the Word of Wisdom, windows of personal revelation are opened to us, and our souls are filled with divine light and truth. If we keep our bodies undefiled, the Holy Ghost "shall come upon [us] and . . . dwell in [our] heart[s]" (D&C 8:2) and teach us "the peaceable things of immortal glory" (Moses 6:61).

## Word of Wisdom for the Mind

Our Heavenly Father opened the windows of heaven and gave his children the Word of Wisdom to warn against consuming substances that can damage and destroy our physical bodies. He likewise has, through prophets, cautioned against consuming the steady diet of evil that is relentlessly offered in today's media, especially magazines, movies, the Internet, videocassettes, DVDs, video games, and television. The windows of computer monitors and television screens can bring to us very useful information, but they can also bring information that is evil, degrading, and destructive.

The Lord has warned repeatedly against the evils and designs of conspiring men in our day who would enslave us to our appetites and passions by tempting and tantalizing us with obscene images, words, and music. Through his servants, the Lord has cautioned us strongly not to take into our minds thoughts that can harm our spirits.

Since 1950, Church leaders speaking in general conference have counseled us some seventy-five times against consuming unhealthy media fare. In recent years, as standards of public decency and morality have declined and as public media have reflected and often led that decline, these words of loving concern from inspired shepherds of the Lord's flock have come with more frequency and greater urgency. The watchmen on the tower have raised a warning voice.

I add my own voice. I suggest that we pay greater heed to voices of warning that our Father in Heaven has raised against the forces of Satan, which come so easily and so pervasively into our homes through the media. I think of all the words of counsel and direction that we have received on this matter as constituting collectively a "word of wisdom for the mind." Just as we exercise great care about what we take into our bodies through our mouths, we should exert a similar vigilance about what we take into our minds through our eyes and ears.

## Gift of the Holy Ghost

The gift of the Holy Ghost may be likened to a sure, personal compass to provide lifesaving vision, wisdom, and insight as a spiritual window. The Holy Ghost gives us clear guidance and direction in a world of unanchored faith. President James E. Faust expressed his assuring testimony that "the Spirit of the Holy Ghost is the greatest guarantor of inward peace in our unstable world. . . . It will calm nerves; it will breathe peace to our souls. . . . It can enhance our natural senses so that we can *see more clearly*, hear more keenly, and remember what we should remember. It is a way of maximizing our happiness" ("The Gift of the Holy Ghost—A Sure Compass," *Ensign,* May 1989, 32–33; emphasis added).

## Worthy Worship

Windows must be washed regularly to clean away dust and dirt. If left to accumulate without regular cleaning, thickening grime can block out light and darken the window. Just as earthly windows need consistent, thorough cleaning, so do the windows of our spirituality.

Weekly sacrament meeting attendance helps us keep our personal windows of heaven free from the obscuring haze of earthly distractions and temptations. By partaking of the sacrament worthily to renew our baptismal covenants, we clarify our view of life's eternal purpose and divine priorities. The sacrament prayers invite personal introspection, repentance, and rededication as we pledge our willingness to remember our Savior, Jesus the Christ. This commitment to become like Christ, repeated weekly, defines the supreme aspiration of Latter-day Saint life.

Frequent temple attendance, as our circumstances allow, is another way to keep our spiritual windows clean. Worship in the house of the Lord will keep our view of what matters most clear and sharp, focused crisply, and free from the dust of the world.

## Testimony

I testify that the windows of heaven are, indeed, open. President Gordon B. Hinckley is the Lord's living prophet today. Joseph Smith is the Prophet of the Restoration. Jesus is the Christ, the Lord and Savior of all mankind. Our Heavenly Father lives and loves each of His children. The Lord has restored the network of eternal truth. We can open the windows of heaven to our personal view. Through these divine windows, we can gaze with the Savior "upon the wide expanse of eternity" (D&C 38:1), a universe without horizons, "worlds without end" (D&C 76:112).

*(Adapted from an October 1995 general conference address)*

# 18

## GROWING INTO THE PRIESTHOOD

### *Introduction*

I love the young men of the Aaronic Priesthood. Some will find it hard to believe, but it doesn't seem all that long ago since I was a young man. When I was a deacon, the ominous signs of the Great Depression began to appear. Tens of thousands of Americans lost their jobs. Money was scarce, and families had to do without. Some young people did not ask their mothers, "What's for dinner?" because they knew all too well that their cupboards held very little.

My parents were hardworking. They made every penny stretch as far as possible. That was probably the major reason everything they gave me was always two or three sizes too large.

I was twelve years old when I received my first pair of ice skates, so large that I had to stuff a third of the toe space with cotton.

When I took them out of the box, I looked up and said, "Mother, I can't skate with these."

"Be grateful for what you have, Joseph," she said. And then, the phrase I had become so accustomed to hearing, "Don't worry; you'll grow into them."

A year later, what I wanted more than anything else were football shoulder pads and a helmet. On Christmas morning, I opened my packages and there they were, shoulder pads and a helmet, except they were sized to fit Goliath—who, by the way, was six cubits or about nine feet tall.

"Mother, they're too big," I said.

"Be grateful for what you have, Joseph," she said again, adding her familiar "Don't worry; you'll grow into them."

Prior to high school I played a lot of neighborhood football. When I put on the new equipment, the shoulder pads hung so far over my shoulders that about the only things they protected were my elbows.

Even though I stuffed cotton and newspaper in the helmet, it jostled every time I took a step. When I ran, it would turn and turn until the only way I could see where I was going would be to look out through the ear hole.

One time I rambled for a long gain at full speed right into a tree. Each time I was tackled, the helmet would spin 180 degrees, and I'd get up looking like my head had spun with it. Then I would have to repack the cotton and newspaper as best I could, put it back on, and head back to the huddle.

My father was truly a great man. I remember one day putting my feet in my father's shoes. I was amazed at the size. *Will I ever be big enough to fill his shoes? Can I ever grow into the man my father is?* I wondered.

I think back on those days with some tenderness. Curiously enough, I also look back with tenderness to my dear mother's encouraging words, "Don't worry, Joseph; you'll grow into them."

In a similar way, we all need to learn how to "grow into" our responsibilities as priesthood bearers.

## The Great Possibilities of Youth

First, I want to assure young men that the Lord has his eye upon you. He loves you. He knows you. He knows your triumphs and your trials, your successes and your heartaches.

He knows that at times you look at the challenges you face and think they're too big to handle. He is, however, willing and ready to help you as you grow into the men you are to become.

You may think at times the duties you have as Aaronic Priesthood bearers are insignificant or unimportant, but I assure you they are not.

Everything you do in the Aaronic Priesthood has a spiritual purpose and is important to the Lord. Whenever you exercise the priesthood, you are on the Lord's errand, doing the Lord's business. You go as His servant, bearing His authority, to act in His name.

I remember when my father, who was also my bishop, laid his hands upon my head to confer upon me the Aaronic Priesthood. I felt something special that day. In the coming weeks, that feeling returned as I passed the sacred emblems of the sacrament to the members of our ward, whom I looked up to as my ideals. It came to my mind that I was doing the very thing the Savior had done at the Last Supper.

I would like to share with you five principles that if lived and incorporated into your lives while you are young, will assure happiness and peace throughout your lives, no matter what trials and temptations come your way. These principles are revealed by the Lord as counsel to all of us who are striving to grow into the kind of men He would have us be.

## Five Principles for Bearers of the Aaronic Priesthood

*First, place Heavenly Father first in your life.* Remember the words of Alma to his son Helaman: "O, remember, my son, and learn wisdom in thy youth; yea, learn in thy youth to keep the commandments of God" (Alma 37:35). The Savior reminded us of that priority when He taught that the first and greatest commandment is, "Thou shalt love the Lord thy God with all thy heart, and with all thy soul, and with all thy mind" (Matthew 22:37).

If you are to succeed in life and in the priesthood, it is essential that you know and understand that our Heavenly Father loves you like a son, because He is the Father of your spirit. That makes you His literal son, spiritually begotten of Him.

As such, you have inherited the potential to become like Him, and His greatest desire is that you grow in this life line upon line and qualify yourself for the privilege of returning to His presence. Remember, it is God's work and glory to bring to pass your immortality and eternal life (see Moses 1:39).

God's love is complete and without limit for you and for all mankind (see John 3:16). He is perfectly just and merciful (see 2 Nephi 9:17; Mosiah 29:12; Deuteronomy 4:31; Alma 42:15). He is perfectly kind and understands your circumstances and condition (see Isaiah 54:8; 3 Nephi 22:8). He knows you better than you know yourself.

Because your Heavenly Father is perfect, you can have complete faith in Him. You can trust Him. You can keep His commandments by continually striving to do so.

"Does that mean all of God's commandments?" you might ask. Yes! All of them!

Joseph Smith said, "[God] never will institute an ordinance or give a commandment to His people that is not calculated in its nature to promote that happiness which He has designed, and which will not end in the greatest amount of good and glory to those who become the recipients of his law and ordinances" (*History of the Church,* 5:135).

God's commandments are not given to limit or punish us. They are exercises that create character and sanctify souls. If we disregard them, we become spiritually flabby and weak and without defense. If we keep them, we can become spiritual giants, strong and bold in righteousness.

Do you take the time each day to review your day's events with your Heavenly Father? Do you express to Him the desires of your heart and your gratitude for the blessings He pours out upon you?

Day-to-day obedience to God's commandments is indispensable, and our obedience protects us during mortality and prepares us for the tremendous adventure that awaits us on the other side of the veil.

*Second, come unto Christ and follow Him as your Savior and Redeemer.* We can come unto Christ as we learn to love Him and as we study the scriptures diligently. How do we show our love for the Savior? He gave us the answer: "If ye love me, keep my commandments" (John 14:15).

Every one of you can read something in the scriptures each day. You should spend some time pondering and studying the scriptures. It is better to read and ponder even one verse than none at all. I challenge each young man to read something in the scriptures every day for the rest of your lives. Few things you do will bring you greater dividends.

Learn of your Savior. Jesus Christ suffered in the Garden of Gethsemane more than any of us can comprehend. Willingly and lovingly, He took upon Himself not only our sins but the pains, sicknesses, and sufferings of all mankind (see Alma 7:11–12). He suffered similarly on the cross, where He gave His life to pay the penalty for our sins if we will repent. And then in His ultimate triumph, He was resurrected and broke the bands of death, making the Resurrection available to all.

The Atonement of Jesus Christ has given the Savior the power to help you grow into the young man He knows you can be. It is through repentance that the Atonement becomes operative in your life.

The more you understand the Atonement and what it means, the less likely you will be to fall prey to temptations of the adversary. No other doctrine will bring greater results in improving behavior and strengthening character than the doctrine of the Atonement of Jesus Christ. It is central to God's plan and is preeminent in the restored gospel.

My sincere testimony as a special witness is that I know Jesus is the Christ, the Only Begotten of the Father, the Creator of heaven and earth, and our Lord and Savior.

*Third, nurture the companionship of the Holy Ghost.* The gift of the Holy Ghost is one of the most precious gifts you can receive in mortality. The Holy Ghost can become your guiding light. The Holy Ghost "will show unto you all things what ye should do" (2 Nephi 32:5). The Holy Ghost can be helpful to you in any righteous endeavor in which you are involved, including in school and among your friends.

However, the principal mission of the Holy Ghost is to testify of our Heavenly Father and His Beloved Son, Jesus Christ. If you are careful in keeping the commandments, the Holy Ghost will help you learn more about Heavenly Father and Jesus Christ. He will enlighten your mind as you ponder and study the scriptures each day.

The promptings of the Holy Ghost may come to you in a still, small voice. You cannot grow into the man you must become unless you first rise above the things of the world that clamor for your attention. For example, some of the world's music is degrading, vulgar, and inappropriate and will drown out the promptings of the Holy Ghost. Bringing into your body substances forbidden by the Lord in the Word of Wisdom will prevent you from feeling and recognizing the promptings of the Holy Ghost.

The failure to live a clean and chaste life deadens the promptings of the Spirit. Take your thoughts to higher levels than the vulgar and immoral. Avoid objectionable television shows and movies, corrupting Internet sites, and all forms of entertainment that portray or encourage immorality and violence. Shun pornography like the deadly, contagious, sin and disease it is. You cannot afford to become addicted to its bondage and slavery. It will drive the Holy Ghost and His influence from your life.

*Fourth, love and revere Joseph Smith as the great prophet of the Restoration.* Since my youth, I have always been impressed by the fact that our Heavenly Father and His Beloved Son, Jesus Christ, would answer the heartfelt prayers of a fourteen-year-old boy who was searching for the truth. Just as He answered Joseph Smith's prayer, our Heavenly Father will answer your prayers in His own time and in His own way.

As you learn more about the Prophet Joseph, you will discover that through him the fulness of the everlasting gospel was restored, including the keys of the priesthood. In addition, you will learn of the greatness of his spirit, the compassion he felt for those who suffered, his grasp of the mysteries of heaven and of the workings of our Heavenly Father and His Son, Jesus Christ, among men.

The more I learn of the Prophet Joseph, the more I love him, the more I yearn to follow his example, the more I appreciate what our Father in Heaven and His Son have done in restoring this gospel that is destined to fill the earth in these the latter-days.

*Fifth, love, follow, and be loyal to God's living prophet.* President Gordon B. Hinckley is the successor and guardian of those priesthood keys that were first restored to the Prophet Joseph Smith. In mortality, only one man at a time holds and exercises all of the priesthood keys; today that man is President Gordon B. Hinckley.

Follow the teachings of our modern-day prophet. He is inspired of the Lord to teach us those things that are necessary for us to live happily and righteously.

## *Love for the Young Men of the Aaronic Priesthood*

My wonderful young brothers in the gospel, I love you and have great respect for you! You have been told often, and I will say it again: You are a chosen generation. You have been raised up by the Lord to carry His Church and Kingdom into the twenty-first century. You have been chosen by the Lord to come forth on this earth when wickedness and evil are very powerful. But you are up to the challenge.

"I have every reason to regard you," said President Gordon B. Hinckley, "as the greatest generation we've ever had in this Church—notwithstanding all of the temptations which you face" ("You Live in Greatest Age of World; Pres. Hinckley Tells Spokane Youth," *Church News,* 4 Sept. 1999, 3).

That does not mean you will not face your share of heartache, challenge, and trial. Since the days when I first stuffed cotton into my ice skates and put on oversized shoulder pads and helmet, my life has been filled with experiences and challenges that seemed at the time too big for me. Even today I can't help but feel, every now and again, that the size of the mantle I have been asked to wear is perhaps too large.

But every day I try to put Heavenly Father first in my life, I try to come unto Christ and follow Him as my Savior and Redeemer, I nurture the companionship of the Holy Ghost, love and revere the Prophet Joseph, and listen to and follow God's prophet today. As I do those things, I am confident the Lord will bless me.

Even after all these years, I can still hear the voice of my mother: "Be grateful for what you have, Joseph. Don't worry; you'll grow into it."

It is my prayer that we may all grow into the priesthood and be the kind of men our Heavenly Father wants us to be.

*(Adapted from an October 1999 general conference address)*

# 19

# IMPROVING OUR PRAYERS

## Commandment to Pray

There may not be a more frequently uttered commandment than that we lift up our hearts and our voices in prayer to our Heavenly Father.

"Pray always," the Lord has commanded to us in these latter-days, "and I will pour out my Spirit upon you, and great shall be your blessing" (D&C 19:38). The Book of Mormon teaches "Ye must pour out your souls in your closets, and your secret places, and in your wilderness" (Alma 34:26).

And the Apostle Paul teaches that we should "Pray without ceasing. [And] in every thing give thanks" (1 Thessalonians 5:17–18).

Jesus the Christ, our exemplar, often prayed to the Father. If the Savior of all mankind felt such a need to supplicate the Father, how much more should we lift up our voices in prayer?

## Separation from the Father

Every human being once lived in heavenly realms, for we are spiritually begotten offspring of God. As His children, we walked with our Heavenly Father. We knew Him. We heard His voice. We loved Him.

And although we were eager to enter mortality and continue our progression, we must have regretted the separation that would accompany it. We must have sorrowed that a veil would cover our eyes and the bright memories of our lives would be cloaked in the forgetfulness of mortality. How we must have yearned to stay close to our Father in Heaven. How freely we must have covenanted to ever reach after Him and commune with Him.

Undoubtedly, the sorrow of our separation from the Father was softened when our Heavenly Father promised that as we sought after Him in prayer, He would reach toward us.

Now we are here. We have no memory of our premortal life. We have forgotten those things we supposed we could never forget. Unfortunately and tragically, we sometimes even forget our Heavenly Father whom we loved so dearly.

## *Effectiveness of our Prayers*

May I invite you to consider the effectiveness of your prayers? How close do you feel to your Heavenly Father? Do you feel that your prayers are answered? Do you feel that the time you spend in prayer enriches and uplifts your soul? Is there room for improvement?

There are many reasons our prayers lack power. Sometimes, they have become routine. Our prayers become hollow when we say similar words in similar ways over and over, so often that the words become more of a recitation than a communication. This is what the Savior described as vain repetitions (see Matthew 6:7). Such prayers, He said, will not be heard.

Our beloved prophet, President Gordon B. Hinckley, has observed that "the trouble with most of our prayers is that we give them as if we were picking up the telephone and ordering groceries—we place our order and hang up. We need to meditate, contemplate, think of what we are praying about and for and then speak to the Lord as one man speaketh to another" (*Teachings of Gordon B. Hinckley*, 469).

Do your prayers at times sound and feel the same? Have you ever said a prayer mechanically, the words pouring forth as though cut from a machine? Do you sometimes bore yourself as you pray?

## Prayer Is Work

Prayers that do not demand much of your thought will likely not merit much attention from our Heavenly Father. When you find yourself getting into a routine with your prayers, step back and think. Meditate for awhile on the things for which you really are grateful. Look for them. They don't have to be grand or glorious; sometimes we should express our gratitude for the small and simple things, such as the scent of the rain, the taste of your favorite macaroni and cheese recipe, the sound of a loved one's voice.

Pondering the things we are grateful for is a healing balm. It helps us get outside ourselves. It changes our focus from our pains and our trials to the abundance of this beautiful world we live in.

Think of those things you truly need. Bring your goals and your hopes and your dreams to the Lord and set them before Him. Heavenly Father wants us to approach Him and ask for His divine aid. Explain to Him the trials and challenges you are facing. Set before Him your righteous desires.

## Prayer Should Be Practical

Our prayers can and should be focused on the practical, everyday struggles of life.

If we are commanded to pray over our flocks, then why should we not pray over our finals? If we are to pray over our crops, then why not other important challenges we face—in our work, our relationships, and certainly our Church assignments.

Some believe that the more eloquent a prayer, the more effective. Too often, these prayers are not so much meant for the ears of the

Almighty as they are for the ears of the audience. Do you want to commune with the Infinite? Then approach Him with reverence and humility. Don't worry so much about whether your words are polished. Worry instead about speaking from your heart. In faith, set before Him your righteous desires and your petitions, knowing that He will hear you.

## Prayers without Faith

Another reason many prayers have little power is that we lack faith. We approach our Heavenly Father as a child might ask something of his or her parents, knowing they will refuse. Without faith, our prayers are merely words. With faith, our prayers connect us with the powers of heaven and can bring upon us increased understanding, hope, and ability. If by faith the worlds were created, then by faith we can create and receive the righteous desires of our heart.

What is faith? Faith is having absolute confidence in that which is in absolute conformity to the will of heaven. When we combine that confidence with absolute action on our part, we have faith.

Faith without works is dead. Sometimes we expect Heavenly Father to answer our prayers when all we have done is uttered a prayer. The doors of heaven will ever be closed to those who, without any effort on their part, simply hold out their hands, waiting for the blessings of heaven to descend upon them.

The legendary football coach Knute Rockne implied the same principle when he said, "I've found that prayers work best when you have big players" (http://www.knuterockne.com/quotes.htm).

The powers of faith are activated by action. We must do our part. We must prepare. We must do all that is in our power, and we will be blessed in our efforts.

Prayer is a private matter between you and Heavenly Father. Both He and you know when you have done what you can. Do not give a thought as to whether or not your best compares with others. In the eyes of Heavenly Father, that doesn't matter.

When you have absolute confidence in things that are in conformity to the will of God and you act with all your power to achieve them, then you will "Ask, and it shall be given you; seek, and ye shall find; knock, and it shall be opened unto you" (Matthew 7:7).

## The Curse of Prosperity

Perhaps one of the great challenges the Church faces in our day is that of prosperity. President Brigham Young said, "The worst fear . . . I have about this people is that they will get rich . . . [and] forget God . . . This people will stand mobbing, robbing, poverty and all manner of persecution, and be true. But my greater fear for them is that they cannot stand wealth" (James S. Brown, *Life of a Pioneer* [Salt Lake City, Utah: George Q. Cannon and Sons, 1900], 122–23).

President Ezra Taft Benson added, "This particular test seems like no test at all . . . and so could be the most deceiving of all tests. Do you know what peace and prosperity can do to a people—it can put them to sleep. . . . On the earth [are] some potential spiritual giants whom [God] saved for some six thousand years to help bear off the Kingdom triumphantly and the devil is trying to put them to sleep" (Ezra Taft Benson, "Our Obligation and Challenge," Regional Representatives Seminar, 30 Sept. 1977, 2–3; unpublished typescript).

Prosperity can deaden us to spiritual things. It can give us the illusion of power. When we are sick, we can go to a doctor and get healed. When we are hungry, we can feed ourselves. When we are cold, we can get warm. In short, most of the problems of life we can solve ourselves—we can answer many of our own prayers.

Because of the relative ease many have in acquiring their daily bread, they can become deceived into thinking they are saviors unto themselves. In their pride and foolishness, they feel they have little need of a Heavenly Father. They think little of the power that created the universe or of the One who gave His life that they might live.

In the Doctrine and Covenants we are warned of these modern-day idolaters: "They seek not the Lord to establish his righteousness, but every man walketh in his own way, and after the image of his own god, whose image is in the likeness of the world" (D&C 1:16).

Such men fulfill the prophecy of Paul, who warned that "in the last days perilous times shall come," times in which men would be "lovers of their own selves, covetous, boasters, proud, blasphemers, disobedient to parents, unthankful, unholy, without natural affection . . . traitors, heady, highminded, lovers of pleasures more than lovers of God; having a form of godliness; but denying the power thereof: from such turn away" (2 Timothy 3:2–5).

Man has ever worshiped the things he loves. That which we love becomes our treasure and when that treasure is the wealth, pleasures, and praise of the world, is it any wonder that the heavens are closed to the prayers of such? Those who worship the things of this world will one day cry to their riches and plead with them to save them. In that day, they will learn the coldness of their god and realize the terrible error of their ways.

## Failure to Serve the Needy

Another reason that our prayers have little power is because we fail to succor those in need. The Book of Mormon teaches, "If ye turn away the needy, and the naked, and visit not the sick and afflicted, and impart of your substance, if ye have, to those who stand in need—I say unto you, if ye do not any of these things, behold, your prayer is vain, and availeth you nothing" (Alma 34:28).

Willingness to aid those in distress around us has ever been the benchmark of the disciples of Christ. Indeed, the Savior taught that our very salvation depends upon the level of our compassion for others (see Matthew 25:31–46). We love to talk of the doctrine of grace—how, because of the atonement of the Savior we can be saved. In spite of our weakness, our sin, our failures, if our hearts are humble and pure and we repent—in spite of all our weakness, we know it is "by grace that we are saved, after all we can do" (2 Nephi 25:23).

In the end, we are all beggars. We cannot merit the blessings of eternity. We can only do the best we can, cleave unto the Spirit, and depend upon the grace of a merciful Heavenly Father for His blessings.

How like unto this is our response to the poor and the distressed? In like manner, they plead with us directly or indirectly for our succor. If we turn our backs upon them can we, in turn, suppose that our Heavenly Father will be merciful to us?

As we are to those in need, so our Heavenly Father will be to us in our time of need.

## King David and Prayer

In the Old Testament we read that David was one who understood adversity and the need to rely upon his Heavenly Father. As a youth, he faced and conquered the giant Goliath. Afterwards, the jealous King Saul sought to take his life. David fled with a small band and was constantly hunted by the king. During day or night, his life was in jeopardy. And through this experience, he understood his dependence upon his Heavenly Father.

In Psalm 37, David reveals an inspired process for active prayer and faith. It is a step-by-step process that may serve as a pattern for us to follow as we seek to increase our faith and improve the efficacy of our prayers.

### Worry Not

"Fret not," is the first step (v. 1). *Fret* means to worry or to brood about something. The first thing we must do is stop worrying. When we worry about the future, we create unhappiness in the present.

Righteous concern may lead us to appropriate action, but worrying about things we cannot control can paralyze and demoralize us. Instead of worrying, focus on doing all that you can and then leave the worrying to your Heavenly Father. If your heart is right with Him, He will take care of the worry and the fear. We must learn to fret not.

## Trust in the Lord

The second step, according to David, is to, "Trust in the Lord" (v. 3). Why should we trust in Him? Because He is our loving and all-wise Father in Heaven. Because He is the giver of all good gifts. Because He knows us and wants us to be happy, successful, and to return to Him. God is in His heavens, He is perfect, He loves us.

I remember the many times my dear mother trusted in our Heavenly Father for my safety. I played quarterback at East High School and running back at the University of Utah. During all that time I don't think my mother ever stopped praying for my safety. She trusted in our Father in Heaven, depending on Him to protect me from major injury during the games. Although I had my share of bumps and bruises, I never had a major injury.

I suppose my mother breathed a sigh of relief when I told her that I was going to leave the football field for a season. I met with my beloved bishop, Marion G. Romney, to express a desire to serve a full-time mission. But that short, worry-free season soon ended when I was called to serve in the German/Austria Mission. Three months after I arrived in Salzburg the name of the mission was changed to the Switzerland/Austria Mission.

The year was 1937, and I arrived in Salzburg, Austria, at the very time Hitler was amassing 300,000 troops on the border for his "anschlus" or his invasion of Austria.

How often my mother and father gathered the family to kneel in prayer and plead for my safety I do not know. What I do know is that I felt the influence of those prayers. I trusted my Heavenly Father would hear their prayers. I trusted in my prayers that He would preserve my life.

A month before Hitler invaded Austria, I was transferred to Switzerland. My testimony is our prayers had been answered.

"Trust in the LORD with all thine heart; and lean not unto thine own understanding," we read in the scriptures. "In all thy ways acknowledge him, and he shall direct thy paths" (Proverbs 3:5, 6).

## Do Good

The third step outlined in Psalm 37 is "do good" (v. 3). We do good because we are followers of Christ. We do good because we are members of His Church. We do good because we are obedient to His commandment to love our neighbor as ourselves. We do good because we have made solemn covenants to serve as a light unto the world. Our Heavenly Father expects our actions to serve as a living testimony to our words. As we do good, the Lord can bless our efforts.

This is not to say that we must never make a mistake for "all have sinned, and come short of the glory of God" (Romans 3:23). The Lord requires that we seek Him with humble heart, that we repent of our sins, and that we continue to do the best that we can. As we make mistakes, we should learn from them and strive not to repeat them. As we do so, we become ever more Christlike, ever more as men and women of God.

As our actions contradict our professions of faith, our prayers become weak. When we do good, the Lord can work through us and magnify our efforts.

## Delight in the Lord

The fourth step is that we "delight" in the Lord (v. 4). What a wonderful doctrine! Instead of worrying or grumbling that our prayers have gone unanswered, we should delight ourselves in the Lord. Be grateful. Be happy. Know that the Lord, in His time, will bring about all your righteous desires, sometimes in ways we predict, others in ways we could not have possibly foreseen. What a wonderful recipe for happiness and peace.

Those who delight in the Lord even in times of adversity will carry with them through their trials an inner and abiding peace. The next time you are tempted to grumble, think of this passage and, instead, delight yourself in the Lord. Your step will be a little lighter, your worries a little less oppressive, and people may even want to be around you more.

## Commit Thy Way unto the Lord

The fifth step is to "Commit thy way unto the Lord." No matter your worries, commit yourself to keeping His commandments. Brethren, honor your priesthood. Sisters, cleave unto the principles of light and truth.

## Rest in the Lord

The sixth step is to "rest in the Lord" (v. 7). Sometimes the hardest thing we can do is wait. The Lord has His own timetable and, although it may frustrate us, His timing is always perfect. When we rest in the Lord, we allow Him to work His will for us in His own time and in His own way.

Rich blessings are promised to those who pray in this manner: "So shalt thou dwell in the land, and verily thou shalt be fed" (v. 1). The Lord, "shall give thee the desires of [your] heart" (v. 4). "He shall bring it to pass" (v. 5). "And he shall bring forth thy righteousness as the light, and thy judgment as the noonday" (v. 6).

## Prayer and Light

Prayer is the way we commune with the Infinite. Prayer is a time of gratitude. A time of introspection. A time of emotion—sorrow, joy, enlightenment, and peace.

The more time we spend in righteous prayer, the more our beings will be filled with light. "And if your eye be single to my glory," the Lord has promised, "your whole bodies shall be filled with light, and there shall be no darkness in you; and that body which is filled with light comprehendeth all things" (D&C 88:67).

The more our souls are filled with light, the more we resemble our Father in Heaven and the more capable we are of enjoying the fruits of the Spirit. This light grows within us, often slowly. It banishes the darkness of this mortality. It sets to flight fear and doubt and all desire to do evil. It fills the soul with love, peace, and unspeakable joy.

The challenge of this mortality is to come out of the darkness into the light. Through prayer, the light of the Spirit can distill upon us line upon line, precept upon precept until, as Brigham Young taught, the Holy Spirit, "opens the vision of the mind, unlocks the treasures of wisdom, and [we] begin to understand the things of God" (*Journal of Discourses,* 1:241).

The things of God can only be understood by the Spirit of God. The Apostle Paul teaches that "the natural man receiveth not the things of the Spirit of God: for they are foolishness unto him: neither can he know *them,* because they are spiritually discerned" (1 Corinthians 2:14).

In the Book of Mormon, we learn again and again of people who fell away from the light and embraced darkness: "Because of their unbelief they could not understand the word of God; and their hearts were hardened" (Mosiah 26:3).

As we commune with our Father in humble prayer, our hearts receive the gentle outpouring of the Holy Spirit. "That which is of God is light," the Lord tells us, "and he that receiveth light, and continueth in God, receiveth more light; and that light groweth brighter and brighter until the perfect day" (D&C 50:24).

Those who do not have this light ever struggle with disbelief. They cannot understand the things of God because their souls have little light.

On the contrary, as our souls become filled with light, we begin to understand clearly things that once were dark.

Think back on Joseph Smith's account of his experience with darkness and light. You will recall that as a boy of fourteen, he became confused by the claims and counterclaims of the various exponents of religion. His inability to discern the truth was compounded by "priest contending against priest, and convert against convert; so that all their good feelings one for another, if they ever had any, were entirely lost in a strife of words and a contest about opinions" (JS–H 1:6).

Joseph continued his narrative:

> During this time of great excitement my mind was called up to serious reflection and great uneasiness; but though my feelings were deep and often poignant, still I kept myself aloof from all these parties, though I attended their several meetings as often as occasion would permit. . . . but so great were the confusion and strife among the different denominations, that it was impossible for a person young as I was, and so unacquainted with men and things, to come to any certain conclusion who was right and who was wrong. . . .
>
> In the midst of this war of words and tumult of opinions, I often said to myself: What is to be done? Who of all these parties are right; or, are they all wrong together? If any one of them be right, which is it, and how shall I know it?
>
> While I was laboring under the extreme difficulties caused by the contests of these parties of religionists, I was one day reading the Epistle of James . . . which reads: "If any of you lack wisdom, let him ask of God, that giveth to all men liberally, and upbraideth not; and it shall be given him."
>
> Never did any passage of scripture come with more power to the heart of man than this did at this time to mine. It seemed to enter with great force into every feeling of my heart. . . .
>
> So, in accordance with this, my determination to ask of

God, I retired to the woods to make the attempt. . . . I kneeled down and began to offer up the desires of my heart to God. I had scarcely done so, when immediately I was seized upon by some power which entirely overcame me, and had such an astonishing influence over me as to bind my tongue so that I could not speak. Thick darkness gathered around me, and it seemed to me for a time as if I were doomed to sudden destruction.

But, exerting all my powers to call upon God to deliver me out of the power of this enemy which had seized upon me, and at the very moment when I was ready to sink into despair and abandon myself to destruction—. . . . I saw a pillar of light exactly over my head, above the brightness of the sun, which descended gradually until it fell upon me.

It no sooner appeared than I found myself delivered from the enemy which held me bound. When the light rested upon me I saw two Personages, whose brightness and glory defy all description, standing above me in the air. One of them spake unto me, calling me by name and said, pointing to the other— *"This is my Beloved Son. Hear Him!"* (JS–H 1:8–17.)

Joseph asked the Personages which of all the sects was right—and which he should join.

I was answered that I must join none of them, for they were all wrong; . . .

He again forbade me to join with any of them. . . .

When I came to myself again, I found myself lying on my back, looking up into heaven. When the light had departed, I had no strength; but soon recovering to some degree, I went home. (JS–H 1:20.)

Lorenzo Snow writes of such an experience of his own:

Some two or three weeks after I was baptized . . . I began to reflect upon the fact that I had not obtained a *knowledge* of the truth of the work . . . and I began to feel very uneasy. I laid aside my books, left the house, and wandered around through the fields under the oppressive influence of a gloomy, disconsolate spirit, while an indescribable cloud of darkness seemed to envelop me. I had been accustomed, at the close of the day, to retire for secret prayer, to a grove a short distance from my lodgings, but at this time I felt no inclination to do so. The spirit of prayer had departed and the heavens seemed like brass over my head. At length, realizing that the time had come for secret prayer. . . .

I had no sooner opened my lips in an effort to pray, than I heard a sound, just above my head, like the rustling of silken robes, and immediately the Spirit of God descended upon me, . . . from the crown of my head to the soles of my feet, and O, the joy and happiness I felt! No language can describe the almost instantaneous transition from a dense cloud of mental and spiritual darkness into a refulgence of light and knowledge, as it was at that time imparted to my understanding. I then received a perfect knowledge that God lives, that Jesus Christ is the Son of God, and of the restoration of the holy priesthood, and the fulness of the Gospel. . . . That night, as I retired to rest, the same wonderful manifestations were repeated, and continued to be for several successive nights. The sweet remembrance of those glorious experiences, from that time to the present, bring them fresh before me, imparting an inspiring influence which pervades my whole being, and I trust will to the close of my earthly existence. (*Biography and Family Record of Lorenzo Snow,* 7–9.)

Such spiritual experiences are available to all who come before their Eternal Father with a broken heart and contrite spirit. One of the things we must do in this mortality is chase away the darkness. We must fill our souls with the light of the Holy Spirit.

## Blessings from Prayer Available to All

The rich blessings that can come into our lives through prayer are available to everyone. The poor have as much access as the rich. The movie star has no advantage over the laborer. We are all equal in the right to approach the throne of our Heavenly King.

The Lord does not care whether we are smart, rich, talented, famous, or skilled. He loves us because we are His children. "Behold, I stand at the door, and knock," the Savior tells us. "If any man hear my voice, and open the door, I will come in to him, and will sup with him, and he with me" (Revelation 3:20).

As we approach our Heavenly Father in the name of Christ, we open the windows of heaven. We can receive from Him truth, light, and knowledge.

Prayer is the doorway through which we commence our discipleship to things heavenly and eternal. We will never be alone so long as we know how to pray.

I leave you my witness that our Heavenly Father lives and answers prayers. Jesus is the Christ. The Prophet Joseph Smith restored the gospel of Jesus Christ to the world. This Church today is led by a prophet of God. I am not alone in proclaiming these truths. Through the power of prayer, millions of people throughout the world add their voice to the growing chorus. God speaks to man today! He directs His Church.

It is my earnest desire that each member of the Church will reexamine his or her own life in the context of prayer. May we ever lift up our voices to our Heavenly Father, that our souls might be filled with celestial light.

*(Based on an address given at a BYU Devotional, 21 January 2003)*

# 20

# Pure Testimony

Concerning testimony, the Psalmist wrote, "The law of the Lord is perfect, converting the soul: the testimony of the Lord is sure, making wise the simple" (Psalm 19:7).

For Latter-day Saints, a testimony is "the assurance of the reality, truth, and goodness of God, of the teachings and atonement of Jesus Christ, and of the divine calling of latter-day prophets. . . . It is knowledge buttressed by divine personal confirmation by the Holy Ghost" (*Encyclopedia of Mormonism*, 4:1470).

Expressions of solemn testimony have long been important to the children of God upon the earth. Individual testimonies have strengthened this Church from its earliest days.

## *Parley P. Pratt and John Taylor*

For example, one evening in April 1836, Elder Parley P. Pratt had retired early with pressing worries and a heavy heart. He didn't know how he was going to meet his financial obligations. His wife had been seriously ill, and his aged mother had come to live with him. A year earlier the house he had been building had gone up in flames.

While he was deep in thought, a knock came at the door. It was Elder Heber C. Kimball, who upon entering the house and filled with the spirit of prophecy, told Elder Pratt that he should travel to Toronto, Canada, where he would "find a people prepared for the fulness of the gospel" and that "many [would] be brought to the knowledge of the truth" (*The Autobiography of Parley P. Pratt,* Deseret Book, 1961, 130–31).

Despite his worries, Elder Pratt departed for Toronto. When he arrived, at first no one seemed interested in hearing what he had to say, but among those he met was John Taylor who had been a Methodist preacher. John received Elder Pratt courteously, but coolly. John Taylor had heard unflattering reports about a new sect, their "golden bible," and stories of angels appearing to an "unlearned youth, reared in the backwoods of New York" (B. H. Roberts, *The Life of John Taylor,* Bookcraft, 1963, 34).

A wise and deeply spiritual man, John Taylor had been seeking truth all his life. He listened to what Elder Pratt had to say. Among other things, the stranger from America promised that anyone who investigated the gospel could know for himself, through the influence of the Holy Ghost, that the message was true.

At one point John Taylor asked, "What do you mean by this Holy Ghost? . . . [Will it give] a certain knowledge of the principles that you believe in?"

The apostle replied, "Yes, . . . and if it will not, then I am an impostor" (*Journal of Discourses,* 23:51).

Hearing this, John Taylor took up the challenge saying, "If I find his religion true, I shall accept it, no matter what the consequences may be; and if false, then I shall expose it" (B. H. Roberts, *The Life of John Taylor,* 38).

Not only did he accept the challenge, but he "received that Spirit through obedience to the Gospel" (*Journal of Discourses,* 23:51). Soon, he knew for himself what millions of others have since known: that the gospel of Jesus Christ has been restored to the earth.

Eventually, this man who had devoted his life to seeking the truth became the third President of The Church of Jesus Christ of Latter-day Saints.

Over time, much in the world has changed. One thing, however, remains the same: the promise Elder Parley P. Pratt made to John Taylor 164 years ago is just as valid today as it was then; the Holy Ghost will confirm the truths of the restored gospel of Jesus Christ.

## Testimony Is for All

Logic itself affirms that a loving Heavenly Father would not abandon His children without providing a way for them to learn of Him. One of the great messages of the Restoration is that the windows of heaven are open. All who seek to know the truth may, through revelations of the Spirit, know for themselves.

We are blessed to live in an age when apostles and prophets walk the earth, bearing solemn and certain testimony that Jesus Christ is the Son of God. Many members—millions strong—add their voices to the growing chorus, testifying that God once again has spoken to man.

President Joseph F. Smith declared: "Every person should know that the gospel is true, as this is everyone's privilege who is baptized and receives the Holy Ghost. . . . I know that the gospel is true, and that God is with his people; and that if I will do my duty and keep his commandments, the clouds will roll by, and the mists will disappear" (*Gospel Doctrine,* 43).

## Obtaining a Testimony

How does one acquire a personal testimony?

Study the words of Moroni. He lived more than 1,500 years ago. This prophet had watched as his people were slaughtered and utterly devastated by civil war. His nation in ruins, his friends and loved ones slain, his own father—a great general and righteous man—killed.

This great prophet, Moroni, having lost all that he loved, stood alone. The last of his people, he was the final witness to the desolation and heartbreak that results from hatred and rage.

He had precious little time and limited space on his plates to write a few, final words. His own people destroyed, Moroni wrote for our day. To us, he inscribed his precious words of farewell—his final words of counsel.

"Behold, I would exhort you," he wrote of the record he was to bury in earth, there to await a future translation, "that when ye shall read these things . . . ye would remember how merciful the Lord hath been unto the children of men. . . . Ponder it in your hearts. And when ye shall receive these things, I would exhort you that ye would ask God, the Eternal Father, in the name of Christ, if these things are not true; and if ye shall ask with a sincere heart, with real intent, having faith in Christ, he will manifest the truth of it unto you, by the power of the Holy Ghost" (Moroni 10:3–4).

Would that every ear could hear the last testimony of Moroni, this giant among men, this humble servant of God.

Do you want to know the truth of the holy scriptures? Do you wish to break the barriers that separate mortals from the knowledge of eternal verities? Do you wish to know—really know—the truth? Then follow Moroni's counsel, and you will surely find what you seek.

Be sincere. Study. Ponder. Pray sincerely, having faith.

If you do these things, you, too, will be able to stand with the millions who testify that God once again speaks to man on earth.

## Testimony Comes Individually

A testimony of the truth of the gospel does not come the same way to all people. Some receive it in a unique, life-changing experience. Others gain a testimony slowly, almost imperceptibly until, one day, they simply know.

Study the words of President David O. McKay who tells of how, in his youth, he knelt and "prayed fervently and sincerely and with as much faith as a young boy could muster," that "God would declare to [him] the truth of his revelation to Joseph Smith."

President McKay related that when he arose from his knees, he had to admit that, "No spiritual manifestation has come to me. If I am true to myself, I must say that I am just the same . . . boy that I was before I prayed."

I don't know how young David felt in his heart at that time, but I'm sure he must have been disappointed—perhaps frustrated that he didn't receive the spiritual experience that he hoped for. But that didn't discourage him from continuing his search for that knowledge.

The answer to his prayers did come, but not until years later, when he was serving as a missionary. Why was the answer to his prayer so long delayed? President McKay believed that this precious spiritual manifestation "came as a natural sequence to the performance of duty" (*Cherished Experiences from the Writings of President David O. McKay*, Clare Middlemiss, comp., Deseret Book, 1955, 16).

## Testimony Comes by Doing

The Savior taught a similar principle: When the truth of His message was challenged by scoffers, He declared, "If any man will *do* [God's] will, he shall know of the doctrine, whether it be of God, or whether I speak of myself" (John 7:17).

Don't you be discouraged if the answer to your prayer does not immediately come. Continue to study, ponder, pray, exercise faith, and live the commandments.

As to why the answer may be delayed, Moroni offers this counsel: "Dispute not because ye see not, for ye receive no witness until after the trial of your faith" (Ether 12:6).

## Bearing Testimony

I remember as a child listening to the testimonies given by adults in my ward. Those testimonies entered my heart and inspired my soul.

Wherever I go throughout the world—no matter the language, no matter the culture—I thrill to hear the testimonies of the Saints.

Recently, I received a letter from our grandson who is a missionary. He wrote that members "who are reading scriptures and praying are more willing to share the gospel" (letter from Elder Andrew Cannon, 30 August 2000).

I believe he's right. The more we study the scriptures and pray, the more likely we can enthusiastically share our testimonies of the gospel with others.

Remember, Church members who receive a testimony of the gospel are under covenant to "stand as witnesses of God at all times and in all things, and in all places" (Mosiah 18:9). It is clear we have a sacred obligation to obtain referrals for our missionaries. Witnesses have a special knowledge and are to bear testimony of "that which [they] have seen and heard and most assuredly believe" (D&C 52:36). We make simple, clear, direct statements that we know with certainty and surety that the gospel is true because it has been "made known unto [us] by the Holy Spirit of God" (Alma 5:46). In bearing such a testimony, speaking by the power of the Holy Ghost, we are promised that "the Holy Ghost shall be shed forth in bearing record unto all things whatsoever [we] shall say" (D&C 100:8). We are blessed personally when we so testify.

President Boyd K. Packer said, "A testimony is to be *found* in the *bearing* of it. Somewhere in your quest for spiritual knowledge, there is that 'leap of faith,' as the philosophers call it. It is the moment when you have gone to the edge of the light and step into the darkness to discover that the way is lighted ahead for just a footstep or two" (Boyd K. Packer, *That All May Be Edified,* "The Candle of the Lord," 340).

Making a determined and confident public statement of your belief is such a step into the unknown. It has a powerful effect in strengthening your own convictions. Bearing testimony drives your faith deeper into your soul, and you believe more fervently than before.

To those who faithfully bear testimony, the Lord said, "Ye are blessed, for the testimony which ye have borne is recorded in heaven for the angels to look upon; and they rejoice over you, and your sins are forgiven you" (D&C 62:3). I have tried to follow this counsel to bear testimony.

## Personal Testimony

May I tell you how I gained a testimony of the truth and divine nature of this great latter-day work? I'm afraid my experience isn't very dramatic. It is not a story of heavenly hosannas, or thundering shouts. It is not a story of lightning, fire, or flood.

But, I have always known the reality and goodness of God. From my earliest memories it was there—a sure and abiding testimony of this great work. Sometimes that assurance comes when we feel the love of the Savior when we meet his servants. I remember when I was just five years old and my family moved into a new ward. That first Sunday, Bishop Charles E. Forsberg came up to me and called me by name. I knew then.

During the cold and grey days of the Great Depression I remember a wonderful servant of the Savior by the name of C. Perry Erickson. Brother Erickson, a contractor, had a difficult time finding work. He could have shut himself up. He could have become bitter and angry. He could have given up. Instead, when I was twelve he was my Scoutmaster. He spent countless hours helping me and others my age to learn, to grow, and to approach every difficulty with confidence and optimism. Without exception, every one of C. Perry Erickson's Scouts received an Eagle award. I knew then.

Yes, the testimonies of priesthood leaders and faithful ward members helped me to know.

I remember the words of my mother and father. I remember their expressions of faith and love for their Heavenly Father. I knew then.

I knew the reality of the Savior's compassion when, at the request of my father, the bishop of the ward, I delivered food and clothing to the widows and poor of the ward.

I knew, when as a young couple, my wife and I gathered our children around us and expressed our gratitude to our Heavenly Father for our many blessings.

I knew last April, when I heard from this pulpit the words of our prophet, President Gordon B. Hinckley, who called Jesus his friend, exemplar, leader, Savior, and King.

President Hinckley said, "Through giving His life in pain and unspeakable suffering, He has reached down to lift me and each of us and all the sons and daughters of God from the abyss of eternal darkness following death. He has provided something better—a sphere of light and understanding, growth and beauty" ("My Testimony," *Ensign*, May 2000, 71).

Now, I would like to bear my testimony—I know that Joseph Smith saw what he said he saw, that the heavens opened and God the Father and His Son, Jesus Christ, appeared to an unlearned youth, reared in the backwoods of New York.

As a special witness of the name of Jesus Christ in all the world, I promise you that if you seek the Lord, you will find Him. Ask, and you shall receive.

I pray that you may do so and testify to the ends of the earth, that the gospel of our Lord and Savior is restored to man!

*(Adapted from an October 2000 general conference address)*

# PRESS
# ON
## WITH CHARITY

# 21

# THE VIRTUE OF KINDNESS

## Consequences of Unkindness

Many years ago, when I was first called as bishop, I had a desire to visit those who were less active in the ward to see if there was anything I could do to bring the blessings of the gospel more fully into their lives.

One day I met with a man in his fifties who was a fine and respected mechanic. He told me the last time he had been to church was when he was a young boy. Something had happened that day. He had been acting up in class and was being noisier than he should when his teacher became angry, pulled him out of class, and told him not to come back.

He never did.

It was remarkable to me that an unkind word spoken more than four decades earlier could have had such a profound effect. But it had. And, as a consequence, this man had never again set foot inside the church. Neither had his wife or children.

I apologized to him and expressed my sorrow that he had been treated that way. I told him how unfortunate it was that one incident—one word spoken in haste, and so long ago—could have the effect of excluding his family from the blessings that come from Church activity.

"After forty years," I told him, "it's time the Church made things right."

I did my best to do so. I reassured him that he was welcome and needed. I was pleased when this man and his family eventually returned to church and became strong and faithful members. In particular, this good brother became an effective home teacher because he understood how something as small as an unkind word could have consequences that extend throughout a lifetime and perhaps beyond.

## Impact of Kindness

Kindness is the essence of greatness and the fundamental characteristic of the noblest men and women I have known. Kindness is a passport that opens doors and fashions friends. It softens hearts and molds relationships that can last lifetimes.

Kind words not only lift our spirits in the moment they are given, but they can linger with us over the years. One day, when I was in college, a man seven years my senior congratulated me on my performance in a football game. He not only praised how well I had done in the game, but he had noticed that I had been a good sport as well. Even though this conversation took place more than sixty years ago, and even though it's highly unlikely the person who complimented me has any recollection of this conversation today, I still remember the kind words spoken to me then by Gordon B. Hinckley.

The attributes of thoughtfulness and kindness are inseparably linked with President Hinckley. When my father passed away in 1963, President Hinckley came to our home. I'll never forget his kindness. He gave my mother a blessing and, among other things, promised that she had much to look forward to and that life would yet be sweet to her. These words gave comfort and encouragement to my mother and were an inspiration to me.

## Kindness and the Celestial Life

Kindness is the walk and talk of a celestial life. Kindness is how a Christlike person treats others, no matter what the circumstances. Kindness should permeate all of our words and actions in the home, at work, and especially in the Church. A kind soul not only treats other people as children of God with divine worth, but also treats all other living things with respect and caring. As President David O. McKay reminded us: "A true Latter-day Saint is kind to animals, is kind to every created thing, for God has created all" (in Conference Report, Oct. 1951, 180).

Jesus, our Savior, was the epitome of kindness and compassion. He healed the sick, even when it was inconvenient or unpopular to do so. He spent much of His life ministering to the one or few. He spoke compassionately to the Samarian woman who was despised by many. He was kind to all who had sinned, only condemning the sin, not the sinner. He kindly allowed thousands of Nephites to come forward and feel the nail prints in His hands and feet. Yet His greatest act of kindness was found in His atoning sacrifice, thus freeing all from the effects of death and all from the effects of sin, on condition of repentance.

The Prophet Joseph exemplified kindness in his life to all, including young children. One child who was blessed by the Prophet's kindness remembered:

"My older brother and I were going to school, near to the building which was known as Joseph's brick store. It had been raining the previous day, causing the ground to be very muddy, especially along that street. My brother Wallace and I got both feet in the mud, and could not get out, and of course, child-like, we began to cry, for we thought we would have to stay there. But looking up, I beheld the loving friend of children, the Prophet Joseph, coming to us. He soon had us on higher and drier ground. Then he stooped down and cleaned the mud from our little, heavy-laden shoes, took his handkerchief from his pocket, and wiped our tear-stained faces. He spoke kind and cheering words to us and sent us on our way to school rejoicing" (Margarette McIntire Burgess, as in *Best Loved Stories of the LDS People,* Jack M. Lyon, Linda Rurie Gundry, and Jay A. Parry, eds. Deseret Book, 1997, 403).

## Kindness in the Family

There is no substitute for kindness in the home. Kindness is best taught and modeled in the home, as are all the virtues of a Godlike life. Children will learn to be kind more from how they see their parents treat others than from spoken words. This lesson I learned from my father. My parents disagreed at times, but my father always listened and spoke with kindness. As a result, he was a better and wiser man. And he made fewer mistakes, because Mother—more often than not—was right!

I have tried to follow my father's example by treating others with kindness. I have learned to listen—especially to my wife—and to value her opinion. For example, when my wife begins a sentence with the words, "I should think you would . . ." I instantly drop everything and begin searching my conscience for something I may have done wrong. Over the years, I have learned the value of a quick confession. Often, sometimes before my wife has finished her sentence, I have already planned out in my mind a magnificent apology, coupled with a plan to make things right.

In truth, my wife is a model of kindness, gentleness, and compassion. And her insight, counsel, and support have been invaluable to me. Because of her I, too, am a better, wiser, and kinder man.

The things you say, the tone of your voice, the anger or calm in your words, these things are noticed by your children and by others. If you were to treat others disrespectfully, your children would learn that it is an acceptable manner for them to follow as well.

## Avoid Criticism

I often wonder why some feel they must be critical of others. It gets in their blood, I suppose, and it becomes so natural to them, they often don't even think about it. They criticize everything and everyone—the way Sister Jones leads the music, the way Brother Smith teaches a lesson or cuts his lawn.

Even when we think we are doing no harm by our critical remarks, consequences often follow. I am reminded of the boy who handed a donation envelope to his bishop and told him it was for him. The bishop, using this as a teaching moment, explained to the boy that he should mark on the donation slip whether it was for tithing, fast offerings, or for something else. The boy insisted the money was for the bishop himself. When the bishop asked why, the boy replied, "Because my father says you're one of the poorest bishops we've ever had."

## Kindness in the Kingdom

The Church is not a place where perfect people gather to say perfect things, think perfect thoughts, and feel perfect feelings. The Church is a place where imperfect people gather to provide encouragement, support, and service to each other as we press on in our journey to return to our Heavenly Father.

Each of us will travel a different road during this life. Each progresses at a different rate. Temptations that afflict your brother may not trouble you at all. Strengths that you possess may seem impossible to another.

Never look down on those who are less perfect than you. Don't be critical because someone can't lead as well as you, can't read as well as you, can't sing as well as you, can't sew or hoe as well as you.

We are all children of our Heavenly Father. And we are here with the same purposes: to learn to love Him with all our heart, soul, mind, and strength and to learn to love our neighbor as ourselves (see Mark 12:30, 31).

One way you can measure your value in the kingdom of God is to ask yourself, "How well am I doing in helping others reach their potential? Do I support others in the Church, or do I tear them down?"

If you are tearing others down, you are tearing down the Kingdom of God. If you are building others, you are building His Kingdom.

We call each other *brother* and *sister* in the Church. There is more to these terms than mere semantics. Think of it: if we really thought of others as our brother or sister, would we be so quick to criticize them?

One might be tempted to say, "Well, he may be my brother, but that doesn't mean I have to like him."

That may be true. But because he is your brother, don't you think it is the Savior's will that you love him? And if we truly love our brother, doesn't that naturally bring with it a desire to be kind, long-suffering, and even helpful?

## People in Perspective

As spiritually begotten sons and daughters of God, every man, woman, and child—whether in this Church, or in any other, or in no church at all—is part of a grand family. That's something to think about the next time someone cuts in front of you in traffic.

Let us never forget the words of the Savior: "Love your enemies, bless them that curse you, do good to them that hate you, and pray for them which despitefully use you, and persecute you" (Matthew 5:44).

It may also be something to think about the next time you see someone in distress whether near or far.

## The Kindness of James E. Talmage

Elder James E. Talmage, a man who is remembered for his doctrinal teachings, showed great kindness to a neighbor family in distress, who were complete strangers to him. Before he was an apostle, as a young father, he became aware of great suffering at a neighbor's home whose large family was stricken with the dreaded and highly contagious disease of diphtheria. He did not care that they were not members of the Church, rather his kindness and charity moved him to act. The Relief

Society was desperately trying to find people to help, but no one would because of the contagious nature of the disease. When he arrived at the stricken home, James found one toddler already dead and two other young children in great agony from the disease, with the baby of the family also showing symptoms. He immediately went to work, cleaning the filthy house, preparing the young body for burial, cleaning and providing for the other sick children, spending the entire day doing so.

He came back the next morning to find that one more of the children had died the previous night. He wrote in his journal what he did next: "[The little girl was still suffering terribly.] She clung to my neck, . . . offtimes coughing bloody mucus upon my face and clothing . . . yet I could not put her from me. During the half-hour immediately preceding her death, I walked the floor with the little creature in my arms. She died in agony at 10 A.M. So, the three children have departed all within the space of twenty-four hours." He then assisted the family with the burial arrangements and spoke at their graveside services (see complete story in John R. Talmage, *The Talmage Story: Life of James E. Talmage— Educator, Scientist, Apostle,* Bookcraft, 1972, 112–14). Young James did all this for neighbors, a family of strangers, not members of the Church. What a great example of Christlike kindness!

## Kindness Is the Temperament of God

When we are filled with kindness, we also are not judgmental. The Savior taught, "Judge not, and ye shall not be judged; condemn not, and ye shall not be condemned: forgive, and ye shall be forgiven" (Luke 6:37). He also taught that, "with what judgment ye judge, ye shall be judged: and with what measure ye mete, it shall be measured to you again" (Matthew 7:1–2).

The more we treat others with Christlike kindness, the more we ensure the greatest effects of mercy in our own judgment. Be merciful to others so that mercy will be extended to you. Such mercy and kindness will not go unrewarded, whether in this life or the next. Be kind because kindness is the temperament of God.

We are all brothers and sisters, children of our Heavenly Father. He loves them. Shouldn't we as well?

I implore you—love your brothers and sisters wherever and whoever they are. Let unkind feelings and harsh words have no place among us. Let's fill our hearts instead with compassion, patience, and charity.

"But," you ask, "what if people are rude?"

Love them.

"And if they are annoying?"

Love them.

"But what if they offend? Surely I must do something then?"

Love them.

"Wayward?" The answer is the same. Be kind. Love them.

Why? Jude, a half-brother to Jesus, taught, "And of some have compassion, making a difference" (Jude 1:22). Who can tell what far-reaching impact we can have if only we are kind?

## Testimony

The gospel of Jesus Christ transcends mortality. Our work here is but a shadow of greater and unimaginable things to come. The heavens opened to Joseph Smith. He saw the living God and His Son, Jesus the Christ. In our day, a prophet, President Gordon B. Hinckley, walks the earth and provides prophetic direction for our time.

As our Heavenly Father loves us, so too should we love His children throughout the world and show kindness in all we do and say.

May we be models of kindness and compassion. And may we ever live up to the words of the Savior: "By this shall all men know that ye are my disciples, if ye have love one to another" (John 13:35).

*(Adapted from an April 2005 general conference address)*

# 22

## THE TIME TO PREPARE

I would like to consider with you the importance of mortal life as a time of preparation. As Amulek testified, "This life is the time for men to prepare to meet God; yea, behold the day of this life is the day for men to perform their labors" (Alma 34:32).

### Eternal Perspective

As members of The Church of Jesus Christ of Latter-day Saints, we have a special understanding of the eternal nature of our souls. We know that we had a premortal existence. In that realm, we accepted our Heavenly Father's great plan of happiness and chose to follow our Lord and Savior, Jesus Christ. Principles we adopted and for which we contended were (1) agency, the ability to choose good or evil; (2) progress, the ability to learn and become like our Heavenly Father; and (3) faith, faith in our Father's plan and in the Atonement of Jesus Christ that enables us to return to the presence of God. Consequently, we were permitted to enter mortality. Concerning this mortal life, the Master declared of us, "We will prove them herewith [the earth on which we dwell], to see if they will do all things whatsoever the Lord their God shall command them" (Abraham 3:25).

We understand that we will live a postmortal life of infinite duration and that we determine the kind of life it will be by our thoughts and actions in mortality. Mortality is very brief but immeasurably important.

We learn from the scriptures that the "course of the Lord is one eternal round" (1 Nephi 10:19) and that God knows "all things, being from everlasting to everlasting" (Moroni 7:22). We are also eternal beings. Our presence here on earth is an essential step in our loving Heavenly Father's plan of happiness for His children. "[We] are, that [we] might have joy" (2 Nephi 2:25). The Prophet Joseph Smith taught that "happiness is the object and design of our existence; and will be the end thereof, if we pursue the path that leads to it; and this path is virtue, uprightness, faithfulness, holiness, and keeping all the commandments of God" (*History of the Church*, 5:134–35).

Right now, this very moment, is part of our eternal progression toward returning with our families to the presence of our Father in Heaven. President Gordon B. Hinckley taught: "We are here [in this life] with a marvelous inheritance, a divine endowment. How different this world would be if every person realized that all of his actions have eternal consequences. How much more satisfying our years may be if . . . we recognize that we form each day the stuff of which eternity is made" (*Teachings of Gordon B. Hinckley*, 174).

That understanding helps us to make wise decisions in the many choices of our daily lives. Seeing life from an eternal perspective helps us focus our limited mortal energies on the things that matter most. We can avoid wasting our lives laying "up for [ourselves] treasures upon earth, where moth and rust doth corrupt" (Matthew 6:19). We can instead lay up treasures in heaven and not trade our eternal spiritual birthright.

This is the day of our mortal probation. We might compare our eternal journey to a race of three laps around the track. We have completed the first lap successfully and have made wonderful progress. We have started on the second lap. Can you imagine a world-class runner stopping along the track at this point to pick flowers or chase a rabbit that crossed his path? Yet this is what we are doing when we occupy our time with worldly pursuits that do not move us closer to the third lap toward eternal life, "the greatest of all the gifts of God" (D&C 14:7).

In both His Old and New World ministries, the Savior commanded, "Be ye therefore perfect" (Matthew 5:48; see also 3 Nephi 12:48). A footnote to the biblical passage explains that the Greek word translated as *perfect* means "complete, finished, fully developed." Our Heavenly Father wants us to use this mortal probation to "fully develop" ourselves, to make the most of our talents and abilities. If we do so, when final judgment comes we will experience the joy of standing before our Father in Heaven as "complete" and "finished" sons and daughters, polished by obedience and worthy of the eternal inheritance He has promised to the faithful.

The Savior has set the example for us and commands that "the works which [we] have seen [Him] do that shall [we] also do" (3 Nephi 27:21). I have always been impressed by Moroni's powerful invitation that he offered as a valedictory admonition at the end of his earthly ministry: "Come unto Christ, and be perfected in him, and deny yourselves of all ungodliness" (Moroni 10:32).

## We Are Here to Serve

Alma explained to his followers that baptism requires that we serve others, that we "bear one another's burdens, . . . mourn with those that mourn . . . comfort those that stand in need of comfort, and . . . stand as witnesses of God at all times" (Mosiah 18:8–9). We cannot work out our salvation alone. We cannot return to the presence of our Father in Heaven without assisting others. Once we understand that we are all literally brothers and sisters in the family of God, we should also feel an obligation to look after one another's welfare and show our love through deeds of kindness and concern. Charity, "the pure love of Christ," (Moroni 7:47) must motivate us in our associations with every one of our Heavenly Father's children.

As we progress and become more like the Savior, we can strengthen every group with whom we associate, including families and friends. The Lord places us in these communities of Saints where we can learn and apply gospel principles to our everyday lives. These groups are at the same time a school, a proving ground, and a laboratory where we both learn and do as we practice living the gospel.

Writing to the Corinthians, Paul pleaded for unity in the Church and for members to serve one another, "that there should be no schism in the body; but that the members should have the same care for one another. And whether one member suffer, all the members suffer . . . ; or one member be honoured, all the members rejoice" (1 Corinthians 12:25–26; see also vv. 12–17). We are only as strong as each member of the "body," or church, of Christ. We should do all we can to help every member realize his or her divine potential as "heirs of God, and joint-heirs with Christ" (Romans 8:17).

In giving our service to others, we need to remember President Hinckley's counsel to extend the hand of fellowship and to share our love with the hundreds of thousands who join the Church as converts each year. The greatest tool the Lord has to welcome new converts warmly and "keep them in the right way" (Moroni 6:4) is the love each of us extends by taking the time to introduce ourselves to new members, learning their names, listening to them, and learning something about them.

## Strengthening the New Convert

Joining a new church and starting a new life is never easy and often frightening. Each of us needs to be the friend that every new member needs to remain active and faithful in the Church. As these friendships are built, new converts "are no more strangers and foreigners, but fellow-citizens with the saints, and of the household of God" (Ephesians 2:19). When people are baptized, "their names [are] taken" and added to

Church membership records, "that they might be remembered and nourished by the good word of God" (Moroni 6:4).

Referring to the miraculous change that occurs in the lives of new members when they are properly nourished by the good word of God, Elder John A. Widtsoe observed that "very common, ordinary people, who accept the gospel from the lips of some humble Mormon missionary become so changed by those enlightening truths of the gospel that they are not the same people any longer" ("Symbolism in Irrigation," *Improvement Era,* June 1952, 423).

## *Stay on Course*

As we work our way through mortality, we may make mistakes and get off course. If we should continue in our errors, we get farther and farther from where we ought to be.

We can compare our lives with the flight of a spaceship. When its engine is ignited, its trajectory is monitored precisely. Any deviation from its decreed course is corrected immediately. Even a fraction of a degree off course, if not corrected, would carry it many miles from its destination. The longer the correction is delayed, the greater will be the required adjustment. Can you imagine how far off course we can become without course corrections?

The Lord has provided for us prophets, scriptures, parents, and other wise leaders to teach us the course we should be following. They can help us monitor our progress and correct the direction we are going when necessary, much the same as tracking stations monitor a satellite's progress and keep it on the right course. Our course on earth is so important. It is determined by the decisions we make each day. We cannot separate our thoughts and actions now from their effects on our futures.

## The Fabric of Our Lives

We might ask ourselves if we merit the blessings of our Father's plan with the life we are now living. The days of our probation are numbered, but none of us knows the number of those days. Each day of preparation is precious.

I have watched the skilled hands of Navajo women in the American Southwest as they weave intricate patterns into beautiful rugs. They select and prepare each colored thread of yarn very carefully and insert it in precisely the right place. They weave the varied colors artistically into the fabric of the whole to form rugs that eventually conform to the preconceived plan of their creators.

In much the same way, we weave into the fabric of our lives the pattern that we will present as our finished product. Our mortal lives are woven each day as we add our deeds into something intricately beautiful, following the Master Designer's plan. When we make wrong choices, we must live with a blotch in the fabric of our souls or retrace our steps through repentance and remove the errant threads we have woven into our character and replace them with the finer threads that our Maker intended for us to use. This poem illustrates the point:

> My life is but a weaving between my Lord and me;
> I cannot choose the colors He worketh steadily.
> Ofttimes He weaveth sorrow and I in foolish pride,
> Forget that He seeth the upper, and I the under side.
> Not till the loom is silent and the shuttles cease to fly,
> Shall God unroll the canvas and explain the reason why.
> The dark threads are as needful in the Weaver's skillful hand,
> As the threads of gold and silver in the pattern He has
>     planned.
>> (Quoted in Neal A. Maxwell "Premortality, A
>> Glorious Reality" *Ensign*, Nov. 1985, 18.)

The tapestry of our lives is being patterned now. The Lord referred to our life before mortality as our first estate and promised each of us that "they who keep their first estate shall be added upon; and they who keep not their first estate shall not have glory in the same kingdom with those who keep their first estate; and they who keep their second estate shall have glory added upon their heads for ever and ever" (Abraham 3:26).

## Procrastination

Procrastination and indecision can hamper our efforts to prepare for the life after mortality. Elder Joseph Fielding Smith said, "Procrastination, as it may be applied to Gospel principles, is the thief of eternal life—which is life in the presence of the Father and the Son" (*The Way to Perfection*, 10th ed., 1953, 202). In the Book of Mormon we read Amulek's plea: "I beseech of you that ye do not procrastinate the day of your repentance until the end. . . . for that same spirit which doth possess your bodies at the time that ye go out of this life, that same spirit will have power to possess your body in that eternal world" (Alma 34:33–34).

It has been said that "life is such a precious gift, it should be guarded from needless dilution. . . . 'Each day is not just another day but more like a falling drop of water, a golden moment of life's span adding to an increasingly rich pool of living'" (Thomas J. Parmley as quoted in R. Scott Lloyd, "Alumnus 95, Returns to High School," *Church News,* 12 June 1993).

Indecision can immobilize or paralyze us, hindering our preparation in mortality. We can become like the people of Nineveh whom the Lord described to Jonah as "persons that cannot discern between their right hand and their left hand" (Jonah 4:11). The Apostle James observed that "a double minded man is unstable in all his ways" (James 1:8). An old Swiss saying describes such indecision in these words:

*With one foot in,*
*with one foot out,*
*You can't be in,*
*you can't be out—*
*Not warm, not cold,*
*not square, not round,*
*More poor than poor*
*and always bound.*
*For such a man*
*will never know*
*where to begin*
*or where to go.*
(Quoted in Hans B. Ringger,
"Choose You This Day," *Ensign,*
May 1990, 26.)

We cannot be double minded in our relationships with husband or wife, parents or children. Are we waiting to savor the enjoyment of our children after they are a little older and we are not so busy? What about the valued friendships that fade because of the thoughtful, lengthy letters we plan to write but never finish and send? Are we faithful in going to our temples regularly? Consider the books we are going to read, the impulses to kindness we are going to act upon, and the good causes we are going to espouse. Are we always packing our bags with the things we value most in life but never leaving on the trip? Does tomorrow never come? Let us resolve to begin to live today—not tomorrow, but today—this hour while we yet have time.

## The End of Our Probation

We know that death is a necessary transition. It will come sooner or later to each of us. Our mortal bodies will return to earth and our spirits will go to the spirit world. By virtue of the Savior's atoning sacrifice, we all will be resurrected. Each of us will stand before the judgment bar of the great Jehovah and be rewarded according to our deeds in mortality.

If we make every earthly decision with this judgment in mind, we will have used our mortal probation wisely and its days will give us peace in this life and eternal life in the world to come.

I testify that these doctrines are true. You can know of gospel truth by the confirmation of the Spirit whispering to your soul. The Lord said, "If any man will do his will, he shall know of the doctrine, whether it be of God, or whether I speak of myself" (John 7:14–17; see also vv. 14–16).

The Savior lives and loves each of us. This I know with all my heart. We are children of a loving Father in Heaven who has raised up the Prophet Joseph Smith to restore the fulness of the gospel. Our Father in Heaven has also blessed us with a living prophet in our day to guide us back to His loving arms.

*(Adapted from an April 1998 general conference address)*

# 23

# INSPIRED CHURCH WELFARE

What a wonderful celebration Easter is. As we reflect on the life of the Savior and His resurrection, certainly the many images of those who petitioned Him for help come to mind. I can easily imagine the deformed legs of a man unable to walk since birth or the tears flowing down a widow's cheek as she follows the body of her only son as it is carried to its tomb. I see the empty eyes of the hungry, the trembling hands of the sick, the pleading voice of the condemned, the disconsolate eye of the outcast. All of them are reaching toward a solitary man, a man without wealth, without home, without position.

I see this man, the Son of the living God, look on each of them with infinite compassion. With a touch of His holy hand, He brings comfort to the downcast, healing to the sick, liberation to the condemned. With a word, the dead man rises from his bier and the widow embraces her enlivened son.

These and other miraculous acts of mercy and kindness, some widely known, others quietly and privately performed, define for me one of the salient characteristics of the Savior: His love and compassion for the downtrodden, the weary, the weak, the suffering. Indeed, these acts of compassion are synonymous with His name.

Although nearly 2,000 years have passed since the mortal ministry of the Son of God, His loving example and His teachings remain an integral part of who we are as a people and who we are as a church. Today, through its inspired welfare program, The Church of Jesus Christ of Latter-day Saints and its members strive to emulate His example as we seek to relieve suffering and foster self-reliance.

## Scope of Church Welfare

The welfare program of the Church is well known throughout the world. People from all walks of life travel to Church headquarters to see firsthand how the Church cares for the poor and needy without creating dependency on the part of those who receive or bitterness on the part of those who give. A president of a country, after visiting Welfare Square, canceled the remainder of his appointments for the day. "There is something here that is more important than anything else I have on my schedule," he said. "I must stay and learn more."

Over the years, the Church welfare program has grown to meet the ever-increasing needs of an expanding Church. In North America today, more than eighty Church farms produce nutritious food for the needy. More than eighty cannery facilities preserve and package this life-sustaining food. More than one hundred bishops' storehouses stand ready to assist more than 26,000 bishops and branch presidents as they carry out their sacred obligation to seek out and assist the poor and needy in their wards and branches. Fifty Deseret Industries operations offer work and training to thousands. Worldwide, one hundred sixty employment centers help more than 78,000 people find jobs each year. An ever-increasing number of LDS Family Services offices help member couples adopt children and provide counseling to those in need.

I feel certain that the great leaders whom the Lord raised up to pioneer this modern-day welfare effort would be well pleased with the advancement of this inspired program of today.

## The Lord's Way

"It has always been a cardinal teaching with the Latter-day Saints," President Joseph F. Smith wrote, "that a religion which has not the power to save people temporally and make them prosperous and happy here, cannot be depended upon to save them spiritually, to exalt them in the life to come" (*Out West,* Sept. 1905, 242).

The temporal and the spiritual are linked inseparably. As we give of our time, talents, and resources to tend the needs of the sick, offer food to the hungry, and teach the dependent to stand on their own, we enrich ourselves spiritually beyond our ability to comprehend.

The Lord declared in a revelation to the Prophet Joseph Smith: "It is my purpose to provide for my saints. . . . But it must needs be done in mine own way; and behold this is the way that I, the Lord, have decreed to provide for my saints, that the poor shall be exalted, in that the rich are made low" (D&C 104:15–16). The Lord's way consists of helping people help themselves. The poor are exalted because they work for the temporary assistance they receive, they are taught correct principles, and they are able to lift themselves from poverty to self-reliance. The rich are made low because they humble themselves to give generously of their means to those in need.

We teach members to be self-reliant, to do everything possible to sustain themselves, and where help is needed to seek help first from their extended families. When members and their families are doing all they can to provide necessities but still cannot meet basic needs, the Church stands ready to help.

In the Church, the bishop has the specific charge to care for "the poor, the needy, the single parent, the aged, the disabled, the fatherless, the widowed, and others who have special needs" *(Church Handbook of Instructions, Book 1: Stake Presidencies and Bishoprics [2006]:* 17.)

I am aware of how one bishop marshaled his resources to assist a man who came to him for help. The man had been happily married for years, but because of a later addiction to alcohol and drugs he was left without a job, home, or family. Hard years of living on the street had degraded and humiliated him. With tears streaming down his face, he pleaded with his bishop for help.

The ward welfare committee discussed this challenge. One man knew a dentist who might be willing to replace the man's broken front teeth. The Relief Society president suggested that nutritious food from the bishops' storehouse might improve his health. Another suggested that this man needed someone who could spend time with him daily and help him find the strength to overcome his addictions.

As the suggestions streamed in, the bishop realized that an entire ward of concerned brothers and sisters stood ready to help.

Soon the bishop began to notice improvements. Priesthood brethren gave the man a blessing. A charitable dentist replaced his broken teeth. Food from the bishops' storehouse improved his health. A faithful elderly couple agreed to serve as special home teachers. They were with him daily to help him stick to his resolve.

Following established principles, this good brother offered to help others in the ward. Slowly his life began to improve. Gradually the look of desperation and misery gave way to one of joy and happiness. Although it was a painful process, he was able to free himself from his addictions. He became an active member in the Church. A life of destitution and misery turned into one of hope and happiness. This is the Lord's way of caring for those in need.

## The Church and Humanitarian Relief

The Church does not limit its relief efforts to its members but follows the admonition of the Prophet Joseph Smith when he said, "A man filled with the love of God, is not content with blessing his family alone, but ranges through the whole world, anxious to bless the whole human race" (*History of the Church*, 4:227). The Prophet instructed members "to feed the hungry, to clothe the naked, to provide for the widow, to dry up the tear of the orphan, [and] to comfort the afflicted" (*Times and Seasons*, 15 Mar. 1842, 732).

In a little over a decade, the Church has shipped more than 27,000 tons of clothing, 16,000 tons of food, and 3,000 tons of medical and educational supplies and equipment to relieve the suffering of millions of God's children in 146 countries around the world. We do not ask, "Are you members of our church?" We ask only, "Do you suffer?"

We are all aware of Hurricane Mitch, which devastated Nicaragua and Honduras. With terrific force it flooded homes and caused mudslides. More than 10,000 people died and another two million were left homeless. This very strong hurricane filled homes and covered streets with mud that seemed as hard as cement.

Almost immediately following the disaster, the Church began sending life-sustaining food, clothing, medicine, and blankets to help both members of the Church and those of other faiths. Once the shipments arrived at their destinations, Church members came by the hundreds to unload the trucks and assemble the supplies into boxes. The items in each box would sustain a family for a week.

President Gordon B. Hinckley, who is the chairman of the General Welfare Committee, was troubled by the suffering in Central America. One sleepless night he felt a prompting to go and offer his love and support to those who had endured this great loss. The prophet's visit to that area lifted the spirits and gave hope to thousands. "As long as [the Church] has any resources," he told them, "we will stand by you in times of trouble" (Address given in Honduras, 21 Nov. 1998; see also "President Hinckley: 'We Will Not Forget You,'" *Church News*, 28 Nov. 1998, 3, 6–7).

In addition to providing needed supplies in times of disaster and catastrophe, as of 1999, nearly 1,300 members of the Church have accepted calls from the Lord to serve the needy of many nations. Let me give two examples.

Brother David and Sister Dovie Glines, from Ivins, Utah, lived in

Ghana, Africa, where they taught business, computer, and office management skills to those who were seeking to improve their employment.

Brother Mark Cutler is a retired surgeon from Clayton, California. He and his wife, Bonnie, served in Vietnam. Brother Cutler was a consultant and instructor for local physicians. Sister Cutler taught English and medical terminology to the hospital doctors and staff.

## Welfare and the Member

In addition to helping others, families and individual members would do well to review their own level of self-reliance. We may ask ourselves a few questions:

- Are we wise stewards of our money? Do we spend less than we earn? Do we avoid unnecessary debt? Do we follow the counsel of the Brethren to "store sufficient food, clothing, and where possible, fuel for at least one year?" (First Presidency letter, 24 June 1988).
- Do we teach our children to value and not waste what they have? Do we teach them to work? Do they understand the importance of the sacred law of tithing?
- Do we have sufficient education and adequate employment?
- Do we maintain good health by living the Word of Wisdom? Are we free from the adverse effects of harmful substances?

If, in honesty, we answer "no" to any of these questions, we may wish to improve our self-reliance plan. Prophets have provided fundamental guides for us.

First, one of today's evils is the sin of covetousness. Inordinate desire for material possessions can become an obsession that consumes our thoughts, drains our resources, and leads to unhappiness. Some members of the Church are increasingly burdened with unnecessary debt because of this sin. President Heber J. Grant said: "If there is any one thing that will bring peace and contentment into the human heart, and into the family, it is to live within our means. And if there is any one thing that is grinding and discouraging and disheartening, it is to have debts and obligations that one cannot meet" ("Gospel Standards," in Conference Report, Oct. 1938, 57).

"Industry, thrift, self-reliance continue as guiding principles of this effort," President Thomas S. Monson, chairman of the Welfare Executive Committee of the Church, has admonished. "As a people, we should avoid unreasonable debt . . . , 'Pay thy debt, and live' (2 Kings 4:7). What wise counsel for us today" ("Goal beyond Victory," *Ensign,* Nov. 1988, 46).

Second, from the beginning, God has commanded us to work (see Genesis 3:19) and has warned us against idleness (see D&C 88:124). Sadly, many in our world today encourage idleness, especially in the form of mindless, inane entertainment that is found in so much abundance on the Internet, on television, and in computer games.

Third, I commend to you the counsel of President Hinckley when he said: "Get all the education you can. . . . Cultivate skills of mind and hands. Education is the key to opportunity" (*Teachings of Gordon B. Hinckley,* 172). Yes, education is the catalyst that will hone and sharpen our talents, skills, and abilities and cause them to blossom.

Fourth, those who choose to follow the example of the Savior and relieve suffering could look to the amount they contribute to fast offerings. These sacred funds are used for one purpose and one purpose only: to bless the sick, the suffering, and others in need.

Contributing a generous fast offering blesses the givers richly and allows them to become partners with the Lord and the bishop in helping relieve suffering and fostering self-reliance. In our prosperous circumstances, perhaps we should evaluate our offerings and decide if we are being as generous with the Lord as He is with us.

## Conclusion

If the Savior were among us in mortality today, He would be found ministering to the needy, the suffering, the sick. Following this example may be one of the reasons President Spencer W. Kimball said: "When viewed in this light, we can see that [welfare] is not a program, but the essence of the gospel. *It is the gospel in action.* It is the crowning principle of a Christian life" (in Conference Report, Oct. 1977, 123–44).

When the welfare program emerged from its humble beginnings in the midst of the Great Depression, few imagined that, seventy-five years later, it would have blossomed and flourished to the point where it blesses literally millions of the world's needy.

An inspiring, favorite hymn tenderly teaches a lesson in giving.

> *Because I have been sheltered, fed by thy good care,*
> *I cannot see another's lack and I not share*
> *My glowing fire, my loaf of bread,*
> *My roof's safe shelter overhead,*
> *That he too may be comforted.*
> (Hymns, *no. 219*)

The Savior, who set the pattern for us, is pleased with those who "remember in all things the poor and the needy, the sick and the afflicted" (D&C 52:40). He is pleased with those who hearken to His admonition to "succor the weak, lift up the hands which hang down, and strengthen the feeble knees" (D&C 81:5).

*(Adapted from an April 1999 general conference address)*

# 24

## BAND OF BROTHERS

### Bond of Brotherhood

I have been extremely fortunate during my life. I am grateful beyond measure for the rich blessings the Lord has bestowed upon me. Some of the choicest blessings of my life have been the close friendships I have experienced over the years. Often, these friendships have been forged in the fires of shared experience. I think back with fondness on the football teams I played on, the missionaries with whom I served in Austria and Switzerland, the bishoprics and stake presidencies that I served in. I think about my family—the happiness and grief we have shared together and how those moments of tenderness have amplified the love we have for each other.

Most recently, I think about the indescribable bond of brotherhood I have felt within the Quorum of the Twelve Apostles.

Though each of these groups was very different, each had common characteristics. Perhaps we grew close because we struggled so much together, strived together, and achieved together. Perhaps our camaraderie was because we linked arms together in a common journey where we had to depend so completely on each other. Whatever it was we shared, these relationships are the foundation of many of the most precious and rewarding moments of my life.

I wish to call your attention to the importance of establishing a bond of brotherhood in our assignments. Please understand when I speak of "brotherhood" I am not excluding our wonderful and indispensable sisters, who are so essential to our success in the Church. I wish to be inclusive today and ask for you to understand that when I speak of creating a "band of brothers" I am including within that definition our faithful, inspiring, and valiant sisters of all ages.

Establishing a bond of brotherhood is critical to successful church work. If those who serve with you feel this mutual love and trust, the work of the Lord will thrive, and heaven will aid you in your efforts. Fail to establish this bond, however, and you may find your work tedious, toilsome, and unproductive.

## D-Day

Some years ago, Stephen Ambrose wrote a book describing the experience of a company of paratroopers during World War II. The army was developing a new kind of warfare the world had not seen before. They were training men to parachute out of planes, often behind enemy lines and at immense personal peril, and to attack and take strategic objectives critical to the overall success of the war effort.

Easy Company of the 506th regiment, 101st Airborne division was one of those groups. Formed from volunteers, the 130 men began their training in 1942 under the direction of their company commander Lieutenant Herbert Sobel.

The men had been told that their training would be harder than any other in the military. In fact, it was so challenging that two out of three men couldn't make it and either dropped out or were reassigned to a regular army unit.

Lieutenant Sobel made things especially difficult. The men disliked him. He was cruel, arbitrary, and punished the men severely for minor infractions. That, combined with poor judgment when it came to military tactics, caused the noncommissioned officers to vow that they would never follow Sobel into combat.

As a result, Sobel was eventually transferred to a training facility and lost his command.

The night before D-Day, Easy Company parachuted behind enemy lines. Their assignment was to take out a battery of artillery guns. But in the chaos of the drop, only twelve of the 130 men were in position to carry out the mission. Nevertheless, they knew that if they didn't take out those guns, the Allied soldiers storming Utah Beach would take heavy casualties from the artillery.

To make matters worse, the guns were manned and defended by more than 50 elite German paratroopers who had dug a series of trenches about the battery, heavily fortifying it against any kind of assault.

In one of the most well-executed and heroic operations of the war, twelve men of Easy Company assaulted the position, routed the enemy, and destroyed the artillery guns.

In later action, Easy Company took part in the ill-fated Operation Market Garden—an assault of the German forces in Holland and Belgium. Later, they were among the forces that held Bastogne against encircling German Panzer units during the Battle of the Bulge.

By the time the war had ended, the highly decorated Easy Company had taken heavy, heavy casualties. Forty-eight of its members had died.

## Brotherhood in the Scriptures

In the scriptures, we learn of other groups with similar bonds. King Mosiah's sons were heirs to the throne. They could have led lives of comfort and ease. But they abandoned their life of privilege, walked into enemy territory, and preached the gospel to thousands of Lamanites, baptizing many.

The sons of those Lamanites who joined the Church would later enlist in the Nephite army. These Stripling Warriors banded together and fought against great odds. They became known as the Sons of Helaman, and their heroic story has inspired countless thousands since.

Throughout history, the great leaders of the world seem to have had this ability to build a band of brothers around them. Consider the great souls who helped usher in this last dispensation—Joseph, Hyrum, and Samuel Smith; Parley and Orson Pratt; Brigham Young, Heber C. Kimball, Wilford Woodruff. They, also, formed a great band of brothers who, though very different in individual personality and background, were all united in a common goal: to serve their God and to build His kingdom on earth.

## Brotherhood among Missionaries

I have had the opportunity to travel to many parts of the world. I have served on the Missionary Executive Council of the Church. I have seen successful missions, and I have also witnessed missions that have struggled. Where missions, have been successful, there is a spirit of love and brotherhood. More often than not, when a mission struggles, the bands that hold the missionaries together are weak.

One of the key tasks Church leaders face is to establish this spirit of brotherhood among those who serve with them. Without this sense of loyalty, sacrifice, and love, the work will not only be less successful but will also be much less rewarding.

Admittedly, this is easier to talk about than to accomplish. Some people seem to have a natural ability to lead. They inspire people and bring out the best that is in them. They have an ability to infuse people with vision that transcends their own lives and inspire greatness within them.

I'm not sure there is a recipe that can turn an ordinary administrator into a great leader. But I am certain that there are principles these great leaders have in common.

*The first principle is never forget the value of a great cause.*

Captain Moroni lived during a time when evil men were conspiring to destroy the liberty and lives of his countrymen. How did he rally the people of his day? He rent his coat and wrote upon it, "In memory of our God, our religion, and freedom, and our peace, our wives, and our children" (Alma 46:12–13).

Moroni knew the power of a great cause.

We cited earlier the Stripling Warriors whose commander was Helaman, the oldest son of the prophet Alma. As you remember, Helaman was the one Alma entrusted with the sacred records. I suppose Helaman was more of a scholar than a warrior. But he lived in a time of conflict and war and, when the 2,000 sons of converted Lamanites took up their weapons of war, they asked that Helaman be their leader.

Every student of the Book of Mormon knows their story. These young men had great faith. They were obedient. Although "they never had fought, yet they did not fear death" (Alma 56:47). Their confidence in the Lord was unshakeable, "Behold our God is with us," they said, "and he will not suffer that we should fall" (Alma 56:46).

After many battles and although every one of them had received wounds, not one soul of them perished (see Alma 57:21).

These young men knew why they were fighting. They understood the nature of their sacrifice. Of them, Helaman wrote: "They did think more upon the liberty of their fathers than they did upon their lives" (Alma 56:47).

They knew the value of a great cause.

Average leaders use the carrot and the stick to motivate those around them. Great leaders communicate a great vision that captures the imagination and fires the hearts and minds of those they lead. Average leaders inspire people to punch a time clock. Great leaders inspire industry and passion.

Lieutenant Sobel, the first commanding officer of Easy Company, maintained order because his men feared him. He was cruel to them and embarrassed them for trivial reasons merely to maintain his authority. Sobel's men obeyed him, but they hated him for it and did all they could to sabotage his command.

You can get people to work by using threats or by promising rewards. But if you want to create a band of brothers, you must inspire those who work with you and encourage them to give their all in a great cause.

And we have a great cause. What greater cause is there than being in the service of the Eternal Father and building His kingdom on earth?

## *The second principle is to understand your priorities.*

It's easy to get caught up in details. The Savior condemned the Pharisees because they spent so much time on the minor aspects while omitting the weightier matters of the law, such as judgment, mercy, and faith (see Mathew 23:23).

If someone were to ask you who we are as a people, what would you say? Who are we as members of The Church of Jesus Christ of Latter-day Saints?

The answer, I believe, is a simple one given to us by the Savior Himself. We are a people who love the Lord with all our heart, soul, and mind. And we are a people who love our neighbor as ourselves (see Matthew 22:35–39).

This answer satisfies many of the questions asked about why we do what we do. Why does the Church ask so much of its members? Because we love the Lord and we love our neighbor. Why do we do temple work? Missionary work? Welfare work? Because we love the Lord and we love our neighbor.

What priorities should you have as leaders? The answer is simple: Love the Lord and love your neighbor.

What should you teach those with whom you serve? Teach them to love the Lord and to love their neighbor.

A mission president could spend hours and hours talking about door approaches, discussion techniques, or tracking every aspect of missionary work, but that would be merely hacking at the leaves unless the missionaries truly love the Lord and genuinely love His sons and daughters.

That is who we are as a people. That is why we do what we do.

## *The third principle is to settle into the harness.*

No great cause ever succeeded without great effort.

One of the reasons the men of Easy Company volunteered for hazardous duty was because when they went into combat, they wanted to be next to someone they could trust—someone who wouldn't do something foolish that could get them killed. They didn't want to be next to someone who was lazy or who hadn't paid attention during training or who wasn't physically capable of what was required. These men had worked to the limits of human capacity and, because of this shared experience, they were not only good at what they did, but they shared a common bond.

From the days of Adam and Eve until now, our Heavenly Father has commanded that we work. Work is the foundation of success and creation. It is the secret of every successful enterprise. Even so, there are some who go to great lengths to avoid work. In fact, a few people I have known have worked exceptionally hard to get out of work. This is something I have never understood. My father was a hard worker and he taught me to be the same.

Have you heard about the professor of psychology at the University of Chicago who spent twenty-five years studying the answer to one question: "What makes people happy?"

He wanted to find out what distinguishes those who live fulfilling and joy-filled lives from those who live lives of quiet desperation.

He surveyed artists and cab drivers, physicians and farmers, and after twenty-five years, he published his findings.

After all his research, he concluded: "The best moments [in our lives] usually occur when a person's body or mind is stretched to its limits in a voluntary effort to accomplish something difficult and worthwhile" (Mihaly Csikszentmihalyi, *Flow: The Psychology of Optimal Experience*, Harper Perennial, 1990, 3).

What makes a person happy?

One of the key ingredients is the simple thing we call work.

Some of the most fulfilling moments of our lives are when we establish worthwhile goals and work toward achieving them.

I know that some stop listening when they hear about goal setting. But I have found the process to be exhilarating.

Each night, I think about my goals and what I want to accomplish the next day. And then I write down on a 3 by 5 card the key things I can do to bring me closer to my goals.

Teach those you lead to give their best effort. Teach them to settle into the harness and work with their might. As they do so, they will find joy in their service.

## *The fourth principle is "fear not."*

When I was a young boy I had a dog called Ruff. We lived in a rural area and so we let the dog run free, but the problem with Ruff was that he got into the habit of chasing people as they rode or walked past our home. I would yell at him to stop, but Ruff never did. I was worried that he might bite someone.

One day, Ruff decided to chase a policeman.

That was a mistake.

Ruff went after the police officer and started nipping at his heels, but the policeman, instead of just speeding away like everyone else, drew his service revolver, aimed it at Ruff, and fired.

He shot my dog in the foot, and a surprised Ruff came limping home.

After that day, he was never the same. Whenever he heard a loud noise, Ruff would tuck in his tail and run like the wind.

He used to come to my father's business and hang out around the store. Sometimes he would bother the customers. Soon, we learned that all we had to do to get old Ruff to leave was to take out a paper sack, blow air into it, and then pop it.

When Ruff heard that pop, he'd dash away, making a beeline for home. I never saw a dog run so fast.

I've noticed something over the years. People sometimes act like old Ruff. Fear can do that to you. Sometimes, fear makes us run away from things—things like setting and achieving goals, developing relationships that last a lifetime, or becoming the people we know we should become. Sometimes fear can even paralyze us to the point where we don't even try.

Fear can be a thick fog that smothers our dreams. It can be a cage that keeps us from reaching our destiny. It can be a weight that restrains our every step.

The difference between human beings and my dog, Ruff, is that you and I have the power of reason. I'm not sure old Ruff was capable of telling the difference between the sound of a pistol and the sound of a paper bag being popped, but we can.

Time after time, the men of Easy Company knew fear. A few days after D-Day, they were walking down a road toward a French village when a German machine gun opened fire on them. In spite of their training, the men ducked for cover and froze. The company commander, Dick Winters, knew if they stayed there, his men would be cut down. Lieutenant Winters stood up in the middle of the road, away from cover, bullets whistling all around him and ordered his men to move out.

His men stared at him, not believing what they were seeing—but only for an instant. The courage of their commanding officer inspired them. Then they moved out.

Because of Lieutenant Winters' bravery, the men survived.

We may not be immune to being afraid, but we do not have to succumb to it.

There are some who give up on the great goals of their lives because of fear. Many missionaries never reach their potential because they are frozen, ducking for cover at the side of the road.

Often, what they need more than anything else is to feel someone else's courage.

Too often, we fail to act because we are frozen by fear. Harold Brown is a good friend of mine. Brother Brown once said that "it is better to face fear once than to live in its shadow always."

I believe he is right.

We are surrounded and uplifted by the faith of our members and by the hand of heaven. If only we could see that, our fears would have far less influence over us.

The Apostle John encouraged us with these words: "Greater is he that is in you," he said, "than he that is in the world" (1 John 4:4).

Move forward with faith, believing you will succeed! Don't let fear of failure stop you from greatness. Let your example of courage inspire those around you to fear not.

## The fifth principle is to press on in faith.

Joseph Smith has always been a great example of perseverance to me. From the time he was a young man he was persecuted, mocked, and reviled. And yet he pressed on. He watched as loved ones died. He was cursed and threatened by enemies, he was betrayed by friends. In spite of innumerable hardships he pressed on.

One night, a mob of forty men stormed the Prophet's house and pulled him and Sidney Rigdon outside. Emma, Joseph's wife, screamed and pleaded with the men to stop, but they did not listen. The mob tried to force nitric acid down the Prophet's throat. They stripped him and covered his body with tar and feathers.

He survived and managed to stumble back to his house where a terrified Emma was waiting. It took his friends the entire night to scrape the tar from his skin.

The following day, this heroic prophet rose and spoke to those who had assembled for the Sunday meeting. Among those present in the congregation were members of the mob who had assaulted him the night before.

Joseph Smith never looked back. From the day he was called of the Father and the Son, he pressed on.

Through sickness, suffering, ridicule, and betrayal, he pressed. He pressed on until the day he gave his life as a testimony to the restored gospel.

Louis Pasteur once said, "Let me tell you the secret [that] has led me to my goal. My strength lies solely in my tenacity" (René J. Doubox, *Luis Pasteur: Freelance of Science,* [Norwalk, Connecticut: Easton Press, 1950], 63). May we understand the wisdom of his words.

To all who enter the Lord's service as leaders in His Church, I say you are about to embark on a great adventure. The journey may be difficult, but think for a moment on the glory of the destination.

I testify that we are sons and daughters of the Eternal God. We are heirs to all He has. We are destined to become kings and queens.

We stand as witnesses to God the Father and His Son, Jesus Christ. We are the heralds of a glorious new era: the second coming of Jesus Christ. We work tirelessly to bring about resplendent Zion. We are citizens, ambassadors, and soldiers of the Lord God of Israel.

And with such a great vision shall we sleep when the trumpet is sounded?

With such a great call, shall our steps falter when our Lord and Master calls us to duty?

When we work together in a bond of brotherhood, when we love each other and are loyal and faithful to the great cause to which we have been called, the impossible becomes possible.

Stephen Ambrose titled his history of Easy Company, "Band of Brothers" because of the bond of fellowship these men felt for each other. This sort of brotherhood happens when a group of people give their heart, might, mind, and strength to a cause greater than themselves. The men of Easy Company weren't great because they were trying to stand out as individuals. They were great because they worked together.

One of the men who served in that elite fighting group remembered a conversation he had with his grandson.

"Grandpa," the little boy asked, "were you a hero in the war?"

The old soldier thought about the question for a moment and then replied, "No, but I served in a company of heroes" (*Band of Brothers*, 307).

You and those with whom you serve each have the potential to be heroes. As you give inspired leadership and give those who serve with you a vision of the great cause, help them set their priorities, encourage them to settle into the harness, overcome their fears, and press on in faith, you will create your own company of heroes.

Every day, hundreds of thousands of faithful members lift up their hearts in prayer, asking that this great work will go forward. They plead that the hearts of the great and small will be softened. They ask that doors—some so great they open to an entire nation, others so humble they open to a single heart—will be opened. With the commission we bear and that kind of support, we will find the success and joy that come when a band of brothers embarks on a heavenly cause.

*(Adapted from an address given at the*
*Seminar for New Mission Presidents, 26 June 2006)*

# 25

# LIVE IN THANKSGIVING DAILY

We've all met those who seem to radiate happiness. They seem to smile more than others, they laugh more than others, just being around them makes us happier as well.

Now think of someone you know who isn't happy at all. Perhaps they seem ten years older than they are, drained of energy, perhaps they are angry or bitter or depressed.

What is the difference between them? What are the characteristics that differentiate the happy from the miserable? Is there something that unhappy people can do to be happier? I believe there is.

## The Ungrateful Man

Let me relate a story to illustrate this observation.

A long time ago in a faraway village, lived a man who everyone did their very best to avoid. He was the type of person who believed that there was only one competent person in the world and that one person was himself. Consequently, he was never satisfied with anything. His shoes never fit right. His shirt never felt comfortable. When his food wasn't too cold, it was too salty, and when it wasn't too hot, it was too bland.

If a field wasn't sowed by him, it was not sowed well. If he didn't close the door, the door was not closed properly.

In short, he made a career of frowning, lecturing, criticizing, and mumbling about the incompetence of every other person in the rest of the world.

Unfortunately, the man was married, which made matters all the worse. No matter what his wife did, in his eyes it was wrong. No matter how the unfortunate woman cooked, sewed, cleaned, or milked the cow it was never satisfactory, and he let her know it.

She tried very hard to be a good wife, but it seemed the harder she tried the less she pleased him. Finally, one evening, she could take no more.

"I'll tell you what we'll do," she told him, "tomorrow, I will do your chores and you will do mine."

"But you can't do my chores," the man replied. "You don't know the first thing about sowing, hoeing, and irrigating."

But the woman was adamant. And on top of that, she was filled with a righteous anger that frankly astonished and frightened the poor man to the point where he didn't dare disagree.

So, the next morning, the wife went off to the fields and the man began the domestic chores. After thinking about it, he had actually convinced himself he was looking forward to it. Once and for all, he would demonstrate to his wife how things were properly done.

Unfortunately, not everything went according to plan. In fact, nearly everything the man touched turned into disaster. He spilled the milk, let the pig into the house, lost the cow, burned the dinner, and ultimately set the house on fire with himself still inside.

When his wife returned, she discovered her husband sitting on a pile of ashes, smoke still rising from his clothes. But the woman wasn't the type to rub things in. She helped him up, wiped the soot from his beard, fixed him a little something to eat, and then prepared a bed of straw for them to sleep on.

From that day forward, the man never complained about anyone or anything else for as long as he lived.

What do you suppose this story teaches us?

For one thing, it teaches that those who complain make their own and other's lives miserable. It teaches humility. It reminds us that "Pride goeth before destruction, and an haughty spirit before a fall" (Proverbs 16:18). It teaches us not to judge others until we walk in their shoes for awhile.

It also illustrates a quality that the Roman orator Cicero claimed was "not only the greatest virtue, but also even the mother of all the rest" (*The Macmillan Book of Proverbs, Maxims, and Famous Phrases,* sel. and arrang. by Burton Stevenson, [New York: Macmillan, 1948], 102).

It is a quality I have found in every happy person I know. It is a quality that instantly makes a person more likable and more at peace. Where there is an abundance of this quality, there is happiness. Where there is an absence, there is often sadness, resentment, and futility.

The virtue I am speaking of is gratitude.

In our story, it was the absence of gratitude that made the man miserable. His inability to appreciate others caused him to be critical of their efforts. Not only did he not empathize with them, he could not allow himself to acknowledge their contributions.

The disasters that confronted him surely made him humble, but more particularly, they made him appreciate and be grateful for his wife.

## Gratitude

Gratitude is a mark of a noble soul and a refined character. We like to be around those who are grateful. They tend to brighten everything around them. They make others feel better about themselves. They tend to be more humble, more joyful, more likable.

You might be surprised to know that to be grateful is a commandment of the Father. "Thou shalt thank the Lord thy God in all things" (D&C 59:7), the Lord has commanded in these latter days. He has also said, "In nothing doth man offend God, or against none is his wrath kindled, save those who confess not his hand in all things, and obey not his commandments" (D&C 59:21).

In the Book of Mormon we learn that we should "live in thanksgiving daily" (Alma 34:38). Isn't that a wonderful thought? To live in thanksgiving daily? Can you imagine how your life would improve if you lived in thanksgiving daily? Can you imagine how your life would improve if others did the same? Do you think the world would be a happier place? Less stressful? Less angry? More spiritual?

President Joseph F. Smith proclaimed, "The grateful man sees so much in the world to be thankful for, and with him the good outweighs the evil. Love overpowers jealousy, and light drives darkness out of his life. Pride destroys our gratitude and sets up selfishness in its place. How much happier we are in the presence of a grateful and loving soul, and how careful we should be to cultivate, through the medium of a prayerful life, a thankful attitude toward God and man!" (*Gospel Doctrine,* 5th ed. Deseret Book, 1939, 263).

Think of someone you know who is truly happy. If you will, grade them on this principle: Do they live in thanksgiving daily?

Now think of someone you know who is unhappy or resentful. Does this person live in thanksgiving daily?

It is difficult to even imagine a resentful person who is grateful or a grateful person who is resentful. Elder Gordon B. Hinckley said that "Absence of gratitude is the mark of the narrow, uneducated mind. It bespeaks a lack of knowledge and the ignorance of selfsufficiency. It expresses itself in ugly egotism and frequently in wanton mischief. . . . Where there is appreciation, there is courtesy, there is concern for the rights and property of others. Without [appreciation], there is arrogance and evil" (in Conference Report, Oct. 1964, 117).

## If Only . . .

I believe that many people are unhappy because they have not learned to be grateful. Some carry the burden of bitterness and resentfulness for many years. Some pass their days as though suffering a deep sadness they cannot name. Others are unhappy because life didn't turn out the way they thought it would.

"If only I had money," some might say to themselves, "then I could be happy."

"If only I were better looking."

"If only I were smarter."

"If only I had a new car, a college degree, a job, a wife, hair that wasn't so frizzy, or in my case, more hair or were twelve inches taller."

If we only look around us, there are a thousand reasons for us not to be happy, and it's simplicity itself to blame our unhappiness on the things we lack in life. It doesn't take any talent at all to find them. The problem is, the more we focus on the things we don't have, the unhappier and more resentful we become.

Over the course of my years, I have met thousands of people. I have dined with the prosperous as well as the poverty-stricken. I have conversed with the mighty and with the meek. I have walked with the famous and the feeble. I have run with outstanding athletes and those who are not athletically blessed.

One thing I can tell you with certainty is this: you cannot predict happiness by the amount of money, fame, or power a person has. External conditions do not necessarily make a person happy. Those who have had Church assignments in Africa report that despite the abject poverty, the people are generally very happy. In fact, often the external things so valued by the world are the cause of a great deal of misery in the world.

Those who live in thanksgiving daily, however, often are among the world's happiest people. And they make others happy as well.

## J. Golden Kimball

Years ago, Elder J. Golden Kimball was traveling with one of the presiding Brethren in Southern Utah. In those days, meetings often didn't have a time limit; they went on as long as the speaker wanted to speak. (For those of you looking for something to be grateful for, perhaps I've just given you one idea.)

One fast Sunday, Elder Kimball and his companion had been preaching nearly all day. Everyone was hungry, especially Elder Kimball, who felt that he "was pretty nearly dead."

Finally, at about four o'clock in the afternoon, the presiding apostle turned and said, "Now, Brother Kimball, get up and tell them about the *Era*."

The *Era* magazine had just been launched, and the Brethren wanted to encourage subscriptions. Elder Kimball reluctantly approached the microphone and then, after a short pause said, "All you men that will take the *Era* if we will let you go home, raise your right hand" (in Conference Report, Apr., 1932, 78).

There was not a single man who did not raise his hand that day and subscribe to the *Era*.

You see, the power of gratitude is immense.

## *Rulon Gardner*

Rulon Gardner grew up in the small town of Afton, Wyoming. He is one of nine children. His mother and father are faithful members of the Church and instilled proper values in their children.

But because Rulon was so large, his classmates teased him and called him names. These taunts troubled young Rulon, but he never became angry or resentful. He could have withdrawn and become bitter. Like so many others, he could have counted all the things that were going wrong and simply given up.

Instead, he used the insults as motivation. He determined he would use his size to his advantage. He would make something of himself.

"I would go out, as a kid," Rulon said, "and I could barely pick up a bale of hay. By the time my senior year came around, I was grabbing four bales of hay at a time, each 100 pounds. Just grabbing them and walking with them and seeing how physically strong I could be" (reported by Alan Robinson, The Associated Press, Sydney, Australia, 28 Sept. 2000).

He would milk cows twice a day, often in sub-zero temperatures. He lifted frozen bales of hay to feed the cows. At times, he would carry a newborn calf into the safety of a warm barn. He would get up early in the morning, do his chores, then go to school. After school, he would either go to wrestling or football practice, then back to the farm to do more chores.

Rulon found that his size wasn't a disadvantage for him as an athlete; in fact, it was an asset. Wrestling, particularly came easy to him, and he became the Wyoming heavyweight state champion. After graduating from high school, he decided that perhaps he might be good enough to compete in the Olympic games.

In Atlanta in 1996, due to a miscommunication, he arrived at the weigh-in twenty-two seconds too late and missed his chance to compete. Again, Rulon could have despaired. He could have cursed his luck. He could have become embittered and resentful.

But do you know what he did?

He worked harder. Instead of burying himself in self-pity, he began speaking at youth firesides about his experience. "I missed the Olympic games by twenty-two seconds," he would tell his eager listeners. "Don't you let anything keep you from your goals."

After four years of hard work, Rulon Gardner hoped to compete in the 2000 Olympic games in Sydney, Australia. The only trouble was, he couldn't afford the trip. That's when the members of his hometown rallied to his side. They held bake sales and potluck dinners and raised enough money to allow Rulon and his family to make the trip to Sydney.

This time he did not miss the weigh-in. He advanced through the preliminary rounds until he reached the final obstacle to his gaining a gold medal.

That obstacle was a man the world called the Siberian Bear, Alexandre Kareline. This huge man is considered by most to be the greatest

Greco-Roman wrestler in the history of the sport. Not only had he not lost a single match in thirteen years, but no one had even scored a point on him in over a decade. Kareline had won the gold medal in three previous Olympic Games and was the heavy favorite to win an unprecedented fourth gold medal.

But at the end of the gold-medal match, it was the farm boy from Afton, Wyoming, who stood triumphant in what many consider the greatest upset of the summer Olympic games.

"The reason I think I won," Rulon said, "is because I work harder than anyone else, train harder. And everyday I live my life, I do everything I need to do to put my life in order" (Ibid.).

Waving an American flag, a grateful Rulon Gardner thanked his family, his God, and his hometown of Afton, Wyoming, for their helping to make that remarkable moment possible.

Winning the gold medal in such a stunning way made Rulon an instant celebrity. Sometimes, this sort of attention changes people. Sometimes people become conceited and self-centered. Sometimes they forget those to whom they owe the most. But not Rulon Gardner.

Recently, while a guest on an evening television talk show, Rulon was invited by the host to watch some highlights from his Olympic victory. Without warning, the picture changed to a live shot from Afton, Wyoming. It seemed that the entire population of the town had assembled in the high school gymnasium. They cheered and shouted and held up signs that said, "Rulon's got milk!" and "My uncle rocks!"

As this man—one of the strongest men in the world—looked into the television monitor at the faces of the people he loved, tears of gratitude came to his eyes.

In a letter written to his stake president, Rulon Gardner said, "The Lord has given me the chance to work for all my dreams. I feel the Church has helped me to focus and live my life in the ways that have helped me to train and become an Olympic champ. . . . I am blessed . . .

to be a member of The Church of Jesus Christ of Latter-day Saints" (letter to President Val J. Call, Afton Wyoming Stake, 20 Oct. 2000).

Rulon Gardner knows what it means to be grateful and as a result knows what it is to be happy.

Gratitude turns a meal into a feast and drudgery into delight. It softens our grief and heightens our pleasure. It turns the simple and common into the memorable and transcendent. It forges bonds of love and fosters loyalty and admiration.

Living in thanksgiving daily is a habit that will enrich our lives and the lives of those we love. But how do we make this part of who we are? May I suggest three things that may help as we strive to live in thanksgiving daily?

### First, we must open our eyes

I agree with Robert Louis Stevenson who wrote, "The man who forgets to be thankful has fallen asleep in life" (*The Letters of Robert Louis Stevenson*, ed. Bradford A. Booth and Ernest Mehew, [New Haven: Yale University Press, 1994], 4:1257). Unfortunately, because the beauties of life are so abundant, sometimes we take them for granted.

Our minds have a marvelous capacity to notice the unusual. However, the opposite is true as well, the more often we see the things around us—even the beautiful and wonderful things—the more they become invisible to us.

That is why we often take for granted the beauty of this world—the flowers, the trees, the birds, the clouds—even those we love.

Ironically, because we see things so often, we see them less and less.

Those who live in thanksgiving daily, however, have a way of opening their eyes and seeing the wonders and beauties of this world as though seeing them for the first time.

I encourage you to look around you. Notice the people you care about. Take in the beauty of your surroundings. Inhale the fragrance of the flowers and listen to the song of the birds. Notice and give thanks for the blue of the sky and the whiteness of the clouds. Enjoy every sight, every smell, every taste, every sound.

Folliott S. Pierpoint gave poetic utterance to this notion when he wrote:

*For the beauty of the earth,*
*For the beauty of the skies,*
*For the love which from our birth*
*Over and around us lies,*
*Lord of all, to thee we raise*
*This our hymn of grateful praise.*
(Hymns, *no. 92)*

When we open our eyes and give thanks for the bountiful beauty of this life, we live in thanksgiving daily.

## Second, we can open our hearts

If we are to be truly happy, we must let go of the negative emotions that bind our hearts and fill our souls instead with love, faith, and thanksgiving.

Anger, resentment, and bitterness stunt spiritual growth. Would you bathe in impure water? Then why do we bathe our spirits with negative and bitter thoughts and feelings?

You can cleanse your heart. You don't have to harbor thoughts and feelings that drag you down and destroy your spirit.

You can repent of uncleanness. That is the miracle of Christ's atoning sacrifice. You can become clean. You can cleanse your heart of impurity.

Begin the process today. Repent of those things you should repent of. Drink deeply of the living waters of the gospel. These latter-days are a time of great spiritual thirst. Many in the world are searching, often desperately, for a source of refreshment that will quench their yearning for meaning and direction in their lives. The Lord provides the living water that can quench the burning thirst of those whose lives are parched by a drought of truth.

Pray with all your heart. Consider the love your Heavenly Father has for all His children. Open your hearts to His cleansing word. Feast on the words of holy writ. Cherish the messages of modern-day prophets and apostles. Forgive others who have offended you. Don't waste another moment wallowing in self-pity. Every day, drain from your heart the feelings of resentment, rage, and defeat that do nothing but discourage and destroy. Fill your heart instead with those things that ennoble, encourage, and inspire.

The great Book of Mormon prophet Nephi certainly had reason to be resentful. Hated by his brothers, bound and beaten and nearly murdered, he had plenty to be bitter about. After his father died, Nephi must have felt completely alone. He surely felt threatened. He surely felt discouraged. He surely felt troubled. But when it comes time for him to communicate his feelings, what does he write?

"My soul delighteth in the things of the Lord; and my heart pondereth continually upon the things which I have seen and heard" (2 Nephi 4:16).

Yes, his path had been difficult. Yes, his heart groaned because of mistakes he had made, but he did not allow himself to linger in negativity. "Rejoice, O my heart," he told himself, "and give place no more for the enemy of my soul, Do not anger again because of mine enemies. Do not slacken my strength because of my afflictions. Rejoice, O my heart, and cry unto the Lord, and say: O Lord, I will praise thee forever; yea, my soul will rejoice in thee" (2 Nephi 4:28–30).

## Third, open our arms

One of the best ways we show our gratitude is to bless the lives of those around us. The great King Benjamin taught his people, that "If you should render all the thanks and praise which your whole soul has

226

power to possess, to that God who has created you, and has kept and preserved you, and has caused that ye should rejoice, . . . If ye should serve him with all your whole souls yet ye would be unprofitable servants" (Mosiah 2:20–21).

And how do we render thanks unto God? King Benjamin tells us that as well. "And behold, I tell you these things that ye may learn wisdom," he says, "that ye may learn that when ye are in the service of your fellow beings ye are only in the service of your God" (Mosiah 2:17).

How do we live in thanksgiving daily? By opening our arms to those around us. When was the last time you told someone you love how much they mean to you? When was the last time you expressed your gratitude to someone who has always been there for you, someone who has sacrificed for you, someone whose heart has always been filled with hopes and dreams for you?

When was the last time you unselfishly reached out to help another in need? Every time we cheer another's heart, every time we ease another's burden, every time we lift a weary hand, we show our gratitude to that God to whom we owe all that we have and all that we are.

A few years ago, a mother and father from the Republic of Georgia faced a terrifying reality. The doctors told them their baby had a heart defect and, unless he had surgery, he would die. Because they did not have adequate facilities in Georgia, the mother and father walked across their country and all the way to Yerevan, Armenia, seeking medical help for their child.

The Armenian doctors examined the child and agreed that the baby needed heart surgery. They knew how to perform the surgery, they had the necessary facilities, but they couldn't perform the operation because they didn't have the right tubing. As much as they wanted to help, there was nothing they could do. They told the couple to take their baby home to die.

As you know, the Church—through its humanitarian service arm—sends millions of pounds of food, clothing, and medical and educational materials throughout the world each year. As it so happened, Elder and Sister Sangster were serving a humanitarian mission in Armenia, and they had just received a container of medical supplies.

You may have already guessed that tucked away in this container of medical supplies was a box of precisely the kind of tubing needed for this child's operation.

When the doctors were given the tubing, they rushed the baby into surgery and performed the operation.

That's a wonderful story and one that repeats itself daily as a result of the tremendous humanitarian help that is given to many nations in the world. The great welfare effort given by the Church benefits members and nonmembers during times of need. It reaches out to care for others. But what happened later makes this an even better story. One day, soon after the surgery, Elder and Sister Sangster heard a knock at their door. When they opened it, this loving mother and father fell to their knees and wept as they thanked the Sangsters and their Church for supplying the precious tubing that had helped save the life of their child.

The blessings that come from opening our arms to others are among the choicest this earth has to offer, and such service contributes to our happiness.

As we strive to open our eyes, hearts, and arms, our step will become a little lighter, our smile will become a little brighter, and the darkness that sometimes broods over our lives will become a little whiter. Don't be discouraged if you haven't been an especially grateful person. Rejoice and think of the impression you will make on those who thought they knew you. Think of how delightfully surprised they will be.

Be grateful.

Every day is a new canvas. A new opportunity. President Gordon B. Hinckley has said, "My plea is that we stop seeking out the storms and enjoy more fully the sunlight. I am suggesting that as we go through life, we 'accentuate the positive.' I am asking that we look a little deeper for the good, that we still our voices of insult and sarcasm, that we more generously compliment and endorse virtue and effort" (*Standing for Something,* Times Books, 2000, 101).

Choice blessings of happiness await those who live in thanksgiving daily. "He who receiveth all things with thankfulness," the Lord has promised, "shall be made glorious; and the things of this earth shall be added unto him, even an hundred fold, yea, more" (D&C 78:19).

Don't wait to begin. Open your eyes, open your hearts, and open your arms. I promise that as you do so, you will feel greater joy and happiness. Your life will have a new level of meaning. You will forge relationships that will transcend this life and endure through the eternities.

I am grateful for this experience of mortality. I am grateful for the gospel and for the life and testimony of the Prophet Joseph Smith. I am grateful for my wonderful wife, my dear children and grandchildren. I am grateful for the support and love shown to me by countless friends and members of the Church throughout the world. I am grateful for life and even more grateful for the glorious promise of eternal life to come.

Not everyone can be a star quarterback, not everyone can be the CEO of a Fortune 500 company, not everyone can win a gold medal at the Olympics, but everyone—*everyone*—can live in thanksgiving daily.

*(Adapted from an address given at a BYU Devotional, 31 October 2000)*

# 26

## DOCTRINAL PRINCIPLES RELATING TO THE FAMILY

(Note: The reader will notice that no reference is made in this chapter to "The Family: A Proclamation to the World," the Church's definitive statement on doctrinal principles relating to the family. This talk was first given prior to its issuance but contains principles consistent with that inspired declaration.)

### Parents Are Not Perfect

I remember attending a sacrament meeting in which one of our granddaughters spoke before leaving on her mission. Our hearts, along with those of her dear parents, swelled with loving pride as she enthusiastically declared to the assembled congregation, "I was *truly* 'born of goodly parents' (1 Nephi 1:1)!" After a brief pause, she went on to add, "But they're *not* perfect." And her parents and grandparents swallowed hard as the lump of emotion in our throats was suddenly transformed into a healthy helping of humble pie.

Of course, in overcoming the trials of mortality, none of us is perfect. But we all ought to be constantly striving to heed the Savior's admonition to become such, to conform our lives to the example He and our Father have set for us (see 3 Nephi 12:48). Our children are especially astute observers of how we conduct ourselves in our marriages and of how we carry out our personal and family responsibilities. They watch closely how we, their parents, govern ourselves and our households, and they are keenly attuned to the overall tone and tenor that we create in our homes. They do, indeed, watch every move we make, and we would do well to remember that their eyes and ears are constantly upon us, always measuring the distance between what we preach and what we practice.

Perhaps better than anyone else, our children know that we are not perfect. However, if we clearly understand the foundation principles of family life and honestly strive to conduct ourselves accordingly, we will earn the love, respect, and gratitude of our children, in spite of our weaknesses. We will find joy, happiness, and peace in grappling with the day-to-day challenges of this life, and we will qualify for the blessings of eternal life, "which gift is the greatest of all the gifts of God" (D&C 14:7).

## Family–Foundation Element of the Gospel

There can be no doubt that family is a foundation element of the restored gospel of Jesus Christ. President Howard W. Hunter instructed the Saints to place foremost emphasis on their families. "We encourage you to make family life a *preeminent* focus," he said. "In the Church, families will never be 'out of style' or 'out of date'" (*Teachings of Howard W. Hunter*, ed. Clyde J. Williams, [Salt Lake City: Utah: Bookcraft, 1997], 143; emphasis added). The First Presidency has issued two letters directed to the members of the Church with the clear purpose of strengthening families. The first letter admonishes us to worthily attend the temple. The First Presidency promises that, "As more members of the Church attend the temple, they *and their families* will enjoy needed blessings" ("Temple Worthiness and Temple Attendance," Message of the First Presidency, 25 Aug. 1994; emphasis added). The second letter reaffirms the promised blessings of love at home, obedience to parents, faith in the hearts of youth, and power to combat evil and temptations "to those who faithfully hold family home evenings" ("Family Home Evening," Message of the First Presidency, 30 Aug. 1994; emphasis added). Obviously, the Lord is concerned about strengthening families.

In contrast to the confusion that reigns in the world, the teachings of the gospel are clear. While Satan's lies and contentions sweep the earth in a whirlwind of falsehoods, the doctrine of our Heavenly Father stands unassailable—as true today as it has been since the beginning of time and as it will be throughout all eternity. I would like to review some five foundation principles of doctrine regarding the family. My list is certainly not comprehensive, but it should prove instructive. These five correct principles offer us constancy upon which we can build firm foundations for living in a turbulent world. They are:

- Families on earth are an extension of the family of God
- Marriage is ordained of God
- The power to create life is a gift from God
- Parents are responsible for teaching their children the laws of God
- The family can become an eternal unit through the power of God

## God at the Center of Family Life

"God, who created all things by Jesus Christ" (Ephesians 3:9) must be at the center of family life. Faith in a living, loving Heavenly Father brings meaning to our existence and focuses our hearts and minds on that which matters most. We must "believe in God; believe that he is, and that he created all things, *both* in heaven and in earth" (Mosiah 4:9; emphasis added). We can cope with the chaos of a troubled world only when we have a testimony, an abiding witness, that God "has all wisdom, and all power, *both* in heaven and in earth; [and that] man doth not comprehend all the things which the Lord can comprehend" (Ibid.; emphasis added).

As we examine each of these foundation truths, I will review the doctrine as set forth in the scriptures and expounded by latter-day prophets. Where instructive, I will contrast revealed knowledge with Satanic deception. I will discuss some of the commandments and words of counsel associated with each principle. Wise practices should result as our understanding of correct principles shapes the daily course of governing ourselves and our homes. It is my belief that families will be strengthened and happiness will increase as we teach these truths by the power of the Spirit to all members of the Church that they may gain a more profound testimony of these elementary doctrines.

From my own experience, I believe that the brethren of the Church seem to be more in need than the sisters of deepening their faith and knowledge of these basic truths. I pray that we will work mightily to teach all members of the Church, with special emphasis on the brethren, to increase their commitment to living in accord with correct principles of godly family life.

## Families on Earth Are an Extension of the Family of God

In the premortal life we lived as male and female spirit beings, as the male and female children of heavenly parents (see *Messages of the First Presidency* [Pres. Joseph F. Smith & counselors], vol. 4, 1909, 203). Enoch, Abraham, Job, Jeremiah, and Alma all testified of our premortal existence. Paul's writings in the New Testament refer to our divine heritage, and the Lord Himself makes this truth plain in revelations given to Joseph Smith ("Man, Antemortal Existence of," Topical Guide, 305).

The earth was created and is sustained by God as a place where His children, male and female (see Moses 2:27; Genesis 1:27, 5:2; Matthew 9:4) may dwell and gain experience. The Lord teaches clearly in the Doctrine and Covenants that family life is ordained of God, "and all this that the earth might answer the end of its creation" (D&C 49:16). President N. Eldon Tanner explained that, "The whole purpose of the creation of the earth was to provide a dwelling place where the spirit children of God might come" ("The Role of Womanhood," in Conference Report, Oct. 1973, 126). That statement was endorsed and sent in pamphlet form to all members of the Church by President Spencer W. Kimball and his counselors. Paul proclaimed, "The Spirit itself beareth witness with our spirit, that we are the children of God: And if children, then heirs; heirs of God, and joint-heirs with Christ" (Romans 8:16–17).

According to our Father's "great plan of happiness" (Alma 42:8), as explained in the restored gospel of Jesus Christ, the family is the vehicle of individual progress toward eternal life. We are accountable as individuals, but we will be exalted as families. It's no surprise, then, that Satan is vigorously—and in many ways, viciously—attacking the family. In general conference of April 1994, Elder Neal A. Maxwell enumerated these disturbing trends:

- In ten years, one-half of all children born in America will be illegitimate.
- More and more children have no functioning fathers. Already 70 percent of our juvenile criminals come from fatherless homes.
- Less than half of the children born today will live continuously with their own mother and father throughout childhood.
- Fifty-five percent of American children under the age of six have both parents or their only parent working in the labor force ("Take Especial Care of Your Family," *Ensign*, May 1994, 88–89).

These trends, if not corrected, will result in devastating consequences for our society.

I could cite other frightening statistics, on divorce rates, teen pregnancy, and single-parent households, but the point is clear enough. Satan is doing all he can to destroy our Father's children and to frustrate His great plan of happiness by attacking the fundamental unit of both mortal and eternal life—the family.

We have heard and read a great deal about the controversy surrounding the United Nations International Conference on Population and Development held in Cairo, Egypt. While some progress was laudable, much of what was heatedly debated centered on population-control policies that Satan masked under the guise of an increasingly popular talking point called "sustainable growth."

In public debate in this country and in most developed nations, there are few voices who cry out in the wilderness of the "sustainable growth" intellectual landscape. But an occasional voice of inspired reason can be heard. A recent *Forbes* magazine editorial asserts that people are an asset, not a liability, and accurately calls "preposterous" the broadly accepted premise that curbing population growth is essential for economic development. The editorial goes on to argue persuasively that, "Free people don't 'exhaust' resources. They create them" (*Forbes,* 12 Sept. 1994, 25).

As part of its coverage of the Cairo conference, *U.S. News & World Report* published an article that reviewed research by agricultural experts who have concluded that the earth is capable of producing food for a population of at least 80 billion—eight times the 10 billion expected to inhabit the earth by the year 2050. One study estimates the earth's gross productive potential to be sufficient to feed as many as 1,000 billion people. The article cited experts who lay most of the blame for scarcity on political instability and failed governmental agricultural and economic policies ( "10 Billion for Dinner, Please," *U.S. News & World Report,* 12 Sept. 1994, 57–60).

Surely, "the earth is full, and there is enough and to spare" (D&C 104:17) declared the Lord, if we follow God's plan and learn to be wise stewards. God, the Father of us all, has provided this earth as a place where His children can live in families to gain bodies and experience that will prepare us to return to our heavenly home. Let us pray for the day when the governments of all the earth will hearken unto the gospel of Christ, which elevates family life to its proper and divine function as the principal mechanism for perfecting the souls of all God's children.

## *Marriage Is Ordained of God*

From the beginning of time on this earth, eternal marriage between a man and a woman has been fundamental to God's plan for the happiness and joy of His children. In the early years of this dispensation, the Prophet Joseph Smith taught that marriage began in the Garden of Eden. In the *History of the Church,* we read the Prophet's own account of his teachings regarding the marriage of Adam and Eve, which he proclaimed while performing the marriage of Newel Knight and Lydia Goldthwaite in Nauvoo:

> I requested them to rise, and join hands. I then remarked that marriage was an institution of heaven, instituted in the garden of Eden; that it was necessary it should be solemnized by the authority of the everlasting Priesthood. . . .
>
> I then pronounced them husband and wife in the name of God, and also pronounced upon them the blessings that the Lord conferred upon Adam and Eve in the garden of Eden. (*History of the Church,* 2:320.)

President Harold B. Lee taught that the union of Adam and Eve "was a marriage performed by the Lord. . . . He made them one, not merely for time, [or] for any definite period; they were to be one throughout the eternal ages" (*Decisions for Successful Living,* Deseret Book, 1973, 125).

The Lord could not have spoken more plainly when he declared, "whoso forbiddeth to marry is not ordained of God, for marriage is ordained of God unto man" (D&C 49:15). The exaltation of man or woman can be obtained only within the bounds of and by obedience to the terms and conditions of the new and everlasting covenant of marriage (see D&C 131:1–4, 132:15–19; 1 Corinthians 11:11). From the beginning, man and woman have been incomplete without the other: "And I, the Lord God, said unto mine Only Begotten, that it was not good that the man should be alone; wherefore, I will make an help meet for him" (Moses 3:18; see also Genesis 2:18). An early Church leader wrote, "Man, in his fulness, is a twofold organization—male and female. Either being incapable of filling the measure of their creation alone, it requires the union of the two to complete man in the image of God" (Franklin D. Richards and James A. Little, *A Compendium of the Doctrines of the Gospel,* Deseret Book Company, 1925, 117; see also

Genesis 1:26–27). Paul wrote, "Nevertheless neither is the man without the woman, neither the woman without the man, in the Lord. For as the woman is of the man, even so is the man also by the woman; but all things of God" (1 Corinthians 11:11–12).

And, in marriage, God intends that man and woman become one; united, bound, and sealed together for all eternity: "For this cause shall a man leave father and mother, and shall cleave to his wife: and they twain shall be one flesh? Wherefore they are no more twain, but one flesh. What therefore God hath joined together, let not man put asunder" (Matthew 19:5–6; see also Genesis 2:24; Moses 3:24). Eternally and equally yoked, man and woman are commanded to work together to provide for themselves and their children: "Adam began . . . to eat his bread by the sweat of his brow, as I the Lord had commanded him. And Eve, also, his wife, did labor with him" (Moses 5:1).

Let's look carefully at the revealed roles of man as husband and father and woman as wife and mother in a god-like marriage. The Apostle Paul taught that the wife should "reverence her husband" (Ephesians 5:33). Paul further explained that "the husband is the head of the wife, even as Christ is the head of the church" (Ephesians 5:23). The wife has a clear duty to sustain her husband, but only insofar as he fulfills his duty to govern the home according to Christ's teachings of love and selfless sacrifice. If the husband begins "to exercise control or dominion or compulsion upon [his wife], in any degree of unrighteousness, . . . Amen to the . . . authority of that man" (D&C 121:37).

A woman is "a co-partner with God in bringing his spirit children into the world" (N. Eldon Tanner, "The Role of Womanhood," in Conference Report, Oct. 1973, 123). The First Presidency, in President Heber J. Grant's administration, declared: "Motherhood is near to divinity. It is the highest, holiest service to be assumed by mankind. It places her who honors its holy calling and service next to the angels" (Message of the First Presidency, in Conference Report, Oct. 1942, 12–13).

The Lord commands husbands, "Thou shalt love thy wife with all thy heart, and shalt cleave unto her and none else" (D&C 42:22). The Apostle Paul taught: "Husbands, love your wives, even as Christ also loved the church, and gave himself for it" (Ephesians 5:25). Other teachings of Paul counsel, "Husbands, love your wives, and be not bitter against them" (Colossians 3:19) and "Let the husband render unto the wife due benevolence" (1 Corinthians 7:3). Peter taught: "Likewise, ye husbands, dwell with them according to knowledge, giving honour unto the wife, as unto the weaker vessel, and as being heirs together of the grace of life; that your prayers be not hindered" (1 Peter 3:7). The man who presides by virtue of priesthood authority must do so in righteousness, "only by persuasion, by long-suffering, by gentleness and meekness, and by love unfeigned" (D&C 121:41).

Husbands and fathers must provide for their own. In a revelation given in 1832, the Lord declared that "Women have claim on their husbands for their maintenance, until their husbands are taken" (D&C 83:2; see also 1 Timothy 5:8) and that "All children have claim upon their parents for their maintenance until they are of age" (D&C 83:4). In the Book of Mormon, Captain Moroni refers to "the sacred support which we owe to our wives and our children" (Alma 44:5).

In April 1994, Elder Boyd K. Packer addressed the role of fathers in his general conference message. He said:

> Your responsibility as a father and a husband transcends any other interest in life. . . . You are to devote, even sacrifice yourself to the bringing up of your children in light and truth. That requires perfect moral fidelity to your wife, with no reason ever for her to doubt your faithfulness. Never should there be a domineering or unworthy behavior in the tender, intimate relationship between husband and wife. Your wife is your partner in the leadership of the family and should have full knowledge of and full participation in all decisions relating to your home. Lead

your family to the Church, to the covenants and ordinances. ("The Father and the Family," *Ensign,* May 1994, 20–21.)

A successful marriage is dependent upon an uncompromising commitment to living in complete harmony with the third principle in this doctrine, which is:

## The Power to Create Life Is a Gift from God

God blessed the male and female he had created and commanded them, "Be fruitful, and multiply, and replenish the earth" (Moses 2:28; Genesis 1:28). In 1942, the First Presidency said, "The Lord has told us that it is the duty of every husband and wife to obey the command given to Adam to multiply and replenish the earth, so that the legions of choice spirits waiting for their tabernacles of flesh may come here and move forward under God's great design to become perfect souls . . . No loftier duty than this can be assumed by mortals." (Message of the First Presidency, in Conference Report, Oct. 1942, 12–13).

God has placed within us the sacred power of procreation. It is indeed a power. Our passions are strong, of necessity, to urge us into parenthood. Without this potent drive, God's purposes would be frustrated. This power is so sacred, however, that it is hedged about and safeguarded by commandments and covenants. The seventh commandment, "Thou shalt not commit adultery" (Exodus 20:14) is designed to deter our departure from God's plan. It is protective counsel. The Lord applied this commandment not only to our actions but also to our hearts when He said: "Ye have heard that it was said by them of old time, Thou shalt not commit adultery: But I say unto you, That whosoever looketh on a woman to lust after her hath committed adultery with her already in his heart" (Matthew 5:27–28). I have always found it to be good counsel, brethren, that when we look upon a woman, we ought to focus our attention on her eyes, the windows of her soul. Such a focus helps prevent the wandering, long look that can so often lead to inappropriate thoughts.

In our day, the Lord has reaffirmed the commandment to keep our thoughts and hearts under control and undefiled when he said: "I have said before, he that looketh on a woman to lust after her, or if any shall commit adultery in their hearts, they shall not have the Spirit, but shall deny the faith and shall fear" (D&C 63:16). How often have we seen this prophecy fulfilled in the lives of suffering Saints? In our service as the Lord's under-shepherds, we have all witnessed the heartbreak resulting from disobedience. We "have seen the sorrow, and heard the mourning of the daughters of [the Lord's] people . . . because of the wickedness and abominations of their husbands" (Jacob 2:31).

The Lord is insistent that we diligently obey the commandments associated with the fourth principle, which is:

## Parents Are Responsible for Teaching Their Children the Laws of God

"The whole purpose of the creation of the earth was to provide a dwelling place where the spirit children of God might come. . . . The whole purpose of mothers and fathers should be to live worthy of this blessing and to assist God the Father and his son Jesus Christ in their work" (N. Eldon Tanner, "The Role of Womanhood," in Conference Report, Oct. 1973, 126). With this great honor "comes the tremendous responsibility of loving and caring for those children so they might learn . . . what they must do to return to their Heavenly Father" (Ibid., 124). Parents are commanded to bring up their children in light and truth (see D&C 93:40), teaching them to understand the principles of the gospel, to pray and walk uprightly before the Lord (see D&C 68:25, 28), and to love one another and serve one another (see Mosiah 4:14–15). "This [sacred assignment] of being a parent cannot . . . be . . . shifted to other shoulders. . . . [T]here is no real way through any impersonal agency or institution that we as parents can impersonalize the personal responsibility which the Lord has given us"

("Off to School," a "Spoken Word" by Elder Richard L. Evans, endorsed by President David O. McKay and counselors and sent by letter dated 10 September 1951 to stake presidents and bishops with the request that it reach all families). "We must do everything we can to strengthen the ties that bind, to strengthen our homes, and to prepare ourselves by exemplary living to teach our children the ways of God, which is the only way for them to find happiness here and eternal life hereafter" (Tanner, "The Role of Womanhood," 124).

In our own family, we have worked hard to teach our children the gospel of Jesus Christ and to let them know, by our deeds, that we love them with all our hearts. We have great joy in our posterity. Our children and grandchildren and their companions fill our lives with satisfaction. May I share a quiet personal moment from our family that helps articulate the emotions that are so difficult to express.

One day at home, our youngest daughter, Lis, turned to us and with all sincerity and great feeling, said, "Thanks, Mom and Dad, for having me." How we were touched. Her love-filled expression of gratitude brought us near to tears. Lis is our eighth child and is blessed with great purity of heart. Our family happiness would be significantly diminished if she were not a part of our lives. We are so grateful that we welcomed as many spirits into our home as the Lord saw fit to send us. And we are humbly grateful that our imperfect but diligent efforts to teach our children the laws of God have borne good fruits that reward us well beyond anything we could have imagined when we were going through the struggles and trials that all young parents must face.

Finally, our Father's great plan of happiness is crowned with this glorious truth:

## The Family Can Become an Eternal Unit through the Power of God

The doctrine of the Church is unique in this regard, for we alone teach that God lives in an eternal marriage relationship and that we may obtain like status. Through the sealing ordinance and by honoring our covenants, we can enjoy the blessings of eternal life. The Lord has assured the obedient that they "shall pass by the angels, and the gods, which are set there, to their exaltation and glory in all things, . . . which glory shall be a fulness and a continuation of the seeds forever and ever. Then shall they be gods, because they have no end; therefore shall they be from everlasting to everlasting, because they continue" (D&C 132:19–20).

The strait and narrow way leads "unto the exaltation and continuation of the lives" (D&C 132:22). Abraham has achieved this promise and this exaltation. The Lord tells us concerning Abraham's seed, that "both in the world and out of the world should they continue as innumerable as the stars" (D&C 132:30). Exaltation is the continuation of the family in eternity. Indeed, as President David O. McKay said, "I picture heaven as a continuation of the ideal home" (in Conference Report, Apr. 1964, 5). He was not speaking metaphorically. This is literally true. We are to become "perfect, even as [our] Father which is in heaven is perfect" (Matthew 5:48). The essence of godhood then is to receive the sealing ordinance, keep sacred covenants, and with our loved ones enjoy the blessings of eternal increase. The Savior proclaims that "by this law is the continuation of the works of my Father, wherein he glorifieth himself" (D&C 132:31).

We must teach these foundation principles in more of our meetings. Eternal family life is the work and the glory of our Heavenly Father. President Boyd K. Packer put it well when he said, "The ultimate purpose of every teaching, every activity in the Church is that parents and their children are happy at home, sealed in an eternal marriage, and linked to their generations" ("The Father and the Family," 19).

May we teach these foundation principles of the family to our brothers and sisters with all diligence!

*(Adapted from a talk given in a General Authority training meeting, 4 October 1994)*

# 27

## EARTHLY DEBTS, HEAVENLY DEBTS

The Gospels record that nearly everywhere the Savior went, He was surrounded by multitudes of people. Some hoped that He would heal them; others came to hear Him speak. Others came for practical advice. Toward the end of His mortal ministry, some came to mock and ridicule Him and to clamor for His crucifixion.

One day a man approached the Savior and asked Him to intervene in a family dispute. "Master, speak to my brother," he pleaded, "that he divide the inheritance with me."

The Savior refused to take sides on this issue, but He did teach an important lesson. "Beware of covetousness," He told him, "for a man's life consisteth not in the abundance of the things which he possesseth" (Luke 12:13, 15).

Covetousness is one of the great afflictions of these latter days. It creates greed and resentment. Often it leads to bondage, heartbreak, and crushing, grinding debt.

The number of marriages that have been shattered over money issues is staggering. The amount of heartbreak is great. The stress that comes from worry over money has burdened families, caused sickness, depression, and even premature death.

## Earthly Debts

In spite of the teachings of the Church from its earliest days until today, Latter-day Saints still sometimes fall victim to many unwise and foolish financial practices. Some continue to spend, thinking that somehow, the money will become available. Somehow they will survive.

Far too often, the hoped-for money does not appear.

Remember this: debt is a form of bondage. It is a financial termite. When we make purchases on credit, they give us only an illusion of prosperity. We think we own things, but the reality is our things own us.

Some debt—such as incurred to acquire a modest home, expenses for education, perhaps for a needed first car—may be necessary. But never should we enter into financial bondage through consumer debt without carefully weighing the costs.

We have often heard that interest is a good servant but a terrible master. In a wise statement, President J. Reuben Clark Jr. described debt this way: "Interest never sleeps nor sickens nor dies; it never goes to the hospital; it works on Sundays and holidays; it never takes a vacation. . . . Once in debt, interest is your companion every minute of the day and night; you cannot shun it or slip away from it; you cannot dismiss it; it yields neither to entreaties, demands, or orders; and whenever you get in its way or cross its course or fail to meet its demands, it crushes you" (in Conference Report, Apr. 1938, 103).

The counsel from other inspired prophets in our time on this subject is clear, and what was true fifty or one hundred fifty years ago is also true today.

President Heber J. Grant said, "From my earliest recollections, from the days of Brigham Young until now, I have listened to men standing in the pulpit. . . . urging the people not to run into debt; and I believe that the great majority of all our troubles today is caused through the failure to carry out that counsel" (in Conference Report, Oct. 1921, 3).

President Ezra Taft Benson said: "Do not leave yourself or your family unprotected against financial storms. Build up savings" ("Pay Thy Debt, and Live . . . ," in *Speeches of the Year,* 1962 [Provo: Brigham Young University Press, 1963], 10).

President Harold B. Lee taught that: "Not only should we teach men to get out of debt but we should teach them likewise to stay out of debt" (*The Teachings of Harold B. Lee,* ed. Clyde J. Williams [Salt Lake City, Utah: Bookcraft, 1996], 315).

President Gordon B. Hinckley declared: "Many of our people are living on the very edge of their incomes. In fact, some are living on borrowings. . . . I urge you to be modest in your expenditures; discipline yourselves in your purchases to avoid debt to the extent possible. Pay off debt as quickly as you can, and free yourselves from bondage" ("To the Boys and to the Men," *Ensign,* Nov. 1998, 53–54).

Many have heeded this prophetic counsel. They live within their means, they honor the debts they have incurred, and they strive to reduce the burden they owe to others. I congratulate you who are doing so, for the day will come when you will reap the blessings of your efforts and understand the value of this inspired counsel.

However, others struggle when it comes to finances. Some are victims of adverse and often unforeseen events that have financially damaged them. Others are in financial bondage because they have not learned to discipline themselves and control their impulses to spend. Consequently, they have made unwise financial choices.

May I suggest five key steps to financial freedom for your consideration.

## First, Pay Your Tithing

Do you want the windows of heaven opened to you? Do you wish to receive blessings so great there is not room enough to receive them? (see Malachi 3:10). Always pay your tithing and leave the outcome in the hands of the Lord.

Obedience to God's commandments is the foundation for a happy life. Surely we will be blessed with the gifts of heaven for our obedience. Failure to pay tithing by those who know the principle can lead to heartache in this life and perhaps sorrow in the next.

## Second, Spend Less Than You Earn

This is simple counsel but a powerful secret for financial happiness. All too often a family's spending is governed more by their *yearning* than by their *earning*. They somehow believe that their life will be better if they surround themselves with an abundance of things. All too often all they are left with is avoidable anxiety and distress.

Those who live safely within their means know how much money comes in each month, and even though it is difficult, they discipline themselves to spend less than that amount.

Credit today is so easy to obtain. In fact, it is almost thrust upon us. Those who use credit cards to overspend unwisely should consider eliminating them. It is much better that a plastic credit card should perish than a family dwindle and perish in debt.

## Third, Learn to Save

Remember the practice of Joseph of Egypt. During times of prosperity, he saved up for a day of want (see Genesis 41:47–57).

Too often, people assume that they will never be injured, get sick, lose their jobs, or see their investments evaporate. To make matters worse, often people make purchases today based upon optimistic predictions of what they only hope will happen tomorrow.

The wise understand the importance of saving today for a rainy day tomorrow. They have adequate insurance that will provide for them in case of illness or death. Where possible, they store a year's supply of food, water, and other basic necessities of life. They set aside money in savings and investment accounts. They work diligently to reduce the debt they owe to others and strive to become debt free.

It is my testimony that the preparations you make today may one day be to you as the stored food was to the Egyptians and to Joseph's father's family.

## Fourth, Honor Your Financial Obligations

From time to time, we hear stories of greed and selfishness that strike us with great sorrow. We hear of fraud, defaulting on loan commitments, financial deceptions, and bankruptcies. We hear of fathers who financially neglect their own families. We say to men and women everywhere, if you bring children into the world, it is your solemn obligation to do all within your power to provide for them. No man is fit to be called a man who gathers around himself cars, boats, and other possessions while neglecting the sacred financial obligations he has to his own wife and children.

Latter-day Saints are a people of integrity. It is part of our code of conduct to honor our debts and behave honestly in our dealings with our fellowmen.

Let me tell you the story of one man who sacrificed greatly to maintain his own financial integrity and honor.

In the 1930s, Fred Snowberger opened the doors of a new pharmacy in northeastern Oregon. It had been his dream to own his own business, but the economic turnaround he had hoped for never materialized. Eight months later, Fred closed the doors of his pharmacy for the last time.

Even though his business had failed, Fred was determined to repay the loan he had secured. Some wondered why he insisted on repaying the debt. Why didn't he simply declare bankruptcy and have the debt legally forgiven?

But Fred did not listen. He had said he would repay the loan, and he was determined to honor his word. His family made many of their own clothes, grew much of their food in their garden, and used everything they had until it was thoroughly worn out or used up. Rain or shine, Fred walked to and from his work each day. And every month, Fred paid what he could on the loan.

Years passed and finally the wonderful day arrived when Fred made the last payment. He delivered it in person. The man who had loaned him the money wept and, with tears streaming down his face, said, "You not only paid back every penny, but you taught me what a man of character and honesty is."

To this day, nearly seventy years after Fred signed his name to that note, descendants of Fred and Erma Snowberger still tell this story with pride. This act of honor and nobility has lived through the decades as a cherished example of family integrity.

## Fifth, Teach Your Children to Follow Your Example

Too many of our youth get into financial difficulty because they never learned proper principles of financial common sense at home. Teach your children while they are young. Teach them that they cannot have something merely because they want it. Teach them the principles of hard work, frugality, and saving.

If you don't consider yourself informed well enough to teach them, all the more reason for you to begin learning. Abundant resources are available—from classes, books, and other resources.

There are among us some who have been blessed abundantly with enough and to spare. Our Heavenly Father expects that we do more with our riches than build larger barns to hold them. Will you consider what more you can do to build the kingdom of God? Will you consider what more you can do to bless the lives of others and bring light and hope into their lives?

## Heavenly Debts

We have considered earthly debts and our duty to repay them. But there are other debts—debts more eternal in nature—that are not so easy to repay. In fact, we will never be able to repay some of them. These are heavenly debts.

Our mothers and fathers gave us life and brought us into this world. They gave us the opportunity to obtain mortal bodies and experience the joys and sorrows of this bounteous earth. In many cases, they set their own comforts, dreams, and desires aside for the sake of their children. How fitting it is that we honor them and show by word and deed our love for them and our gratitude.

We also owe a great debt to our ancestors who have preceded us and who wait beyond the veil for those ordinances that will allow them to continue their eternal progression. This is a debt we can repay for them in our temples.

What a debt we owe to the Lord for restoring His divine church and true gospel in these latter-days through the Prophet Joseph Smith. From his youth until his martyrdom, Joseph devoted his days to bringing to mankind the gospel of Jesus Christ that had been lost. We owe our deepest gratitude to him and to all the men who have succeeded him in the sacred calling to preside over His Church.

How can we ever repay the debt we owe to the Savior? He paid a debt He did not owe to free us from a debt we can never pay. Because of Him, we will live forever. Because of His infinite atonement, our sins can be swept away, allowing us to experience the greatest of all the gifts of God: eternal life (see D&C 14:7).

Can such a gift have a price? Can we ever make compensation for such a gift? The Book of Mormon prophet King Benjamin taught "that if you should render all the thanks and praise which your whole soul has power to possess. . . . [and] serve him with all your whole souls yet ye would be unprofitable servants" (Mosiah 2:20–21).

We have earthly debts and heavenly debts. Let us be wise in dealing with each of them and ever keep in mind the words of the Savior: "Lay not up for yourselves treasures upon earth, where moth and rust doth corrupt, and where thieves break through and steal: But lay up for yourselves treasures in heaven" (Matthew 6:19–20). The riches of this world are as dust compared to the riches that await the faithful in the mansions of our Heavenly Father. How foolish is he who spends his days in the pursuit of things that rust and fade away. How wise is he who spends his days in the pursuit of eternal life.

Know within your hearts that Jesus the Christ lives. Be at peace, for as you draw near to Him, He will draw near to you. Let not your hearts be weary, but rejoice. Through the Prophet Joseph Smith, the gospel is restored once again. The heavens are not sealed. As in ancient days, we have a man who communicates with the Infinite. A prophet walks the earth in our day and at this time.

*(Adapted from an April 2004 general conference address)*

# 28

# THE LAW OF THE FAST

Two thousand years ago, upon the sand and stones of Galilee walked a man that few recognized for who He truly was: the Creator of worlds, the Redeemer, the Son of God.

A lawyer approached Him and asked, "What is the greatest commandment?" Jesus answered: "Thou shalt love the Lord thy God with all thy heart, and with all thy soul, and with all thy mind. This is the first and great commandment. And the second is like unto it, Thou shalt love thy neighbour as thyself. On these two commandments hang all the law and the prophets" (Matthew 22:37–40).

Through the Prophet Joseph Smith, the Lord has established His Church once again among men. The Church of Jesus Christ of Latter-day Saints, restored to the earth in these latter days, is centered on those commandments the Savior proclaimed as the greatest: to love our Heavenly Father and to love our fellowmen. To the members of His latter-day Church, our Savior said, "If thou lovest me thou shalt serve me and keep all my commandments" (D&C 42:29).

One way we show our love is through observing the law of the fast. This law is based upon a primary yet profound principle—a simple practice—that, if observed with the proper spirit, will help us draw closer to our Heavenly Father and strengthen our faith, while at the same time help us ease the burdens of others.

In The Church of Jesus Christ of Latter-day Saints, members are encouraged to fast whenever their faith needs special fortification and also to fast regularly once each month on a designated fast day. On that day, we go without eating or drinking for two consecutive meals, commune with our Heavenly Father, and contribute a fast offering to help the poor. The offering should be at least equal to the value of the food that would have been eaten. Typically, the first Sunday of each month is designated as fast Sunday. On that day, members who are physically able are encouraged to fast, pray, bear witness to the truthfulness of the gospel, and pay a generous fast offering. "The law of the fast," taught Elder Milton R. Hunter, "is probably as old as the human family. . . . In ancient times, prophet-leaders repeatedly gave to church members the commandment to observe the law of fasting and praying" (*Will a Man Rob God?* 207–08).

## Fasting and Prayer

In the scriptures, fasting is almost always linked with prayer. Without prayer, fasting is not complete fasting: it's simply going hungry. If we want our fasting to be more than just going without eating, if we desire also the spiritual benefits of the fast, we must also lift our hearts, our minds, and our voices in communion with our Heavenly Father. Fasting, coupled with mighty prayer, is powerful. It can fill our minds with the revelations of the Spirit. It can strengthen us against times of temptation.

Fasting and prayer can help us develop courage and confidence. It can strengthen our character and build self-restraint and discipline. Often when we fast, our righteous prayers and petitions have greater power. Testimonies grow. We mature spiritually and emotionally and sanctify our souls. Each time we fast, we gain a little more control over our worldly appetites and passions.

Fasting and prayer can help us in our families and in our daily work.

THE LAW OF THE FAST

They can help us magnify our callings in the Church. President Ezra Taft Benson taught: "If you want to get the spirit of your office and calling as a new president of a quorum, a new high [councilor], a new bishop [or, I might say, a Relief Society president]—try fasting for a period. I don't mean just missing one meal, then eating twice as much the next meal. I mean really fasting, and praying during that period. It will do more to give you the real spirit of your office and calling and permit the Spirit to operate through you than anything I know" (*The Teachings of Ezra Taft Benson*, 331–32).

## Fasting and the Poor

The Prophet Joseph Smith taught: "Let this be an [example] to all saints, and there will never be any lack for bread: When the poor are starving, let those who have, fast one day and give what they otherwise would have eaten to the bishops for the poor, and every one will abound for a long time . . . And so long as the saints will all live to this principle with glad hearts and cheerful countenances they will always have an abundance" (*History of the Church*, 7:413).

Book of Mormon prophets taught the law of the fast: "Behold, now it came to pass that the people of Nephi were exceedingly rejoiced, because the Lord had again delivered them out of the hands of their enemies; therefore they gave thanks unto the Lord their God; yea, and they did fast much and pray much, and they did worship God with exceedingly great joy" (Alma 45:1).

The powerful combination of fasting and prayer is exemplified by the four sons of Mosiah. They faced overwhelming odds, yet worked miracles in bringing thousands of the Lamanites to a knowledge of the truth. They shared the secret of their success, which was that they "searched the scriptures" and "they had given themselves to much prayer, and fasting." What was the result? "They had the spirit of prophecy, and the spirit of revelation, and when they taught, they taught with power and authority of God" (see Alma 17:2–3).

When we fast, we of course experience hunger. And for a short time, we literally put ourselves in the position of the hungry and the needy. As we do so, we have greater understanding of the deprivations they might feel. When we give to the bishop an offering to relieve the suffering of others, we not only do something sublime for others, but we do something wonderful for ourselves as well. King Benjamin taught that as we give of our substance to the poor, we retain "a remission of [our] sins from day to day" (Mosiah 4:26).

Another Book of Mormon prophet, Amulek, explained that often our prayers have no power because we have turned our backs on the needy (see Alma 34:28). If you feel that Heavenly Father is not listening to your petitions, ask yourself if you are listening to the cries of the poor, the sick, the hungry, and the afflicted all around you.

Some look at the overwhelming need in the world and think, *What can I do that could possibly make a difference?*

I will tell you plainly one thing you can do. You can live the law of the fast and contribute a generous fast offering.

Fast offerings are used for one purpose only: to bless the lives of those in need. Every dollar given to the bishop as a fast offering goes to assist the poor. When donations exceed local needs, they are passed along to fulfill needs elsewhere.

As an Apostle of the Lord Jesus Christ, I have traveled the world testifying of Him, and in those travels I have witnessed the suffering and need of millions of our Heavenly Father's children. Far too many in the world today—thousands upon thousands of families and individuals—experience want each day. They hunger. They ache with cold. They suffer from sickness. They grieve for their children. They mourn for the safety of their families. These people are not strangers and foreigners but children of our Heavenly Father. They are our brothers and our sisters. They are "fellowcitizens with the saints, and of the household of God" (Ephesians 2:19). Their fervent prayers ascend to heaven pleading for respite, for relief from suffering. At this very hour on this very day, some members even in our Church are praying for the miracle that would allow them to surmount the suffering that surrounds them. If, while we have the means to do so, we do not have compassion for them and spring to their aid, we are in danger of being among those the prophet Moroni spoke of when he said, "Behold, ye do love money, and your substance, and your fine apparel, . . . more than ye love the poor and the needy, the sick and the afflicted" (Mormon 8:37).

## Example of My Father

How well I remember my father, the bishop of our ward, filling my small red wagon with food and clothing and then directing me—as a deacon in the Church—to pull the wagon behind me and visit the homes of the needy in our ward.

Often, when fast-offering funds were depleted, my father would take money from his own pocket to supply the needy in his flock with food that would keep them from going hungry. Those were the days of the Great Depression, and many families were suffering.

I remember visiting one family in particular: a sickly mother, an unemployed and discouraged father, and five children with pallid faces, all disheartened and hungry. I remember the gratitude that beamed in their faces when I walked up to their door with my wagon nearly spilling over with needed supplies. I remember how the children smiled. I remember how the mother wept. And I remember how the father stood, head bowed, unable to speak.

These impressions and many others forged within me a love for the poor, a love for my father who served as a shepherd to his flock, and a love for the faithful and generous members of the Church who sacrificed so much to help relieve the suffering of others.

In a sense, you too can bring to a needy family a wagon brimming with hope. How? By paying a generous fast offering.

Parents, teach your children the joys of a proper fast. And how do you do that? The same as with any gospel principle—let them see you live it by your example. Then help them live the law of the fast themselves, little by little. They can fast and they can also pay a fast offering if they choose. As we teach our children to fast, it can give them the power to resist temptations along their life's journey.

## Fast Offering—How Much?

How much should we pay in fast offerings? The measure of our offering to bless the poor is a measure of our gratitude to our Heavenly Father. Will we, who have been blessed so abundantly, turn our backs on those who need our help? Paying a generous fast offering is a measure of our willingness to consecrate our substance to relieve the suffering of others.

Brother Marion G. Romney, who was the bishop of our ward when I was called on a mission and who later served as a member of the First Presidency of the Church, admonished: "Be liberal in your giving, that you yourselves may grow. Don't give just for the benefit of the poor, but give for your own welfare. Give enough so that you can give yourself into the kingdom of God through consecrating of your means and your time" ("The Blessings of the Fast," *Ensign*, July 1982, 4).

The deacons in the Church have a sacred obligation to visit the home of every member to collect fast offerings for the poor. President Thomas S. Monson once related to me how he, as a young bishop, began to sense that the young deacons in his ward were complaining about having to get up so early to collect fast offerings. Instead of calling the young men to task, this wise bishop took them to Welfare Square in Salt Lake City.

There, the boys met a disabled woman operating the switchboard. They saw a blind man placing labels on cans, and an elderly brother stocking shelves. As a result of what they saw, President Monson said a penetrating silence came over the boys as they witnessed the end result of their efforts to collect the sacred funds that aided the needy and provided employment for those who otherwise would be idle.

## *Blessings of the Fast*

As members of the Church, we have a sacred responsibility to assist those in need and to help relieve their heavy burdens. Observance of the law of the fast can help people of all nations. President Gordon B. Hinckley asked: "What would happen if the principles of fast day and the fast offering were observed throughout the world[?] The hungry would be fed, the naked clothed, the homeless sheltered. . . . A new measure of concern and unselfishness would grow in the hearts of people everywhere" ("The State of the Church," *Ensign,* May 1991, 52–53).

Fasting in the proper spirit and in the Lord's way will energize us spiritually, strengthen our self-discipline, fill our homes with peace, lighten our hearts with joy, fortify us against temptation, prepare us for times of adversity, and open the windows of heaven.

Listen to the rich blessings prophesied for those who live the law of the fast: "Then shalt thou call, and the Lord shall answer; thou shalt cry, and he shall say, Here I am. . . . The Lord shall guide thee continually, and satisfy thy soul in drought . . . and thou shalt be like a watered garden, and like a spring of water, whose waters fail not" (Isaiah 58:9, 11).

As we live the law of the fast, we not only draw nearer to God through prayer, but we feed the hungry and care for the poor. Each time we do so, we fulfill both of the great commandments upon which "hang all the law and the prophets" (Matthew 22:40).

I bear witness that He who had compassion for the "least of these" (Matthew 25:40) looks with love and compassion upon those today who seek to "succor the weak, lift up the hands which hang down, and strengthen the feeble knees" (D&C 81:5). I raise my voice in testimony and promise that those who live the law of the fast will surely discover the rich blessings that attend this holy principle.

*(Adapted from an April 2001 general conference address)*

# 29

# LIFE'S LESSONS LEARNED

Lately I have reflected on many of the wonderful experiences I've had in my life. As I have expressed gratitude to my Heavenly Father for these marvelous blessings and opportunities, I have realized, perhaps more than ever before, how critical the formative years of my life were.

Many of the most important and life-changing moments of my life occurred when I was a young man. The lessons I learned then formed my character and shaped my destiny. Without them, I would be a very different man and in a very different place than I am today. In the hope it will be helpful and encouraging, I would like to briefly reflect about some of these experiences and what I learned from them.

I'll never forget one high school football game against a rival school. I played the wingback position, and my assignment was to either block the linebacker or try to get open so the quarterback could throw me the ball. The reason I remember this particular game so well is because the fellow on the other side of the line—the man I was supposed to block— was a giant.

I wasn't exactly the tallest athlete in the world. But I think this other guy may have been. I remember looking up at him, thinking he probably weighed as much as two of me. Keep in mind, when I played we didn't have the protective gear that players have today. My helmet was made of leather, and it didn't have a face guard.

The more I thought about it, the more I came to a sobering realization: if I ever let him catch me, I could be cheering for my team the rest of the season from a hospital bed.

Lucky for me, I was fast. And for the better part of the first half, I managed to avoid him.

Except for one play.

Our quarterback dropped back to pass. I was open. He threw the ball, and it sailed toward me.

The only problem was that I could hear a lumbering gallop behind me. In a moment of clarity, I thought that if I caught the ball there was a distinct possibility I could be eating my meals through a tube. But the ball was heading for me, and my team was depending on me. So I reached out, and—at the last instant—I looked up.

And there he was.

I remember the ball hitting my hands. I remember struggling to hang on to it. I remember the sound of the ball falling to the turf. After that, I'm not exactly sure what happened because the giant hit me so hard I wasn't sure what planet I was on. One thing I did remember was a deep voice coming from behind a dark haze: "Serves you right for being on the wrong team."

William McKinley Oswald was my high school football coach. He was a great coach and had a profound influence on my life. But I think he could have learned his method of motivating players from an army drill sergeant.

That day, during his half-time speech, Coach Oswald reminded the whole team about the pass I had dropped. Then he pointed right at me and said, "How could you do that?"

He wasn't speaking with his indoor voice.

"I want to know what made you drop that pass."

I stammered for a moment and then finally decided to tell the truth. "I took my eye off the ball," I said.

The coach looked at me and said, "That's right; you took your eye off the ball. Don't ever do that again. That kind of mistake loses ball games."

I respected Coach Oswald, and in spite of how terrible I felt, I made up my mind to do what coach said. I vowed to never take my eye off the ball again, even if it meant getting pounded to Mongolia by the giant on the other side of the line.

We headed back onto the field and started the second half. It was a close game, and even though my team had played well, we were behind by four points late in the fourth quarter.

The quarterback called my number on the next play. I went out again, and again, I was open. The ball headed toward me. But this time, the giant was in front of me and in perfect position to intercept the pass.

He reached up, but the ball sailed through his hands. I jumped high, never taking my eye off the ball: stabbed at it; and pulled it down for the game-winning touchdown.

I don't remember much about the celebration after, but I do remember the look on Coach Oswald's face.

"Way to keep your eye on the ball," he said.

I think I smiled for a week.

I have known many great men and women. Although they have different backgrounds, talents, and perspectives, they all have this in common: they work diligently and persistently toward achieving their goals. It's easy to get distracted and lose focus on the things that are most important in life. I've tried to remember the lesson I learned from Coach Oswald and prioritize values that are important to me so that I can keep my eye focused on things that really matter.

I urge you to examine your life. Determine where you are and what you need to do to be the kind of person you want to be. Create inspiring, noble, and righteous goals that fire your imagination and create excitement in your heart. And then keep your eye on them. Work consistently toward achieving them.

"If one advances confidently in the direction of his dreams," wrote Henry David Thoreau, "and endeavors to live the life which he has imagined, he will meet with a success unexpected in common hours" (*Walden*, ed. J. Lyndon Shanley, Princeton University Press, 1971, 323).

In other words, never take your eye off the ball.

Another lesson I learned on the football field was taught to me at the bottom of a pile of ten other players. It was the Rocky Mountain Conference championship game, and the play called for me to run the ball up the middle to score the go-ahead touchdown. I took the handoff and plunged into the line. I knew I was close to the goal line, but I didn't know how close. Although I was pinned at the bottom of the pile, I reached my fingers forward a couple of inches and I could feel it. The goal line was two inches away.

At that moment I was tempted to push the ball forward. I could have done it. And when the referees finally pulled the players off the pile, I would have been a hero. No one would have ever known.

I had dreamed of this moment from the time I was a boy. And it was right there within my reach. But then I remembered the words of my mother. "Joseph," she had often said to me, "do what is right, no matter the consequence. Do what is right and things will turn out okay."

I wanted so desperately to score that touchdown. But more than being a hero in the eyes of my friends, I wanted to be a hero in the eyes of my mother. And so I left the ball where it was—two inches from the goal line.

I didn't know it at the time, but this was a defining experience. Had I moved the ball, I could have been a champion for a moment, but the reward of temporary glory would have carried with it too steep and too lasting a price. It would have engraved upon my conscience a scar that would have stayed with me the remainder of my life. I knew I must do what is right.

The Light of Christ helps us to discern right from wrong. When we allow temptations to drown out the still voice of our conscience—that is when decisions become difficult.

My parents taught me to react quickly when temptation comes and to say "No!" instantly and emphatically. I recommend that same counsel to you. Avoid temptations.

Another lesson I learned was the joy of service to others. I have written previously of how my father, who was the bishop of our ward, had me load up my wagon and deliver needed food and supplies to the homes of families that were in need. He wasn't alone in his desire to reach out to those in distress.

Seventy-five years ago, Bishop William F. Perschon presided over the Fourth Ward of the Pioneer Stake in Salt Lake City. He was a German immigrant, a convert to the Church, and he spoke with a heavy accent. He was a fine businessman, but what most distinguished him was his great compassion for others.

Each week during priesthood meeting, Bishop Perschon had the Aaronic Priesthood bearers recite the following phrase: "Priesthood means service; bearing the priesthood, I will serve."

It wasn't merely a slogan. When widows needed assistance, Bishop Perschon and the Aaronic Priesthood were there to help. When a chapel was being built, Bishop Perschon and the Aaronic Priesthood were there. When the sugar beets and potatoes at the welfare farm needed weeding or harvesting, Bishop Perschon and the Aaronic Priesthood were there.

Later, William Perschon served in the stake presidency, where he influenced a young bishop by the name of Thomas S. Monson. In the 1950s, Bishop Perschon was called to preside over the Swiss-Austrian Mission and played an instrumental role in building the first "overseas" temple, located in Bern, Switzerland.

You could scarcely think of Bishop Perschon without thinking of his concern and compassion for others and his untiring commitment to teach that same quality to others. Of the young men in the Aaronic Priesthood over whom he presided as bishop, twenty-nine went on to become bishops themselves. Ten served in stake presidencies. Five became mission presidents, three accepted calls as temple presidents, and two served as General Authorities (Elder Glen L. Rudd, letter to President Thomas S. Monson, 5 Feb. 1987).

That is the power of a great leader. That is the power of service.

Although I didn't fully understand it at the time, it is clear to me now that these lessons—and many others I learned as a youth—served as the foundation upon which the rest of my life has been built.

We all possess spiritual gifts. Some are blessed with the gift of faith, others the gift of healing. In the body of the Church, all of the spiritual gifts are present. In my case, perhaps one of the spiritual gifts for which I am most grateful is that I have been blessed with an obedient spirit. When I heard wise counsel from my parents or Church leaders, I listened and tried to make it part of my thoughts and actions.

I urge you also to cultivate the gift of an obedient spirit.

The Savior taught that "whosoever heareth these sayings of mine, and doeth them, I will liken him unto a wise man. And every one that heareth these sayings of mine, and doeth them not, shall be likened unto a foolish man" (Matthew 7:24, 26).

How do we know if we are wise or foolish?

The answer is found in how we respond when we hear inspired counsel. We obey.

That is the test of wise or foolish.

What does it profit us if we listen to wise counsel and do not heed the words? Of what use is experience if we do not learn from it? What good are the scriptures if we do not cherish the words and incorporate them into our lives?

President Gordon B. Hinckley has promised that "[Heavenly Father] will shower down blessings upon those who walk in obedience to His commandments" (in Conference Report, Apr. 1995, 95).

I add my voice to his.

I testify that Jesus is the Christ, the Savior of all mankind. I testify that God is close at hand. He cares about us and loves us, His children. Prophets, seers, and revelators guide the progress of the restored Church of Jesus Christ. President Gordon B. Hinckley stands as a latter-day prophet to the Church and to the world.

I give thanks to my Creator for this wonderful life where each of us has the opportunity to learn lessons we could not fully comprehend by any other means. May we set righteous goals and work to achieve them, do what is right, and reach out in love to those around us is my prayer.

*(Based on an April 2007 general conference address)*

# 30

# JOSEPH SMITH'S FIRST VISION

## Introduction

I wish to call your attention to a subject that is near and dear to my heart and which I hope will become near and dear to your heart as well. I refer to the First Vision and the Prophet Joseph Smith. This is a most sacred event and ranks among the most glorious and rare events ever to take place in the history of the world. And to think that it was initiated by a humble fourteen-year-old farm boy in rural upstate New York. If you young people ever think that you are insignificant or unimportant, just think of what Joseph Smith did as a young boy. The Lord can and does work through young people to accomplish His purposes because you are humble and can be taught by Him.

## Why the Lord Chose Joseph Smith

Why do you think that the Lord chose young Joseph Smith to usher in the dispensation of the fulness of times? I have often thought about this. There are several reasons. I will mention two. First, Joseph Smith was foreordained in the premortal life to be the great Prophet of the Restoration. He was hand-picked by our Heavenly Father to be the instrument through which the gospel was to be restored to the earth after the long Apostasy. Just as Joseph Smith was foreordained to perform his great mission, each of us is foreordained to serve and perform a special mission. It will take diligence and faithfulness on your part to discover what that mission is, but I am sure it is important to you, your family, and the Church.

Second, Joseph was chosen because he was young and humble. Many people wonder why the Lord would choose such a young boy to restore the true Church. Some people feel that God would logically choose someone who is knowledgeable in theology and the scriptures. Joseph Smith, on the other hand, was unlearned in the ways and things of the world. He had little education. That is precisely why the Lord chose him. God needed someone who was unsullied; someone who was teachable and not darkened with the various traditions of the world. I am amazed at the great trust that the Lord had in Joseph Smith. He placed upon him enormous responsibilities. Joseph proved his mettle. The Lord gave him line upon line and precept upon precept. That is how the Lord will work with each of you. He loves you greatly, but He wants you to demonstrate that you can be trusted. That is why He gives you assignments you may view as small and insignificant—to see if He can trust you. If you prove yourself, then He will give you more. It is the greatest honor to be trusted of the Lord.

## The Story of the First Vision—Sacred History

I never tire of hearing the story of the First Vision. To make a point, I would like you to once again consider Joseph's divine experience.

Joseph lived as any boy of the nineteenth century on the American frontier. He helped his parents who farmed the land in an effort to make a living and provide for their sizeable family. According to Joseph, about the time he turned twelve years old, he began to think about religion and became interested in spiritual things. He said: "My mind became seriously impressed with regard to the all important concerns for the welfare of my immortal soul" (1832 account. See *Opening the Heavens:*

*Accounts of Divine Manifestations, 1820–1844,* ed. John W. Welch, BYU Press and Deseret Book: 2005, 4). After a few years of such pondering on spiritual things, Joseph experienced the religious revival atmosphere in his neighborhood. Preachers would go from town to town and get the people excited about religion. They were all trying to convert the people to their specific beliefs. Many of his neighbors and even some family members joined various denominations. This confused Joseph. He felt inclined to affiliate as well but wanted to make the right choice and join God's true church. He observed the great diversity of teachings and correctly reasoned that God could not be the author of that confusion. He finally decided that he would look in the Bible for direction. He learned in the Bible that God does not change and that truth does not change and rightfully concluded that God's church would teach and practice the truth, whatever that was. As he was thinking about these things, he opened one day their large family Bible to the passage with which we are all familiar: "If any of you lack wisdom, let him ask of God, that giveth to all men liberally and upbraideth not; and it shall be given him" (James 1:5). He said of that reading: "Never did any passage of scripture come with more power to the heart of man than this did at this time to mine. It seemed to enter with great force into every feeling of my heart. I reflected on it again and again, knowing that if any person needed wisdom from God, I did; for how to act I did not know, and unless I could get more wisdom than I then had, I would never know; for the teachers of religion of the different sects understood the same passages of scripture so differently as to destroy all confidence in settling the question by an appeal to the Bible" (JS–H 1:12).

Joseph decided that he would take James at his word. He would ask God. He decided that he needed to be alone so he chose a spot in the forest near his home. According to Joseph, before he went to pray, he chose the spot and marked it with his axe, so he would know where to find it (1843 account. Ibid., 25). It was there that he knelt down and began to pray.

He relates that he was immediately overcome by the powers of darkness, which is reasonable to believe. Given what was about to transpire, Satan would naturally do all in his power to prevent the First Vision. Satan doubtless knew who Joseph Smith was. He might even have been present when Joseph Smith was foreordained in the Grand Councils in our premortal existence—foreordained to perform this great work. The veil is not drawn for Satan because he has no body. Therefore, he has the advantage of knowing who we are and knows of our premortal greatness. If there was anything he could do to prevent this from happening, he was going to do it. And so he unleashed all of his evil power on the young Joseph. The darkness was so great and powerful that Joseph felt he was going to die. He could not speak. He was filled with doubt and fear.

We must remember that Satan also knows each of us. He knows what great things we are to accomplish in this life. His mission is to keep us from our divine potential. Joseph learned very vividly of the reality of the adversary and his powers. Yet, more important, he learned that God is more powerful than Satan. Joseph called upon God with great faith and energy and was finally delivered from the evil powers.

What happened next was marvelous. A pillar of light, brighter than the sun, gradually fell upon him. God, our Heavenly Father, the great Elohim, the Almighty God, stood before him. And by His side was God's Only Begotten Son; the resurrected Lord, Jesus Christ; our Savior and Redeemer.

Joseph said that as this light was descending toward him it increased in brightness and magnitude. By the time it reached the tops of the trees, he said, he thought the whole forest was going to catch fire and be burned. However, the great light did not burn the forest, and he felt encouraged that he would be able to endure in the midst of such a powerful light (Ibid., 21). Imagine what it would have been like, to have been there and to have seen this great vision.

In a moment, Joseph Smith knew more about God and Jesus Christ than everyone living on the earth combined. He knew firsthand that God lives and has a tangible body of flesh and bones. He knew and saw firsthand Jesus Christ and probably viewed His scars from the Crucifixion. Finally, after centuries of darkness, a special witness of God and Jesus Christ stood on the earth. The long Apostasy was finally over.

After the Father introduced his Son, Jesus Christ, to Joseph with the words, "This is my Beloved Son, Hear Him," what was the first thing that Jesus told Joseph Smith? Joseph relates: "He spake unto me saying, 'Joseph, thy sins are forgiven thee. Go thy way, walk in my statutes, and keep my commandments. Behold, I am the Lord of Glory. I was crucified for the world that all those who believe on my name may have eternal life'" (Ibid., 8). I find it fascinating that the first thing said to Joseph was that his sins were forgiven him. This teaches us that repenting and receiving forgiveness for our sins is of utmost importance to the Lord. This also teaches us that the Lord knows each of us personally and desires our improvement and happiness. I can't imagine the joy in Joseph's heart as he heard directly from Jesus Christ that his sins were forgiven him. I testify that just as Joseph Smith received that assurance, we can receive such an assurance by the power of the Holy Ghost, if we repent. Peace and joy will fill our hearts. It is worth every effort to live clean, righteous lives, to receive such an assurance from God.

As we know, the Savior also told the boy Joseph that he was to join none of the churches because His true church was not presently on the earth. Joseph was also told that he would be the instrument through which the fulness of the gospel would be restored. What else happened in the First Vision? Well, we do not know exactly, but Joseph did leave some clues. In one account, Joseph relates that he saw many angels during the First Vision (1835 account. Ibid., 8). He also said that there were many things which happened and were taught to him that he could not appropriately write. We may have thought in the past that the First Vision lasted a few minutes. However, it appears to me that it may have lasted more like several hours. As can be expected, after the vision ended,

Joseph was weak, yet filled with unspeakable joy. He entered the grove as a young boy, he left as a man with a mission.

## What Did Joseph Learn from the First Vision?

Joseph learned many important truths from the First Vision, as we have discussed. He became a special witness of Heavenly Father and Jesus Christ. He learned for certain that Jesus is a separate and distinct personage from the Father. He learned that the promise of James is true. He learned of the reality of Satan. But he learned that God is more powerful than Satan. He learned the true nature of God. That is why he said: "It is the first principle of the gospel to know for a certainty the character of God, and to know that we may converse with Him as one man converses with another" (*History of the Church*, 6:305).

Joseph also learned something of himself. He was being prepared for the future, in which he would perform a great mission. The truths he learned in the Sacred Grove during the First Vision made him fearless. Expressing courage, he boldly testified: "I had actually seen a light, and in the midst of that light I saw two Personages, and they did in reality speak to me; and though I was hated and persecuted for saying that I had seen a vision, yet it was true; and while they were persecuting me, reviling me, and speaking all manner of evil against me falsely for so saying, I was led to say in my heart: Why persecute me for telling the truth? I have actually seen a vision; and who am I that I can withstand God, or why does the world think to make me deny what I have actually seen? For I had seen a vision; I knew it, and I knew that God knew it, and I could not deny it, neither dared I do it; at least I knew that by so doing I would offend God, and come under condemnation" (JS–H, 1:25).

## What We Learn from the First Vision

We all stand figuratively in the place Joseph stood. He wanted to know the truth. He then did the only thing that anyone can do to really know the truth. He asked God—the source of truth. We must do the same if we expect to know and understand the truth. We must ask God and be open and humble to receive the answer that comes. We need to know for ourselves that Joseph was a prophet of God, that God and Jesus really appeared to Joseph, and that The Church of Jesus Christ of Latter-day Saints is the true church. I have such a testimony and have been blessed with this knowledge for as long as I can remember.

We must each experience a Sacred Grove. It may be our bedroom, a closet, the chapel, a place in the mountains. We must seek the Lord. We must ask and not become weary in asking. We must seek to know for ourselves the truth. The Lord is bound to answer. You probably will not see a vision of God and Jesus Christ. But the answer will come. The answer will come by the power of the Holy Ghost, by the still, small voice. And the witness of the Holy Ghost can be more penetrating and enduring than even a physical manifestation.

## *Joseph Smith's Place in Our Sacred History*

We call it the First Vision, not just because it was the first of many visions given to Joseph Smith but also because it is first in importance. The First Vision was the inaugural event to open this, the last dispensation, the dispensation of the fulness of times. Next to the Creation, the Fall, and the Atonement and the resurrection of Jesus Christ, no other single event stands in greater importance in the history of the world.

Despite the significance of the First Vision, there are many people who have and who will continue to speak evil of Joseph Smith. He will continue to be ridiculed and criticized. He was told by Moroni that his name would be had for good and evil in the world (see JS–H, 1:33). This remains true today. Some people even say they can accept everything about our Church, *except* Joseph Smith. The fact is, it is impossible to accept the Church and all it teaches without accepting and reverencing the work done by the Prophet Joseph. Either God and Jesus appeared to Joseph Smith and established their latter-day work or they didn't. Either he was a true prophet of God or he wasn't. I testify to you that he was, in fact, one of the greatest prophets who ever lived. I will spend the rest of my days with this burning testimony on my lips.

I recall what George Albert Smith said of those who have ridiculed Joseph Smith: "There have been some who have belittled him, but I would like to say that those who have done so will be forgotten and their remains will go back to mother earth, if they have not already gone, and the odor of their infamy will never die, while the glory and honor and majesty and courage and fidelity manifested by the Prophet Joseph Smith will attach to his name forever" (in Conference Report, Apr. 1948, 181–82).

It is my hope and my prayer that you may develop a great love and appreciation for the Prophet Joseph Smith. May you ever be found defending him and testifying to others of the truthfulness of the divine work that God established through him. May you know of the truth that God, the Father, and His Beloved Son, Jesus Christ, appeared to the young boy Joseph Smith, and in doing so brought about an end to the great Apostasy and changed the history of the world. I testify that Joseph was the mighty prophet of the Restoration. The Book of Mormon is the word of God. This is the true church.

*(Adapted from an address to the youth*
*of the Bonneville First Ward, January 2002)*

# 31

# THE TEMPLE

President Joseph F. Smith said, "The time will come, perhaps not in my days, nor in the next generation, when temples of God, dedicated to the holy ordinances of the gospel and not to the worship of idols, will be erected in diverse countries of the earth. For this gospel must be spread over all the world until the knowledge of God covers the earth as the waters" (quoted in Spencer W. Kimball, *The Miracle of Forgiveness*, 33).

The Prophet Joseph Smith declared: "The greatest responsibility in this world that God has laid upon us is to seek after our dead" (*History of the Church*, 6:313). He further stated: "Those Saints who neglect it in behalf of their deceased relatives, do it at the peril of their own salvation" (*History of the Church*, 4:426).

## Why Temples?

The temple is the house of the Lord, a place where we can feel His influence. It is a holy place where the most sacred ordinances of the gospel are performed. In the temple, God's children receive instruction and make covenants with Him that are necessary to return to His presence.

## Temples, Past and Present

Whenever there have been people on the earth who would listen to the prophets, God has commanded them to build temples. Sometime after the death of the Apostles in New Testament times, temple ordinances were lost from the earth. When the Lord restored the gospel in these latter days, he commanded His people once again to build temples.

## Why Go to the Temple?

Temple service focuses on our relationship with God the Father and His Son, Jesus Christ. When we attend the temple regularly, we grow closer to our Heavenly Father and the Savior. We can become more Christlike as we learn to see our lives from an eternal perspective, obtain instruction through the Spirit, make sacred covenants, and participate in saving ordinances for ourselves and for our deceased ancestors.

A temple exists "that the Son of Man might have a place to manifest himself to his people. . . . And that they may grow up in [the Lord], and receive a fulness of the Holy Ghost, and be organized according to [God's] laws, and be prepared to obtain every needful thing" (D&C 109:5, 15).

A temple is "a place of thanksgiving for all saints; and for a place of instruction for all those who are called to the work of the ministry in all their several callings and offices; That they may be perfected in the understanding of their ministry, in theory, in principle, and in doctrine, in all things pertaining to the kingdom of God on the earth, the keys of which kingdom have been conferred upon you" (D&C 97:13–14).

Regular temple attendance can provide spiritual strength and a feeling of fulfillment for you and your family. It will be an anchor in your daily life, a source of guidance, protection, security, peace, and revelation.

## Ordinances That Lead to Exaltation

It was Jesus Himself who declared: "Except a man be born of water and of the Spirit, he cannot enter into the kingdom of God" (John 3:3). Clearly, we must be baptized and receive the gift of the Holy Ghost in order to return to our Father's presence. To be exalted in the celestial kingdom, we must also receive the ordinances of the temple. These ordinances include the endowment and the sealing of parents and children.

## Ordinances for You and Your Immediate Family

When you first attend the temple for yourself, you receive the endowment, which teaches about the purpose of life and the mission of the Savior. You also enter into covenants—agreements—with the Lord. Once you are endowed, you and worthy members of your family can be sealed together. If each of you lives worthily, these sealing ordinances will unite you and your family for eternity.

President Joseph F. Smith said: "We are not living only for the few miserable years that we spend on this earth, but for that life which is interminable; and we desire to enjoy every blessing throughout these countless ages of eternity, but unless they are secured to us by that sealing power which was given to the Apostle Peter by the Son of God, we cannot possess them. Unless we secure them on that principle, in the life to come we shall have neither father, mother, brother, sister, wife, children, nor friends, nor wealth nor honor, for all earthly "contracts, covenants, bonds, obligations, oaths, vows, connections, and associations, [see D&C 132:7] are dissolved in the grave, except those sealed and ratified by the power of God" (*Journal of Discourses,* 16:250–51).

## Ordinances for Your Ancestors

Most of our ancestors lived when the fulness of the gospel was not found on the earth. Thus, they could not receive the necessary ordinances. Mercifully, our Father in Heaven has provided a way for these ancestors to hear the gospel in the spirit world (see D&C 138). However, the ordinances of the gospel must be performed on earth. So the Lord has directed worthy Church members to be baptized, confirmed, ordained (for men), endowed, and sealed in behalf of their ancestors. This vicarious work can only be done in a dedicated temple.

You are responsible to make sure that ordinances are completed for your ancestors. You can begin by caring about them. As your heart turns toward them, you will want them to receive the ordinances necessary for exaltation. You can receive these ordinances for them. But first you must know who they are and when and where they lived. The Church has many resources to help you identify them. Also, people have been called to help you. When you learn about your ancestors, you can submit their names for temple work. Then you can serve them by receiving the ordinances in their behalf. This service will bring you joy as you bind them together as eternal families.

## How Can I Prepare Spiritually for the Temple?

Temple work is spiritual. You will become motivated and prepared to go to the temple as you prayerfully—

- Strive to understand the doctrine that relates to eternal life
- Live according to gospel principles
- Seek to be led by the Holy Spirit

You will also be led to do the family history work that supports temple activity. President Harold B. Lee declared, "The temple ceremonies are designed by a wise Heavenly Father who has revealed them to us in these last days as a guide and a protection throughout our lives, that you and I might not fail [to merit] exaltation in the celestial kingdom where God and Christ dwell (*The Teachings of Harold B. Lee,* ed. Clyde J. Williams, 1996, 574). There are many miracles occurring in our day. My own beloved mother called her entire posterity together shortly before her passing. She described on that very sacred occasion, as we gathered around her, a most inspirational experience. She said, "For three nights now I have been permitted to have a glimpse into the spirit world. I, therefore, declare to each of you that there is indeed a spirit world beyond the veil. I have seen it. I have been permitted to see the other side. This was a great privilege for me to behold. It was the most glorious and precious experience I have ever had in my entire life. My great wish would be that I might return some day and tell you more about it." Perhaps you can imagine the impact that sacred declaration had on our family. We will never forget that heavenly experience and the testimony she bore.

## Conclusion

We have a great future ahead of us, which will hasten the work so that we are ready for the Savior when He comes again. I testify to you that the work of the Church is the work of the Lord and that there is order in all things, including the basic doctrines and ordinances of the gospel, which every human being who has ever lived upon the earth will have the opportunity to accept.

Let us follow the counsel of President Gordon B. Hinckley, he who has spearheaded the remarkable work of multiplying the number of temples around the world: "I think the Lord expects of us that we will go to the temple and take advantage of the tremendous opportunities to be found in that holy house. . . . Every temple that we build becomes a memorial to the truth that we believe in, the immortality of the human soul. Everything that occurs in those temples is concerned with the eternities, with everlasting life. We wouldn't need a temple if were just getting married for this life. We wouldn't need a temple if all of our efforts were centered in this life. The temple becomes the great bridge from this life to the next and finds expression in the most unselfish kind of service of which I am aware. It is a tremendous opportunity, a marriage for time and all eternity. I don't know whether we can appreciate it to the degree that we really should" (*Church News,* 6 Feb. 1999).

I bear testimony that God lives, that Jesus is the Christ, the Only Begotten of our Heavenly Father, our Redeemer who gave us the great Atonement. May we ponder and resolve to follow His great example and visit His house often.

*(Adapted from remarks given at the Nauvoo*
*Illinois Temple dedication, 28 June 2002)*

# 32

## Sunday Will Come

### Personal Memories

I was born of goodly parents. From my father, Joseph L. Wirthlin, I learned the values of hard work and compassion. He was bishop of our ward during the Great Depression. He possessed a genuine concern for those in distress. He reached out to those in need not because it was his duty but because it was his sincere desire.

He tirelessly cared for and blessed the lives of many who suffered. In my mind, he was an ideal bishop.

Those who knew my father knew how active he was. Someone once told me that he could do the work of three men. He rarely slowed down. In 1938 he was operating a successful business when he received a call from the President of the Church, Heber J. Grant.

President Grant told him they were reorganizing the Presiding Bishopric that day and wanted my father to serve as counselor to Bishop LeGrand Richards. This caught my father by surprise, and he asked if he could pray about it first.

President Grant said, "Brother Wirthlin, there are only thirty minutes before the next session of conference, and I want to have some rest. What do you say?"

Of course, my father said yes. He ended up serving twenty-three years, nine of them as Presiding Bishop of the Church.

My father was sixty-nine years old when he passed away. I happened to be with him when he suddenly collapsed. Soon after, he was gone.

I often think about my father. I miss him.

My mother, Madeline Bitner, was another great influence in my life. In her youth she was a fine athlete and a champion sprinter. She was always kind and loving, but her pace was exhausting. Often she would say, "Hurry up." And when she did, we picked up the pace. Perhaps that was one of the reasons I had quick acceleration when I played football.

My mother had great expectations for her children and required the best from them. I can still remember her saying, "Don't be a scrub. You must do better." *Scrub* was her word for someone who was lazy and not living up to his potential.

My mother passed away when she was eighty-seven years old, and I think about her often and miss her more than I can say.

My younger sister Judith was an author, composer, and educator. She loved many things, including the gospel, music, and archaeology. Judith's birthday was a few days before mine. Every year I would give her a crisp one-dollar bill as my birthday present to her. Three days later she would give me fifty cents as her birthday present to me.

Judith passed away a few years ago. I miss her and think of her often.

## Elisa

And that brings me to my wife, Elisa. I remember the first time I met her. As a favor to a friend, I had gone to her home to pick up her sister, Frances. Elisa opened the door and at least for me, it was love at first sight.

I think she must have felt something, too, for the first words I ever remember her saying were, "I knew who you was."

Elisa was an English major.

To this day I still cherish those five words as some of the most beautiful in human language.

She loved to play tennis and had a lightning serve. I tried to play tennis with her, but I finally quit after coming to the realization that I couldn't hit what I couldn't see.

She was my strength and my joy. Because of her, I am a better man, husband, and father. We married, had eight children, and walked together through sixty-five years of life.

I owe more to my wife than I can possibly express. I don't know if there ever was a perfect marriage, but, from my perspective, I think ours was.

When President Gordon B. Hinckley spoke at Sister Wirthlin's funeral, he said that it is a devastating, consuming thing to lose someone you love. It gnaws at your soul. He was right. As Elisa was my greatest joy, now her passing is my greatest sorrow.

## Comforting Doctrines of Eternal Life

In the lonely hours, I have spent a great deal of time thinking about eternal things. I have contemplated the comforting doctrines of eternal life.

During my life I have heard many sermons on the Resurrection. Like you, I can recite the events of that first Easter Sunday. I have marked in my scriptures passages regarding the Resurrection and have close at hand many of the key statements uttered by latter-day prophets on this subject.

## The Resurrection

We know what the Resurrection is—the reuniting of the spirit and body in its perfect form (see Alma 11:43).

President Joseph F. Smith said "that those from whom we have to part here, we will meet again and see as they are. We will meet the same identical being that we associated with here in the flesh" (*Teachings of Presidents of the Church: Joseph F. Smith,* 1998, 91).

President Spencer W. Kimball amplified this when he said, "I am sure that if we can imagine ourselves at our very best, physically, mentally, spiritually, that is the way we will come back" (*The Teachings of Spencer W. Kimball,* ed. Edward L. Kimball, 1982, 45).

When we are resurrected, "this mortal body is raised to an immortal body . . . [then, we] can die no more; [our] spirits uniting with [our] bodies, never to be divided" (Alma 11:45).

Can you imagine that? Life at our prime? Never sick, never in pain, never burdened by the ills that so often beset us in mortality?

The Resurrection is at the core of our beliefs as Christians. Without it, our faith is meaningless. The Apostle Paul said, "If Christ be not risen, then is our preaching vain, and [our] faith is also vain" (1 Corinthians 15:14), then he added: "If in this life only we have hope in Christ, we are of all men most miserable. But now is Christ risen from the dead, and become the firstfruits of them that slept. For since by man came death, by man came also the resurrection of the dead" (vv. 20–21).

In all the history of the world there have been many great and wise souls, many of whom claimed special knowledge of God. But when the Savior rose from the tomb, He did something no one had ever done. He did something no one else *could* do. He broke the bands of death, not only for Himself but for all who have ever lived—the just and the unjust (see John 5:28–29).

When Christ rose from the grave, becoming the firstfruits of the Resurrection, He made that gift available to all. And with that sublime act, He softened the devastating, consuming sorrow that gnaws at the souls of those who have lost precious loved ones.

## The Savior's Death

I think of how dark that Friday was when Christ was lifted up on the cross.

On that terrible Friday the earth shook and grew dark. Fearsome storms lashed at the earth.

Those evil men who sought His life rejoiced. Now that Jesus was no more, surely those who followed Him would disperse. On that day, His enemies stood triumphant.

On that Friday the veil of the temple was rent in twain.

Mary Magdalene and Mary, the mother of Jesus, were both overcome with grief and despair. The superb Man they had loved and honored hung lifeless upon the cross. On that Friday, the Apostles were devastated. Jesus, their Savior—the man who had walked on water and raised the dead—was Himself at the mercy of wicked men. They watched helplessly as He was overcome by those who hated Him.

On that Friday the Savior of mankind was humiliated and bruised, abused and reviled.

It was a Friday filled with devastating, consuming sorrow that gnawed at the souls of those who loved and honored the Son of God.

I think that of all the days since the beginning of this world's history, that Friday was the darkest.

## Joy of Resurrection Morning

But the gloom of that sad day did not endure.

The despair did not linger because on Sunday, the resurrected Lord burst the bands of death. He escaped the grave and appeared gloriously triumphant as the Savior of all mankind.

And in an instant the eyes that had been filled with ever-flowing tears dried. The lips that had whispered prayers of distress and grief now filled the air with wondrous praise—for Jesus the Christ, the Son of the living God, stood before them as the firstfruits of the Resurrection, the proof that death is merely the beginning of a new and wondrous existence.

## Sunday Will Come

Each of us will have our own Fridays—those days when the universe itself seems shattered and the shards of our world lie littered about us in pieces. We all will experience those broken times when it seems we can never be put together again. We will all have our Fridays.

But I testify to you in the name of the One who conquered death—Sunday will come.

In the darkness of our sorrow, Sunday will come.

No matter our desperation, no matter our grief, Sunday will come.

In this life or the next, Sunday will come.

I testify to you that the Resurrection is not a fable. We have the personal testimonies of those who saw Him. Thousands in the Old and New Worlds witnessed the risen Savior. They felt the wounds in His hands, feet, and side. They shed tears of unrestrained joy as they embraced Him.

After the Resurrection, the disciples became renewed. They traveled throughout the world proclaiming the glorious "good news" of the gospel.

Had they chosen, they could have disappeared and returned to their former lives and occupations. In time, their association with Him would have been forgotten.

They could have denied the divinity of Christ. Yet they did not. In the face of danger, ridicule, and threat of death, they entered palaces, temples, and synagogues, boldly proclaiming Jesus the Christ, the resurrected Son of the living God.

Many of them offered as a final testimony their own precious lives. They died as martyrs, the testimony of the risen Christ on their lips as they perished.

## *The Transforming Power of the Resurrection*

The Resurrection transformed the lives of those who witnessed it. Should it not transform ours?

I testify that we will all rise from the grave. And on that day, my father will embrace my mother. On that day I will once again hold in my arms my beloved Elisa.

Because of the life and eternal sacrifice of the Savior of the world, we will be reunited with those we have cherished.

On that day we will know the love of our Heavenly Father. On that day we will rejoice that the Messiah overcame all that we could live forever.

Because of the sacred ordinances we receive in holy temples, our departure from this brief mortality cannot long separate relationships that have been fastened together with cords made of eternal ties.

It is my solemn testimony that death is not the end of existence. Because of the risen Christ, "death is swallowed up in victory" (1 Corinthians 15:54).

Because of our beloved Redeemer, we can lift up our voices, even in the midst of our darkest Fridays, and proclaim, "O death, where is thy sting? O grave, where is thy victory?" (1 Corinthians 15:55).

When President Hinckley spoke of the terrible loneliness that comes to those who lose the ones they love, he also promised that in the quiet of the night a still, unheard voice whispers peace to our soul: "All is well."

I am grateful beyond measure for the sublime true doctrines of the gospel and for the gift of the Holy Ghost, which has whispered to my soul the comforting and peaceful words promised by our beloved prophet.

From the depths of my sorrow, I rejoice in the glory of the gospel. I rejoice that the Prophet Joseph Smith was chosen to restore the gospel to the earth in this last dispensation. I rejoice that we have a prophet,

President Gordon B. Hinckley, who directs the Lord's Church in our day.

May we understand and live in thanksgiving for the priceless gifts that come to us as sons and daughters of a loving Heavenly Father and for the promise of that bright day when we shall all rise triumphant from the grave.

It is my prayer that we may always know that no matter how dark our Friday, Sunday *will* come.

*(Adapted from an October 2006 general conference address)*

# INDEX

Romney, Marion G.: on serving two
masters, 69; on fast offerings, 256
Running, 114

Sacrament, 24–25
Sacrifices: to follow Jesus Christ, 3–4; of
pioneers, 31–34
Salvation, service and, 189–90
Samaritan woman, 35–37, 105–6
Sangster, Elder and Sister, 227–28
Satan, attack on family of, 234–35
Saving money, 244–47
Savior, Jesus Christ as, 21
Scriptures: Latter-day Saints' belief in,
21–23; help us push forward, 115–16;
coming unto Jesus Christ through,
149–50; testimonies and, 174;
brotherhood in, 206–7
Sealing, 275
Second coming, 12–13, 21
Selfishness, 48
Self-reliance, 198, 201–2
Separation, from Heavenly Father, 154–55
Service: to build kingdom of God, 33–34;
finding happiness through, 48; from
fellow church members, 95; diligence
in, 121; failure to give, 159–60;
testimonies and, 175; James E. Talmage
as example of, 184–85; giving, 189–90;
gratitude and, 226–28; priesthood and,
262–63
Simpson, Robert L., on search for living
water, 36
Slave, 104–5
Smith, George Albert, on belittling Joseph
Smith, 272
Smith, Hyrum, 207
Smith, Joseph, 207; on faith, 27; helps
African-American Saints, 47–48; on
difference between Holy Ghost and gift
of the Holy Ghost, 52; appears to
Brigham Young, 55; on recognizing the
Holy Ghost, 56; on Book of Mormon,
75; finds comfort, 97; as guiding light,
102–5; on learning principles of the
gospel, 113; helps us push forward, 116;
encourages Saints to be diligent, 126;
on perseverance on missions, 129; as
example of enduring to the end,

132–33; on purpose of commandments,
149; loving and revering, 151–52; First
Vision of, 165–66; kindness of,
181–82; on life and happiness, 188;
encourages helping the needy, 199–200;
perseverance of, 213–14; on marriage as
holy ordinance, 235–36; on fasting for
the poor, 253; chosen to restore gospel,
265–66; lessons learned from First
Vision of, 270; place in Church history
of, 271–72; on doing work for the dead,
273
Smith, Joseph F.: on growth of Church,
28–29; on testimonies, 171; on
spiritual and temporal prosperity, 198;
on gratitude and happiness, 219; on
spread of temples, 273; on sealing
ordinance, 275; on reuniting with loved
ones, 281–82
Smith, Joseph Fielding: on life, 117–18; on
procrastination, 193
Smith, Samuel, 207
Snow, Eliza R., on sacrifices of women
pioneers, 32
Snow, Lorenzo: on being happy, 45;
spiritual experiences of, 166–67
Snowberger, Fred, 247–48
Snowman, the horse, 43–45
Sobel, Herbert, 205–6, 208–9
Soil, 84–85
Souls, our stewardship over, 70–71
Sower, parable of, 84–85
Spiritual gifts, 263
Spirituality, climbing to higher, 113
Spiritual thirst, 37–39
Spirit world, Elder Wirthlin's mother sees,
276–77
Stars, numbers of in universe, 98–99
Statue of Liberty, 91
Stevenson, Robert Louis, on gratitude, 224
Stewardship: over our souls, 70–71;
accountability and, 72
Strength, trials as source of, 96
Stripling Warriors, 208
Suffering: finding comfort during, 92–93;
purpose of, 93–94
Surgery, for baby with heart defect, 227–28

Talmage, James E.: on wealth of Peter,